Don Watson's work, both serious and satirical, has appeared in most of Australia's major journals and newspapers and on television, stage and radio. He was speech-writer and adviser to the former Australian Prime Minister, Paul Keating, and is writing a book about the Keating government. He lives in Melbourne.

'Throughout the book, and it is one of the many distinctions, the prose has an almost classical eighteenth-century symmetry, enlivened by the play of sardonic wit . . . A brief review cannot do justice to the qualities of *Caledonia Australis*, especially to a reverberation which sounds beneath the prose, like a ground bass. Instead of ideology there is compassion and sympathy; the judgements are, on the whole, restrained and shaped by the complexities of the issues; and the reader can apply the author's remarks to much of modern Australian life.'

PAUL DE SERVILLE, THE *AGE*

'Watson has an imaginative span, a love of place and a sympathy for his subjects akin to the best in Manning Clark's writing. This is a melancholy book, taking as its theme the public tragedy of the extermination of a people and the private tragedy of one man.'

MICHAEL McKERNAN

'Much of it is sheer impressionism and much of it very effective indeed. His account of the erasure of Aboriginal society is moving and profoundly disturbing; his treatment of the transforming effect of colonisation on the character of the colonists, an ambitious and important theme, should be given serious consideration in Australia and Scotland.'

PROFESSOR ERIC RICHARDS, FLINDERS UNIVERSITY OF SOUTH AUSTRALIA

'Watson has not only thoroughly traced his story back to its Scottish roots, but has told it in such a way that he has restored the tonalities of other times and other places. The writing is terse and often exceptionally good.'

JIM DAVIDSON, ABC

'For [the Scottish settlers] the Presbyterian religion was a view of the world, rather than a series of practices. They came to own a great part of Australia. Watson's book makes clear that to understand them (and Australian history) you have to go back to the world of John Knox and John Calvin. All history is ultimately theological.'

EDMUND CAMPION, THE *BULLETIN*

'Watson is out to crack the shell of myth encasing McMillan today. What emerges is something remarkably like the Calvinist dual personality so familiar from Scottish literature. Angus McMillan was not simply one sort of fellow who pretended to be another sort of fellow. He acted so differently in different contexts that any notion of a morally coherent personality breaks down. The Victorians were quite unable to deal with this scale of inconsistency except by fancies of Satanic possession. Even that was beyond the Victorians of Victoria, Australia, who created a safe, benevolent, kindly McMillan whose name is now commemorated in a 'stretch of water, a mountain, numerous streets, an annual memorial lecture and a motel.'

NEAL ACHERSON, *TIMES LITERARY SUPPLEMENT*

CALEDONIA

Scottish highlanders on the frontier of Australia

AUSTRALIS

A Vintage book
published by
Random House Australia Pty Ltd
20 Alfred Street, Milsons Point, NSW 2061
http://www.randomhouse.com.au

Sydney New York Toronto
London Auckland Johannesburg
and agencies throughout the world

First published by William Collins Pty Ltd, Sydney, in 1984

This Vintage edition published 1997

National Library of Australia
Cataloguing-in-Publication Data

Watson, Don 1949–.
Caledonia Australis

Bibliography
Includes index
ISBN 0 09 183555 0.

1. Scots – Victoria – Gippsland – History – 19th century.
2. Australia – Emigration and immigration - History.
3. Scotland – Emigration and immigration – History – 19th century. I. Title

994.560049163

Design by Yolande Gray
Typeset by Midland Typesetters, Maryborough
Printed by Griffin Press Pty Ltd, Adelaide
10 9 8 7 6 5 4 3 2 1

CALEDONIA AUSTRALIS

Scottish Highlanders on the frontier of Australia

DON WATSON

VINTAGE

CONTENTS

ACKNOWLEDGEMENTS

This book owes much to many people. In Scotland, most of all, Dr Alistair MacLean offered me both his knowledge of the history of the Highlands and Islands, and his hospitality. For this and his assistance through correspondence I wish to thank him. I am grateful for the help I have received from the staffs of the Scottish National Library, the Scottish Records Office, the Museum of National Antiquities, the School of Scottish Studies, Scottish Galleries and the Mitchell Library, Glasgow. Jim Campbell, Janet and Peter Doig, Val Peak, Michelle Myers, the Grays at Braco, Coinneach and Calum MacLean, Donald and Roderick MacPherson, Mike and Angela Hodd, and Ian Perring were, in various ways, good friends of this book. The Australian Academy of the Humanities made travel to the United Kingdom possible for me for the first time, and the Footscray Institute of Technology facilitated a second trip. I wish to thank the staffs of the La Trobe Library, Melbourne, the Mitchell Library, Sydney, and John Thomson at the Australian National Library, Canberra. I was helped in numerous ways by those people in Gippsland who give their time and energy to unravelling and preserving their community's history. Mr John Irving, Mrs Beryl Atkin and the members of the South Gippsland Historical Association and the Port Albert Maritime Museum; Mrs Helen Cowie, Mr John Leslie, Mr Paddy Miles and the Sale Historical Museum; Linda Barraclough and Marion le Cheminant and the East Gippsland Historical Association; Mrs McCarthy and the Valencia Creek Hall Committee; Jim and Nancy Treasure; Mr Phillip Pepper; the Thomsons at Clydebank; the MacLeods at Seaspray; and Bill and Jamie Frew, are just some of them. Peter Gardner was thinking and writing about the Gippsland Aborigines long before I was. My work owes more to him than it is possible for me to convey. John Hooker had sufficient confidence in the project to take it on and support it. Patrick Morgan, Jane Lennon, John MacLaren, the late Peter Kerr, Elaine Dargan, Terry Counihan, Jane Kinsman, John Timlin, Neville White and Jack Hibberd were generous friends and supporters. Tim Robertson translated Strzelecki's letters with panache.

Hilary McPhee always understood what this book is about. For that I want to thank her here.

FOREWORD

In 1840 Angus McMillan, a Scottish Highlander, came down from the Great Dividing Range to a region of lush unspoiled hills and plains in the south-eastern corner of Australia. McMillan called his discovery 'Caledonia Australis': he was trying to reconcile a half-learnt British grandiloquence with Celtic nostalgia. He had both in his head when he looked at the land for he was a newly arrived Highland Briton.

Although hundreds of Highlanders came to settle there, 'Caledonia Australis' never went much further than Angus McMillan's head. The new province was called Gippsland, after a governor, instead. Despite this loss McMillan stayed and prospered for a while. He became in his own lifetime the community's most honoured citizen and, after his death, his services were enshrined in granite monuments by roadsides.

Monuments honour deeds and end questions. They render over incongruities, silence echoes. Although Aborigines still live in fringe communities in Gippsland, their presence awakens no memories in the Europeans. Their history forms no part of European understanding. Nor, for the most part, does the Celtic heritage. The Celts disappeared along with the blacks. The monuments tell no-one what the Highlanders were ever doing there; what habits of mind they brought with them, or what remain. The history of Gippsland skates over the process by which the community came to think of itself as British, or Australian or loyal Australian British.

This book is a retelling of a frontier tale. It is about incongruities. It attempts a leap from Highland history to Australian history. If that is implausible or impossible it is no more nor less than the Highlanders themselves attempted.

The ironies are inescapable. No-one should be surprised when reality mocks the stated intentions of ambitious people, or renders faintly ludicrous the attempts of people uprooted from their own land to make sense of a new one. Irony is often all that we have left.

The end of a frontier era is marked by the emergence of an historical orthodoxy which cannot incorporate the losers. And when those 'passing' societies are examined they are found to be pre-eminently built on charming but preposterous myths. It is this central irony which the title 'Caledonia Australis' is intended to convey.

PREFACE

The art of writing history is to create a context for selected facts. The context becomes the essence of the work because facts, of themselves, have a paradoxical tendency to resist being set down—a tendency to take on distorted meanings. The historian's art, then, is neither that of a reporter nor that of a novelist; it lies in the discovery and construction of the least intrusive context. This is where Don Watson's study of the Scottish Highlanders in Gippsland is so very successful.

The author limits his theme of dispossession to two settings—the desperate poverty of Scotland during the first half of the nineteenth century which led to mass emigration; and the resultant dispossession and impoverishment of an Aboriginal nation when the crofters arrived in Australia. Marshalling his material into a clearly focused narrative, exposing the disparity between what people thought they were doing and what they actually did, his grasp of collective motives is as convincing as his insight into individual quirks. Serious though never solemn, astute yet compassionate, this is history illuminated by a broad perspective. On top of everything else, Dr Watson writes beautifully.

So the story is told of people escaping a life of unbearable hardship in primitive, smoke-filled huts—a life of dispossession, chronic hunger and social humiliation—to risk a voyage halfway round the world.

The heart of the tragedy is that these previously dispossessed Scots should come to inflict dispossession on others. Though many of the individuals who played a part are honoured for their courage and resilience, the subject is tragic. Most horribly, during the last frenzy of massacres, they are shown as gullible folk goaded to bestiality by nothing more than innuendo and rumour. The author, deftly choosing his sources, lets witnesses reveal themselves—often in unintentional ways—and each other. He proves that, contrary to popular prejudice, the Aboriginal clans did not give in without a struggle. They fought back, even when they came to be hopelessly outnumbered.

The consequences remain with us today: fringe communities, health problems, lack of sanitation, deaths in jail (whether these are suicides or not), alcoholism and the overwhelming issue of native land title.

Dr Watson does not allow himself the least sentimental lapse, either concerning victimised clansmen or victimised Aborigines. Though passionate about the subject, this is not an angry book. Nor is it a guilty book. What he offers is an exploration, an enquiry. He unearths detail upon detail and for each one he finds a place, of carefully relative importance, in his pattern. A few facts, of course, assert their own centrality: most dramatic of all being that only 96, of an estimated 2,000–3,000 Kurnai people in the region when the Highlanders arrived in 1841, were left alive to be counted sixteen years later.

The history of modern Australia has not been the simple fable we are usually served up—the birth in 1788, the violent infancy of convict sufferings, the coming-of-age at Gallipoli and so forth. Modern Australia began with a clash of already mature cultures. And the process has gone on multiplying, other mature cultures being added, each reshaped by absorption into a unique mixture. Aboriginal culture remains central to this uniqueness. Defeated though they were, in the short term, the indigenous inhabitants still persistently modify the rest.

Right now, while *Caledonia Australis* makes its reappearance in the bookshops, our nation plunges into another trough of ignorance and racial prejudice, spurred on by people whose behaviour suggests they are as blind to what they do as they are deaf to what has already been done. Don Watson's book, offering an encounter with events in a particular region at a particular time, addresses the great issues by opening up a chapter of our history which very few of us are familiar with—and which we all ought to think about.

I welcome the timely reissue of this fascinating book.

Rodney Hall

INTRODUCTION

My ancestors were pioneers, first settlers in a forest—a quite stupendous forest in the hills between the riverine plains of Gippsland and the swamps of Westernport in eastern Victoria. In 1840 the Polish explorer and philanthropist, Paul Strzelecki, the pastoralist and bunyip aristocrat, James Macarthur, and a small party, including the almost-legendary Aboriginal guide, Charley Tarra, had clawed their way through the forest and nearly perished. The pioneers came thirty years later and, as pioneers are wont to do, soon accomplished a feat of labour which to modern minds is almost beyond imagining. Modern minds are also prone to think that it was a shameful thing to destroy such a wonderful natural creation as that forest, the modern heart might also stop at the dimensions of it: but the minds of the pioneers were full of dreams of cow yards and cream cans and paddocks full of rustling maize, and with God on their side their hearts were unstoppable.

A century after these ancestors of mine ventured into the forest with saws and axes and cut down their first hundred-metre-high mountain ash the shape of my cultural inheritance became clearer to me. The gist of this inheritance seemed to comprise a work ethic and a sense of irony, yoked together like two draught horses—or two brothers, or husband and wife, or a father and son—one grunting and cursing as he labours, the other making grim jokes through clenched teeth. At first glance the two look mutually—even murderously—hostile and out of step. But patient watching reveals a kind of unity, as if mighty labour and mockery feed off each other. In truth it seems to be that Hard Work and Wry Humour—like good and evil, life and death—are the inseparable and inescapable partners of pioneering and have been at least since Job.

For imprinted on the psyches of all pioneers is the knowledge that the Lord and Nature sometimes resist and even mock our efforts to know them or defy them. This is useful and essential knowledge. It makes toil, misfortune and loss bearable. Irony is seeing the joke that the unseen hand is playing—and sharing it. Irony is the informal conversation the pioneer has with God. It is the means by which we forgive him and ourselves.

Our pioneering heritage taught us that the labour of men and women can move mountains, and be defeated by the caprice of a dog. They can tame a wilderness and lose it all to rabbits. As often as not we learned about our heroic forebears as if they *were* comic figures; through stories of their frustration and failures, their eccentricities, and their inability to master animals, trees, machinery and other elements in the pioneer's natural environment.

The serious side was much harder to get at. It tended to come sanitised and in the form of myth and cliché, the two being indistinguishable to young minds and having much the same stupefying effect upon them. The education system taught us that the feats of the pioneers were heroic and beyond question or reproach; and the pioneers' descendants taught us little more than this. The pioneers themselves, when they found a moment to reflect, were not inclined to boast or wonder. Pioneers are nothing if not taciturn (talking wastes energy), and humble (vainglory is a notorious incitement of divine wrath). So it came to pass that clichés, having the virtue of modesty because they have no known author, and economy because they can be used again and again, were the order of the day. Clichés are the verbal equivalent of darned socks and reheated stew and, to a pioneer, just as indispensable.

The words we heard so often still echo in the deeper gullies of our brains: 'things were very different then'; 'there were none of the comforts of course'; 'people made do with what they had—because there was nothing else they *could* do when it was all said and done'; and, 'truth be told, they were happier than we are with all our creature comforts . . .' This was the pioneering past: this, and local histories which were only sometimes reliable and nearly always written in the same Panglossian vein. We were very conscious of these pioneers, but it was only a rare glimpse we got of what their eyes had seen and, rarer still, what their hearts and minds had made of it. We certainly did not see it in those roadside cairns and statues—the clichés set in stone looking out at the landscape unseeing and unthinking.

I began researching these pioneers after attending the funeral of my grandmother. The project grew into something quite unlike the original conception, but the idea of scouring the pioneering legend for signs of life occurred to me while I stood among the weather-beaten old bodies—stiff-necked people, as the Bible says—gathered round her graveside. This grandmother was one reason why I knew my debts to the pioneers and even had some notion of what a blessing this heritage was. However, we also knew that with her we had buried knowledge of ourselves. As the day wore on this became a matter of general regret. 'Another one gone,' they said. 'Soon there will be none left.' They gathered to drink their tea and eat their cake and scones, and speak of cattle markets and illness; they uttered the familiar homilies about the good innings she had had; and, as the chooks settled on their roosts and the magpies fluttered into the cypresses at dusk, they drove off to their homes in the hills where dogs and the TV news were waiting. Someone really should get them down on tape, quite a few of us said; and I don't think there was anyone there who did not feel that these people had more to tell than they had told, or had ever been told about them.

They were selectors, or at least their parents had been. Some of their parents had begun life in Australia working for the squatters, making their own way by phenomenal labour when the Selection Acts made land available to them in the 1870s. They were the product of an attempt to create an Australian independent yeomanry, and if they were not in every sense what the Victorian legislators had in mind, they were at the very least proof that Selection had authored more than the hardship and horse thieves which Australian legend tends to assert. They had survived the odds in peace and war and remained upright, conservative, patriotic, productive—and silent.

But these were characters from the second act. They had taken on the leftovers, filling in the gaps on the map of settlement at the end of Australia's 'squatting age' and, in their sober and penurious ways, providing a perfect contrast to the less restrained egos of the pastoral frontier. The pastoralists had grabbed huge tracts of land; amassed large, if unstable, fortunes, and built monuments to both their courage and their vanity. That, at least, is their story at the first reading. This book is by way of a second reading. Its concern is with the ambiguities; the unanswered and perhaps unanswerable questions about a moment in our history when some men suddenly found themselves with no witness except God: and God having given no sign other than the approval implied in vast holdings and many sheep and cattle, just as suddenly these same men found themselves with the light of Providence smiling on them so brightly and manifestly, everything speaking of their good works, everything pointing to the future they had created, certain events of the past were made a dark corner into which no patriotic citizen would ever shine a light.

Any study of a frontier is likely to ask more questions than it satisfactorily answers. Inevitably, this book is at times impressionistic, speculative and fragmentary. It offers descriptions of the Kurnai tribes who lived in Gippsland and the culture and experience of those who routed them, but it is far from the last word on either subject. It describes events that certainly happened, though in many cases we can do little more than guess at causes, consequences and the order of them. Like most frontier diaries, those to emerge from Gippsland are incomplete and written long after the events took place: yet in this they help describe not just the frontier but the way a country's history is written.

In particular, it is a study of one man who—half steering his way, half being blown—arrived in the new province and from that moment seemed to embody every paradox the frontier could throw up: making its history and being made by it, writing its story and engineering its secrets, living through all manner of triumph and torment and leaving a legend which put his life beyond our reach, ending up a cliché, a block of stone.

My personal interest in pioneers forms part of the context in which this book was conceived. The rest derives from developments in Australian historiography twenty years ago: namely, a renewed interest among historians in Aboriginal history and in exploration.

Exploration had a minor renaissance among Australian historians in the late 1970s, I think primarily because of Ray Erikson's work on Ernest Giles and, somewhat later, Elsie Webster's monumental (and undervalued) study of Ludwig Leichhardt. Erikson not only told an epic tale, he reminded us that exploration had cultural and political dimensions which the 'explorer as hero' phase of history writing had neglected. Erikson's Giles is both a hero and an agent of private interest. Australian explorers were almost always thus: with few exceptions they were sent on missions to extend the realms of sheep and cattle, and science—and even glory—simply followed in their train. Explorers were the ritual preliminary to the main event—the act of settlement and the accumulation of wealth.

Yet before the pastoral interest sent in the flocks and herds and retainers, and convicts and Native Police, and the state sent in commissioners and magistrates, and the churches their ministers and missionaries, the explorer made his own kind of conquest. By naming the rivers and hills and rocks after the icons of his own culture, he began at once to paint out the past and with it the culture and legitimacy of the land's original inhabitants. Naming those lakes and waterfalls and canyons after Wellington and Victoria and the heroes of antiquity, or some wealthy benefactor or great aunt, was an act of stunningly simple effect: with a few strokes, writing the history of the place according to the lights of the explorer and his masters, substituting their ancestors for Aboriginal ones, and establishing permanent and familiar symbols to ease the passage of new settlers from the old world to the new, from the frontier to civilisation.

While Ray Erikson led in these directions, Elsie Webster's painstaking deconstruction—and reconstruction—of the Leichhardt story delved into the place of myth in Australia. Webster showed how hearsay, bad reporting, envy, prejudice, rumour, greed and intellectual fashion swallowed Leichhardt as completely as the desert did, and regurgitated him and swallowed him again—bending and twisting the myth, but never breaking or burying it.

Exploration and myth are inseparable and both depend upon an opposing force. There could be no exploration without the natives: no more than there could be anthropology or missionaries or heroism, to name just three Victorian fashions. There could be no white women in *durance vile*, to name a fourth. There could be no frontier without someone on the other side of it. The Australian Aborigines attacked Giles, Eyre, and Stuart, harassed Warburton, and frightened Mitchell into shooting them. They killed Kennedy and almost certainly Leichhardt. They played their part in the Burke and Wills saga, saving King while Burke died refusing the food they offered him. Giles came to respect Aboriginal knowledge and habits and even adopted some of them. Eyre became their protector. Mitchell ended up an admiring student of their culture and industry. At every step in the history of Australian exploration, the Aborigines were there; in fact and imagination, in reality and myth.

They were in schools too. Contrary to much opinion now, long before the groundbreaking work of Michael Christie, Lyndall Ryan, Judith Wright, Henry Reynolds, Roger Milliss and others inspired some conservative elements to claim that a 'black armbands' school of history was invading the national consciousness and poisoning young minds, Australian secondary school and university students were being taught enough about the conflict to write essays full of umbrage at the terrible things that had been done. As a marker of matriculation history exams and as an academic in the 1970s, I read hundreds of papers which dripped with moral outrage, but were almost devoid of anything which might be called historical knowledge. History teachers brought all the usual applications of logic and evidence to the convicts and the gold rush, squatters and selectors, Federation and the First World War, but the subject of Aborigines was treated as a different exercise—a moral one, a good work-out for young consciences. Indeed, much as they had been at the end of the encounter on the frontier, in our education system the Aborigines were handed over for spiritual instruction.

This was what the new writing on Aboriginal history changed: it put the subject into the realm of fact and interpretation where it properly belongs. And it introduced, as never before, the idea of the frontier. It may have been because they judged there to have been relatively little conflict in the settlement of Australia that some Australian historians were so loath to employ the concept. Some doubtless recoiled as they would from any abstraction, or any subject whose evidence was not strictly reliable. It could even be that the doctrine of *terra nullius,* whose literal meaning was a denial of the Aborigines' very existence, had played upon their minds. Whatever its causes, this strange oversight put the Aborigines at the same disadvantage in the writing of our history as it put them in the battle for the land. The loss, however, was on both sides: the Aborigines lost, with so much else, their proper place in history; and white Australia lost its perspective on the moments of its creation.

That is one reason why those people who in recent times have talked about Aboriginal history as part of a 'guilt industry' have got it so lamentably wrong. They talk as if there had never been a frontier, or as if it was a moral and material void before we made it one. This is both bad history and bad psychology. 'As far back as I can remember there were all sorts of tales in connection with this killing business, and it seemed to me that everyone was more or less ashamed of the affair,' wrote a Gippsland pioneer to the Reverend George Cox early in the twentieth century. If any feelings of collective guilt now exist it is surely because they existed then. And if it makes us face them, far from being debilitating, the study of this history is perhaps the only effective therapy available.

It is not, presumably, because they want to establish a 'guilt industry' in Japan that, fifty years after the Second World War, some Australians feel entitled to tell the Japanese to confront their past; rather it is because they want them to acknowledge the responsibilities that flow from the facts. Perhaps in anger some Australians do want to see the sins of the Japanese fathers visited on Japanese children. In that case they should have no difficulty understanding Aboriginals who want to see the same thing happen here. But the purpose of acknowledging the reality that our forefathers, men just like ourselves except they were more God-fearing and very often more respectable, massacred innocent people and hid or burned the bodies—the purpose of *history* in this case—is the very opposite of recrimination or vengeance. The purpose is to let the children into some of the secrets of their own natures and perhaps spare them the guilt of previous generations.

The publication in 1982 of Henry Reynolds's *The Other Side of the Frontier* did not turn the tide, but it did make a difference. At one level Reynolds's book was a scholarly study of evidence which hitherto had mostly been ignored; at another, it was a contemporary polemic urging Australians to reassess the history of white settlement and recognise, at the very least, that if the Aborigines had regularly required shooting and incarceration, logic demanded that they be accorded something in history more honourable and adult than the role of passive and innocent victims.

For Reynolds and others, establishing the undeniable fact of widespread Aboriginal resistance would shift the foundations of the contemporary debate: Among other things, it meant that the words 'conquest', and 'invasion' could be more readily substituted for European 'settlement'. The High Court of Australia's 1992 determination that *terra nullius,* the doctrine that the Europeans had occupied an empty continent, was a legal fiction and that a native title did exist, and the subsequent implementation of a Native Title Act makes Reynolds's work a landmark study in Australian history.

Reynolds was not the only historian to fill in the picture of an extended struggle on the frontier of Australia. In addition to others I have mentioned, Judith Wright's magnificent (and too little read) *The Cry for the Dead* should have put the broad question of resistance and brutal repression beyond doubt. In his massive *Waterloo Creek,* Roger Milliss provided us with the crimes, the motive, the characters, the psychosis and a superabundance of forensic detail proving coordinated acts of extermination in New South Wales in the 1830s. *Waterloo Creek* (all 1,000 pages of it) was a monumental and ultimately irrefutable addition to the record, but it did not invade the nation's consciousness. The same can be said of Phillip Pepper and Tess D'Araugo's *The Kurnai of Gippsland.* Written after this book and not always agreeing with it, Pepper and D'Araugo established beyond doubt that the claims made here in fact understated the case: the resistance was more concerted and so was the effort at extermination. I missed some of the most crucial evidence. There were more massacres than I acknowledged and there is more evidence for them than I found. Peter Gardner and Patrick Morgan have continued to dredge up documents in the past few years, and Gardner's relentless research is gradually yielding a pattern of behaviour which might well apply right across the Australian frontier.

That is something for historians to bear in mind: behaviour on one part of the frontier was often governed by the experience of another—not to say by experience in the lands from which the frontiersmen came. It was not difficult to see that the deeds done in Gippsland were kept quiet because the Myall Creek criminals had been hanged;

or to draw a faint line between the attitudes which produced those events and attitudes and events in Gippsland. Milliss, though he scarcely mentions Gippsland, makes the faint line unmistakable and in doing so makes it much harder to deny the rumours of widespread killings in that province. In *Waterloo Creek* Milliss paints a picture which Australian history has still not adequately registered—of *calculated* and *systematic* savagery towards the Aborigines. This was two years before the Highlanders of this book rode down from the Monaro into Gippsland. That the Aborigines would lose the battle was inevitable: that they would be all but annihilated was not so certain. But it helps our understanding to learn from Milliss that Lachlan Macalister, the godfather of Gippsland, was recommended by the Sydney establishment as the man most likely to do the sort of job which was ultimately done by James Nunn at Waterloo Creek. As much as common attitudes, common methods may have been at work. At Myall Creek in 1838 the blacks were roped together and cut down with cutlasses and sabres. Around the turn of the century a Mr W. H. Thomas, a schoolmaster at Woodside near Warrigal Creek in Gippsland, together with a Mr Lamb uncovered 'a quantity of human bones and skulls of men, women and children, even to very young children . . .' And 'as a result of careful examination of these it was disclosed that all the skulls were fractured, a piece being broken away at the base of the skull, as though caused by a blow from a tomahawk.'[1]

Caledonia Australis emerged from this sort of historical (and political) debate. It was, to that extent, a book of its time. And so, inevitably, when the New Right turned on what they took to be a Left interpretation of Australian

1 P. D. Gardner, *Gippsland Massacres*, Ngarak Press, Ensay, Victoria, 1993, pp. 58–59.

history, this book tended to be thrown in with the others as a work from a school of historians who hated their own past, morbidly highlighted the worst in it and ignored the best, broke the rules of historical inquiry by applying contemporary liberal norms and values to people of another age and sought under the guise of scholarship to relieve the guilt they felt about the treatment and condition of Aborigines.

A great deal could be said about the motives and reasoning behind this long campaign. To begin with, we can be sure that some people who wrote about Aboriginal Australia were, in various degrees, guilty of the sins alleged—including the sin of guilt. There has been no shortage of anachronistic judgements and polemical overkill in the writing of post-European Aboriginal history in recent times. Some of it may even fall into the category which would be thoroughly loathsome if its opposite were not generally far worse—'political correctness'. But the expression—or affectation—of a deep loathing for political correctness does not put any of us beyond the reach of history, and history's judgement. If the facts are there and can be found they should be found—and they should be known. We might reasonably distrust the judgements of people for whom atrocious acts satisfy political needs or the cravings of their unconscious; but that is no reason to trust those who hide such things or hide from them. It can hardly hurt a mature society to know that its founders were capable of evil as well as good. An immature society can only benefit.

My ambition with this book was always to make a crack in the deep encrustation of myth which surrounds the settlement of Australia: not because I loathe the people who made the myths or of whom the myths were made: on the contrary, aren't we meant to love them? The myths not only keep these people from me but, what is a greater frustration, are inadequate to what I know or imagine about them. It is not that there should be no myths, not that we can live without them, rather that we need better ones to fill the void. If only a handful of young Australians now study their own history it is possibly at least in part because our myths no longer feed them and were never real enough, or big enough, to reproduce themselves.

I still look forward to the day when someone with the stature and subtlety of John Wayne steps onto the Australian screen and, with a look around the mighty landscape, confronts *himself.* That is not to abandon historical verisimilitude. It is not to forsake either the pioneers or the cause of modern Aboriginal Australians. It is not to abandon the irony which, of all the frontier's legacies, appears to have lived the longest. It is only to state the obvious; namely, if we don't confront the possibility of evil as well as the good in creation we are left with a moral and aesthetic void—a great hole where a drama should be.

That is what is most wrong about this charge of 'black armbands': it is based upon a puerile and offensive assumption that to write about these dark events risks losing our respect for the builders of modern Australia. For some advocates of the theory it even seems to follow that those who write about them love their country less than those who pass them by. If these were my motives in writing this book I was not aware of them. I set out to give a more sympathetic portrait of the pioneers than any I had ever encountered. I wanted to give them blood as well as bones; religion, motives, choices, memories, identity, ancestors, an inheritance of their own. My ambition (instinct might be the right word) was to fill the void. I suspect the same is true of much revisionist history, which is, after all, invariably an attempt to find a deeper contemporary meaning in the past.

This book's most fervent advocate could not say it did much to either fill the void in our history or offer some inspiration for improvement. But re-reading it now I can at least say that it proves there was a bigger story to tell about Gippsland than had been previously told, and even a new footnote to be written about Scotland. It does remind us that, while nothing governed their actions as much as the material ambition and financial necessity they shared, the behaviour of settlers on the Australian frontier had other origins—in culture and ideology, religion and memory, and that they had only some of these in common. If the result for the Aborigines was the same, we might say that it hardly matters if Lachlan Macalister seems to have justified his behaviour by one means and Angus McMillan and Patrick Coady Buckley by others. But of course it does matter, both to history and the modern debate. We might easily distance ourselves from the military mind of Macalister or the brutalised Buckley—but it is harder with McMillan. The harder we look at McMillan the more we see the patterns of our collective experience and the elements of our contemporary dilemma. The harder we look at him the more signs we see of the kindness and brutality, self-interest and charity, memory and amnesia, decency and hypocrisy that has characterised public and private dealings with Aboriginal Australia from the beginning to the present day. And the harder we look at the society McMillan came from the more we see how the dispossessed everywhere tend to follow the same path to material and spiritual poverty: in the nineteenth century the Australian Aborigines were not the only ones to be first cast as dangerous and unruly savages, and then left stranded between pity and contempt—and then thrown still further adrift from humanity by Social Darwinism.

Commonsense demands that we judge the behaviour

of men and women according to their circumstances and the mores of their times, but it does not compel us to assume that all men and women will respond identically to those circumstances or observe the mores in equal measure. Difficult as it is to resist them sometimes, the purpose of recognising that people behave differently for different reasons is not to enable us to make comparative moral judgements. It is rather to make historical ones: to find the drama where the void is, to see how like us they are. 'Men of their time' they were—just as the cliché goes—but Angus McMillan was one man and Henry Meyrick another and though they lived at the same time and were squatters on the same frontier, they thought very differently. Meyrick railed against the atrocities he knew his fellow squatters were engaged in, yet the same Meyrick said he would shoot Aborigines down like dingoes if he caught them killing his sheep. McMillan committed the atrocities yet the same man felt constrained in the last years of his life to be the Aborigines' protector. To understand the frontier and what we have inherited from it we need to understand both men, and to do that we might do well to listen to another man of his time, George Dunderdale.

Dunderdale settled in Gippsland in the 1850s. He watched first hand as frontier history was written and he wrote, often with wry judgement, about the irony of it all. Only once or twice does he sound mildly passionate. We live in an 'age of whitewash', he says: 'There is scarcely a villain of note on whose character a new coat has not been laboriously daubed by somebody, and then we are asked to take a new view of it. It does not matter very much now, but I should prefer to whitewash the Aboriginals'. How could George Dunderdale know that by the expression of this simple sentiment he put himself among the category of chroniclers which a century later are labelled guilt mongers?

To Hilary McPhee

The ungodly, in the day of anguish and trouble, shall despair, and curse the Lord God into their hearts. They shall be numbered to the sword, and in the slaughter they shall fall. Their vestments of spiders' webs shall not abide the force of the Lord's wind. This fate shall befall them because they hold the wrong opinions, because they call light darkness, and darkness light.

John Knox
Epistle to the Congregation
of the Castle of St Andrews

PROLOGUE

In July 1837 the Presbyterian cleric John Dunmore Lang, of New South Wales, was given a public breakfast in his hometown, the Clydeside port of Greenock. He was in Scotland to recruit emigrants for the colony from the Highlands. He rose 'amid immense cheering' to say that his work had only just begun. 'Thousands and tens of thousands of destitute Highlanders and Islanders might yet find their way to New Holland,' he said. For Lang, emigration was like planting seeds in more than one plot. God forbid the idea that calamity may ever befall Britain, said Lang; but should the unthinkable occur, 'how animating the thought that in the uttermost ends of the earth there should be a numerous and powerful Nation descended from the ancient state of Britain, still speaking our noble language, still inheriting our British spirit, still exhibiting the power of our holy religion'. Highland society was dying. Lang would take the Highlanders before they withered and plant them in fertile Australian soil.

In Glasgow six months earlier, Sir Robert Peel drove his audience to a frenzy of self-congratulation with a combination of imperial chauvinism and praise for Scots as the embodiment of the British spirit. The Reverend Dr MacLeod, lately Moderator of the Church of Scotland and Lang's main ally and agent in Highland emigration, spoke too. He told the audience that Britain's moral authority rested on Protestantism ('Great Applause'): it was Protestantism which guaranteed 'rational liberty' at home and greatness abroad, and which assured her of remaining, 'despite the grumbling discontent of some of her spoiled children . . . the Queen of all nations'.

The British sometimes affected curiosity about their

manifest superiority. The *Edinburgh Review* and *Quarterly Review* puzzled on it often. Clearly it was the Christian revelation which taught the value of discipline, 'the folly of all passionate and vindictive assertion of supposed rights and pretensions', the substantial advantages of 'honesty and fair dealing over trickery and fraud', the vice of bigotry and the virtue of tolerance. Christianity revealed that goodness was practical. But why was it that the British showed the greatest aptitude to profit from the Christian message? The question was purely rhetorical, of course.

Peel told them in Glasgow that 'no tawdry emblem of revolution' would ever fly over the British Empire. Britain would go forth bearing 'the disposition to improve with the resolution to maintain'—a precise definition of the new doctrine of 'Improvement'. The 'proud King of the British Monarchy shall stand unshackled,' said Peel; he would continue to protect 'the rich from spoliation and the poor from oppression'. The King in fact was in the last stages of physical decay, but Glasgow's Protestant bourgeoisie were undeterred. They were almost delirious with the thought of empire. The whole world was becoming an extension of their own virtue. They stood as one for Sir Robert Peel and waved their handkerchiefs over their heads.

CHAPTER ONE

THE HIGHLANDERS AT HOME

It is said, that there are certain provinces on that side of the country, where the men are truly savage, and have neither law nor religion, and support a miserable existence by what they can catch.

JOREVIN DE ROCHEFORT IN SCOTLAND *c.*1661

The Highlands of Scotland are bounded in the east by the Grampians to within about 65 kilometres of Aberdeen and stretch south as far as Callander. In the west they take in the Hebrides and stretch up the coast from the southerly tip of Kintyre to Cape Wrath. The country is wild and wet. There is almost as much water as there is land, and large stretches of the countryside are barren, mountainous and gloomy. It is forbidding country. It startles the imagination.

The people who lived in the Highlands and Islands thought the people who lived in the south—both Scots and English—were dull, mean, effeminate and torpid. The people who lived in the south—the Sassenachs—were adamant that the Highlanders were barbarians.

The Highlanders and Islanders were a world apart. Above all they were distinguished by their clan society and their language. A clan, Duncan Forbes explained to dimly comprehending southerners after Culloden, was 'a set of men bearing the same surname and believing themselves to be related the one to the other and descended from the same common stock. In each clan there are several subaltern tribes ... but all agree in owing allegiance to the Supreme Chief of the clan or kindred and look upon it to be their duty to support it at all adventures.' Loyalty, that 'honourable principle of fidelity to superiors and their trusts', bound the clan together. The chief set the example and received loyalty in return. It was not a question of priorities or conscious resolution, it was an 'habitual attachment'.

With loyalty went a pervasive pride—not only among chiefs who did not see their domains as inferior to kingdoms because they were small—but also among tacksmen, the traditional holders of the land who were closely related to the chiefs and intensely aware of the purity of their blood. The tacksman combined the roles of proprietor, gentleman and military lieutenant. He sublet the clan's land to the people and organised them for war or cattle thieving. More than this, the tacksman was a linchpin of the clan culture; he was a model of manners and mores, and the bearer of the clan's tradition. And among the common folk too there remained the pride of membership of a clan, a sense of ancestry, which made them feel at least the equal of any outsider. It was a pride calculated to irritate southerners. They were always 'a Donald or a Mac, or some ramification of some clan', the English-born and educated geologist, John MacCulloch, groaned in 1819. They carried more pride than their station should have allowed.

Through four centuries of Norse occupation and the steady encroachments of Norman feudalism in the south, Gaelic society endured. It retained relatively open and egalitarian characteristics, difference in rank being substantially counterbalanced by common membership of a clan, and by knowledge of, and pride in, one's blood. As the Scottish historian Christopher Smout has said, 'Highland society was based on kinship modified by feudalism, Lowland society on feudalism tempered by kinship.' The mode of production could change in the Highlands, and the basic social ordering could change, but the sense of ancestral ties, of the unalterable nature of bloodlines, died hard.[1]

Recognition of one's genealogy not only inspired pride, it was a reminder of basic rights, the most important of which derived from the traditional Gaelic principle that the clansfolk, not the chief or his factors, owned the land. The children of the soil were the proprietors of the soil. That this notion has loomed larger the less it corresponded to reality is not a product of Gaelic romanticism, but of the fact that the land which the Highlanders lost in the late eighteenth and early nineteenth centuries was the source not only of their livelihood, but also of their identity.

The Gaelic language bound the Highlanders together and set them apart from the southern clans; it also did as much as anything else to render them wild and peculiar—not to say barbarous—in the eyes of English speakers. In the Hebrides Gaelic is still spoken as a first language, and the Scottish poets and scholars who use it declare that there is no more musical or precise language. 'That nervous expressive tongue . . . where every word is descriptive and expressive of the object it is affixed to,' wrote John Lanne

1 Maternal and paternal lines are still carefully distinguished in the Hebrides because it is taken for granted that there is a 'difference in the people'. A woman will be known throughout her life as *Bean* ('wife of'—thus *Bean Dhomhnuill, Bean Calum*, or 'wife of Donald', 'wife of Malcolm') but on her death she reverts to her maiden name and her coffin will be inscribed with the name of *her* people. Individuals are always identified by patronymics: that is, one is always the 'son of' (*Mac*) or the 'daughter of' (*Nic*) one's father (thus *Calum Dhomhnuill* is 'Malcolm son of Donald') unless one's mother was the sole provider, or the stronger character, in which case the identification will be through her.

Buchanan, a Presbyterian minister in the Hebrides in 1794.

Their language was matched by their music. Buchanan was especially impressed by the Hebridean islanders whose music he said was distinguished by 'taste and elegance'. 'In their agility in the dance,' he said, 'they stand almost unrivalled by any people.' Such skills were generally learnt at the 'ceilidh', the peculiarly Celtic social gathering. Ceilidhs expressed and maintained Celtic culture through music, song, poetry, saga and folk tale. They fostered arts and the most valued social skills—retentive memories, fluency of composition, sureness and correctness of speech. And, as Buchanan saw it, ceilidhs 'quite incidentally inspired in the young a love of the virtues extolled: hospitality, courtesy and self-forgetful courage'. All this with only a peat fire at the centre of it.

As a means of preserving history and legend and of enlivening everyday life, ballads and work songs were central to Highland culture. The Highlanders accompanied their labours with songs, 'like all primitive people', James Logan observed. He might have added that to some extent the songs reflected a primitive division of labour. The women's songs were often chants devised to accompany hard, monotonous work. The men tended to sing the 'play' songs of hunting and conquest.

The eighteenth-century explorer and naturalist, Thomas Pennant, noticed the sexual division of labour: 'The men are thin but strong; idle and lazy except employed in the chase, or anything that looks like amusement; are content with their hard fare and will not exert themselves further than to get what they deem necessaries. The women are more industrious, spin their own husbands' cloaths, and get money by knitting stockings.'

Southern observers rarely failed to comment on the drudgery of the women's lives—unless it was to reflect on the beauty of their naked feet, the excess of thigh they displayed or the premature ageing of their bodies. 'The common women are in general most remarkably plain, and soon acquire an old look,' Pennant said. By the nineteenth century the condition of women had become a measure of the primitive. However, behind the patriarchy of Highland society there was a good deal that went unseen. Highland men bore the ancient legends of battle but women sometimes fought them. In combat with Agricola's armies or the colonisers of the nineteenth century, the women are recorded as fighting with the men, or sometimes alone when the men bolted for the hills. And always they performed the tasks on which life depended and maintained a culture which reflected their role.

In Celtic culture the story-teller leavened the real world with tales of an imaginary one. Tales of legendary deeds led dwellers in the present away from the mundane business of searching for sheep and scratching the ground. They lent also an historical justification to continuing acts of bravado where rationality might have outlawed them. In a basically oral culture stories and songs were natural extensions of language and repositories of tradition. The laments in particular were works of great power and beauty.

The Scottish Gaels were inveterate legenders and chronically superstitious. Legends and omens gave an intractable natural world a metaphysical dimension. The omens which preceded death suggested that while nature was inscrutable, ambivalent and capricious it was also ultimately fathomable. The 'second sight' granted to a select few was a blessing not so much for the usefulness of specific predictions as for the human purchase on an unpredictable world it provided. It was, after all, of little practical use to know from the signs that someone was soon to drown in a storm; or that the Caledonian Canal would be built; or even 'that the people will degenerate as the country improves'. Second sight changed nothing. It was a view of the preordained. For the seer it was probably as much a curse as a blessing. He who had seen in a dream a poor neighbour encircled by the grey mist was going to find it hard to look him in the eye until death came. Not that the prophets were always reliable. But did it matter?

If poets verses be but stories
So be food and raiment stories.
So is all the world a story;
So is man of dust a story.

Did it really matter, then, that when the great rock fell from the cliff on Skye it did not fall on the Clan MacDonald, as Kenneth MacKenzie, the Brahan Seer, had said it would? It would no doubt get them, right enough.

In Highland society death was neither to be taken lightly nor passed off as nature taking its course; except in the sense that death was a 'prerecognizable destiny'. The living had a responsibility to both the corpse and the spirit, though sometimes the reverence and the rules were drowned in the wakes. Above all the body had to be buried with its kin and very long journeys were frequently made to ensure that this was done. There were elaborate rituals of mourning, including touching the corpse to ward off memories of the death, circling the grave, and the employment of professional mourning women, who it seems were kept in most communities. At funerals the laments were sung by these women as they walked behind the coffin, or they were played to indescribably haunting effect by a piper.

Morbid omens and legends of war and revenge lent credence to the claims of outsiders that scarcely a week passed in the Highlands without some unprovoked atrocity being inflicted by one clan on another. Life, however, was probably not quite so bloody. The notion that they lived in a chronic state of 'reciprocal hostility', or as Samuel Johnson said, 'in the perpetual warfare that characterizes all mountain tribes', is itself legendary stuff. Legends are rarely the work of the people in them. In Highland society, kinship and loyalty were strengthened by these tales of the heroism of ancestors, and the surpassing wickedness of the tribe over the hill. Such military traditions served the lairds well.

Against their reputation for habitual warring, treachery and cattle theft must be weighed the Highlanders' civility and generosity which even their detractors acknowledged. Buchanan, admittedly an almost reverential admirer, wrote of their behaviour during hard times in the late eighteenth century:

> In defiance of the hardships these oppressed people suffer, they retain part of their former state and dignity at their meetings and partings. They address one another by the titles gentleman and lady (*duinvasle* and *beanvasle*) and embrace one another most cordially . . . And they are never known to enter a door without blessing the house and people so loud as to be heard, and embracing every man and woman belonging to the family. They both give and receive news, and are commonly entertained with the best fare their entertainers are able to afford.

In 1824 Dr John MacCulloch discovered 'true civility' was 'really a national feature of the Highlands'. 'Of course,' he said, 'I speak of the lower classes, among whom it is not the result of a code of instruction. It is that true civility which arises from kindness, or good nature . . .' Not that such kindness was always appreciated by travellers of

MacCulloch's ilk. The Highlanders, like the Irish, had a facility for indirectness which bemused and irritated outsiders. It irked MacCulloch to have the shortest route to the next town pointed out to him and then to discover that it took him into an impassable marsh. Perhaps it was a trait of Celtic discourse to prefer the possibilities of conversation to the rapid resolution of a question, perhaps they preferred politely confounding an intruder to drowning him in a peat bog; or perhaps they believed that a man born to be hanged would never be drowned and it was wise to enjoy his company while it was available.

Drowning MacCulloch would have been vulgar in any case, and as MacCulloch recognised, from 'this most abstruse and undefinable faculty, a Highlander is free'. In an age when politeness was passing they were polite—'there would have been a herald and a flourish of trumpets to announce that Dame Partlett had laid an egg'. Politeness was not servility. Few venturers failed to remark on the articulate confidence of the Highlanders, even if they found nothing else to recommend about their society. 'I fear they pity us,' Pennant said in 1771. He was not the first or last invader to recognise this characteristic of a colonised people.

The Highlanders were also polite to fairies (*Daoine Shi*), a 'peevish repining race of beings' who envied the more substantial achievements of humankind. Milk could be used to placate them. During confinements salt strewn around the doorway would generally ward them off. The ancient Celtic practice of passing an infant over the fire was still believed to retain some efficacy at christenings in the nineteenth century. In 1836 James Logan noted that the Highlanders approached 'with veneration' the little green mounds under which the fairies lived.

The fairies were just one entry in the catalogue of the

Celtic supernatural. There was the *gruagach*, a beast in human form which seduced young girls resting from their labours, then turned into a carnivorous horse and ate them—or frightened them out of their wits. Water kelpies lured travellers into their clutches and devoured them before they had time to prepare for eternity. Spunkies blazed mesmeric lights to lure people to their doom in the moss: they thrived on drunks. On the other hand the *urisk* (the Celtic equivalent of the English brownie) was a useful addition to any decent household.

The Highlands were alive with more than Highlanders. They buzzed with myths and legends deriving from centuries of occupation and, if not a mastery of the natural world, a brilliant understanding of it.

Witches were about. Thomas Pennant recorded a marriage in the Highlands in 1771:

> The courtship of the Highlander has these remarkable circumstances attending to it; after privately obtaining consent of the Fair, he formally demands her of the father. The lover and his friends assemble on a hill allotted for that purpose in the parish, and one of them is despatched to obtain permission to wait on the daughter: if he is successful, he is again sent to invite the father and his friends to ascend the hill and partake of a whisky cask which is never forgot. The Lover advances, takes his future Father-in-Law by the hand, and then plights his troth, and the Fair-one is surrendered up to him. During the marriage ceremony, great care is taken that dogs do not pass between them, and particular attention is payed to the leaving of the Bridegroom's left shoe, without buckle or latchet, to prevent witches from depriving him on the nuptial night of the power of loosening the virgin zone.

Marriage customs reflected and reinforced the basic social divisions of the Highlands. Within the common Gaelic culture the clans were determinedly separate. Almost always marriage took place within the clan, so members were joined by blood as well as common interest. The practice tended to ensure harmony within clans *and* animosity between them.[2]

The superstitions with which every aspect of Highland life was imbued did not run counter to much Christian belief—at least not to those parts of it which stressed the wisdom of a virtuous life. Major-General David Stewart wrote in 1825 that Highland superstitions were not only captivating but salutary, 'inculcating in the minds of all, that an honourably spent life entailed a blessing on descendants, while a curse would descend on the successors of the wicked, the oppressor and the ungodly'.

Curses could also be man-made. The Highlanders sometimes used sympathetic magic to destroy their enemies: it was at least hoped that an image of the miscreant stuck with pins would be as effective as a sword.

A rich spiritual life of course does not fill stomachs or keep out the cold. However, it probably helped in times of scarcity, which were not infrequent, as did the close social bonding which the Highlanders enjoyed. Pennant noted an absence of beggars on his visit and attributed this both to the economic system and the charitability of the people. As historian E. P. Thompson has said: 'It is not easy for us to conceive that there may have been a time within a smaller and more integrated community, when it appeared to be "unnatural" that any man should profit from the necessities

2 There was no great reverence for chastity in the old Gaelic culture. Men often competed for women who had become pregnant unchastely. Yet the society appears to have minimised illegitimacy as much through traditional practices as through Calvinist strictures and the relative ease of enforcing marriage in small communities. There were the salutary folk tales which spoke of supernatural consequences; the police-like role of old women in the clan community, and the traditional sport of 'bundling', a regular semi-Platonic tumble between boys and girls.

of others, and when it was assumed that in times of dearth, prices of necessities should remain at a customary level, even though there might be less all round.' The history of the Highlands in the eighteenth and nineteenth centuries offers frequent reminders that such times did exist. Indeed, that ethos did perhaps as much as anything else to mitigate the effects of famines created by a new economic system.

In the Highlands 'the milk and flesh of their flocks and the products of the chase' supplemented ale and whisky and the staples oats and primitive barley (*bere*). Hunting returned rabbits, hare and otters; geese, ducks, plover, woodcock, grouse, pigeon and snipe. The lochs had salmon and the sea both scale and shell fish, seaweed and seals. Cattle produced cash in Lowland markets from about the sixteenth century. They were driven to Crieff and Falkirk each year and often as far south as Norfolk. Washington Irving saw Highland drovers near Perth in 1817; they were dressed in plaids and blue bonnets and carried their staffs under their arms. The cattle realised more than capital. Their blood was combined with oats to produce haggis. It was an abomination to southern palates but it was the most simple and nutritious of dishes for a Highlander. Samuel Johnson found that the Highlanders ate well. He thought their breakfasts were unsurpassed: 'If an epicure could remove by a wish, in quest of sensual gratifications, wherever he had supped he would breakfast in Scotland,' he said. The lack of knives and forks, or the inexpert use of them, he was ready to forgive.

Highlanders were not much concerned by the opinions of the English, unless the opinion was defamatory or if it became law. They did not much mind if Lowlanders thought the plaid loathsomely unfashionable, savage and indecent garb, so long as it kept them warm: it did, by day and night in the home and on the heather. To sleep in the plaid on the heather was 'bliss' said an anonymous eighteenth-century writer: it was 'as soft as a featherbed and much more wholesome'.

Highland houses were often no more than wooden posts interlaced with branches of trees, like wicker work, and covered on the outside with turf. Johnson found crude houses of stone. Where stone or wood was unavailable, Highland houses were constructed of turf alone and must have resembled, as one writer put it, nothing so much as fungi on the surface of the earth. Or graveyard mounds. The Celts seemed to prefer living with an inconvenience to the labour involved in removing it. Pastoral life did not encourage the dextrous arts. A peat fire forever burning in the centre filled the huts and the inhabitants with smoke, and visitors from the south with a mixture of amusement and horror. Around the fire the inhabitants sat, 'brooding . . . till their legs and thighs are scorched to an extraordinary degree'. But the smoke was not without its advantages, or it seemed that way to many Highlanders: it was 'perpetual suffumigation, as potent as that of a magician'. It 'will scarcely suffer the inhabitants to exist, much less the fever', wrote MacCulloch.

Highland medicine, MacCulloch charitably observed, 'is neither very deficient, nor very inefficacious, nor very unreasonable'. Tradesmen and conventional wisdom did much of the work. Bethune, hereditary physician to MacLeod of MacLeod on the Isle of Skye, was a master in the use of herbs. 'I need not work,' he is reputed to have said, 'I possess more wealth in the flower of this knoll, than thou shalt with the palms of thine hands.' One does not have to believe that their homes were cosy, any more than one has to swallow the idea that Highlanders commonly lived to 180, or that pulverised seal liver cured the fluxes, or that a hare eating dung prognosticated a storm, to form the impression that in normal times the clansfolk lived reasonably long and moderately happy lives—despite cohabiting with cows in chimneyless huts.

For centuries the Highlanders lived in what had come to be called the darkness of unreason and pagan superstition; but they were Christians too. They probably received their first Christian instruction from St Ninian who preached among the southern Picts in the fourth century and whose influence in the north is attested by St Ninian's Isle in the Shetland Islands. However, it was an Irishman, St Columba, who planted the Church of Rome in the Highlands when he established his monastery on Iona in the sixth century. Primitive Catholicism coexisted with paganism until Puritan missionaries began entering from the south a thousand years later; and even Presbyterians were sometimes carried off by fairies.[3]

Calvinist missionaries and catechists from the Society in Scotland for the Propagation of Christian Knowledge (SSPCK) advanced into the Highlands in the mid-seventeenth century. They found the people 'ignorant of their own wants—shut out from the world by a strange language—destitute of native literature—the victims of discord and poverty—they were doomed everywhere to remain in darkness, while other men were everywhere awakening to enjoy the day-spring of knowledge'. The Calvinists planted schools and churches. To facilitate the teaching of 'true, rational, Christian knowledge', they decided that Gaelic—'whereby the natives are strangers to the world'—should be extirpated as quickly as possible, so they forbade its use in SSPCK schools; until the missionaries realised

3 If we are to believe the inscription on his tombstone, Dr Robert Kirk was carried off by *Daoine Shi* in the eighteenth century. This was some time after he had translated the Psalms into Gaelic.

that it was much harder to spread their religion in English.

The Calvinists intended to teach the Highlanders that life was a precarious, not to say insignificant, thing.[4] They taught them more than they needed to know. They told them that 'the world twines itself about the soul as a serpent about an eagle, to hinder its flight upward, and to sting it to death': that Satan was forever laying serpents' eggs in the hearts of men so that he might pursue his 'tortuous, wriggling policy': that they were born in sin and no part of them was good: that all their previous practices—pagan or Catholic—were wicked and must be renounced. The Highlanders and Islanders were told that it was wicked to break the Sabbath and that they must stop holding their fairs on that day. In general, however, the Highlanders were not much impressed by this or any other literal application of Calvinist principles, and long after their arrival the missionaries found that 'Ignorance, Popish and even Heathenish superstition, Profaneness, Idleness, Theft and many other Disorders did continue to abound to the offence of God, Scandal of Religion, and Prejudice of the Publick, and great numbers of poor People who might have been useful to the country were lost to themselves and others.'

The Reformation took a peculiarly puritanical form in Scotland. In so far as the Kirk, established in Edinburgh

---

4 An inscription on a nineteenth-century tombstone in the graveyard at St Vigean's on Scotland's south-east coast is a good illustration of the doctrine:

Death rides on every passing breeze
It lurks in every flower
Each season has its own disease
Its peril every hour.

Go home dear friends, shed not a tear
For we must lie till Christ appears
Then grieve no more, but be content
For unto you we were but lent.

in 1560, adhered to the teaching of John Knox and his successor Andrew Melville, it was a rigid theocracy, savage, ridiculous and immensely hypocritical. The Kirk was the vehicle for the Godly Commonwealth, enforcing the teachings of scripture in the belief that they would thus create on earth a mirror image of the kingdom of God in heaven. It was not to be confined to Scotland. The reformers spoke of Presbyterianism conquering not just England but the Roman Church throughout Europe. In this Zion the Church was responsible for 'those faults which the civil doth neglect . . . drunkenness, fornication, excess (be it in apparel or be it in eating and drinking), oppression of the poor . . . wanton words and licentious living'; and for seeing that the State carried out to the letter the Law of Moses, which among other things prescribed the death penalty for murder, blasphemy, perjury, idolatry, adultery and sodomy.

It was not always taken quite so far, although adulterers and fornicators, who were subjected to whipping and long periods of public repentance, or prostitutes who suffered the ducking stool, may have sometimes wondered whether their punishments were much to be preferred to that of homosexuals, who were burnt. Now scripture also made it clear that to oppress the poor was a sin of a magnitude equal to any sexual deviation, which committed the Church to punishing usurers and helping the used. But this was a dictum at odds with the economic reality which Calvinism itself encouraged. For by investing the authority to interpret Divine will with the Presbyters rather than a hierarchy, and in scripture rather than tradition, Presbyterianism gave Divine sanction to the worldly interests of its leaders. Extraordinarily zealous in the prosecution of sexual offenders, the Kirk found little time to prosecute the usurers. One thousand sexual offenders were punished in St Andrews between 1560 and 1600, yet only one usurer was prosecuted in the same period. Providence would surely see fit to punish blaspheming businessmen; bankruptcy or some other misfortune could safely be interpreted as Divine wrath on usury or sharp practice—and success in business, or a generally favourable economic climate was, equally, Divine vindication of worthy business enterprise. As T. C. Smout says, 'By 1790 neither Presbyterian nor Anglican leaders had any time for Puritanism, both believed that the social order was already organised in a way highly satisfactory to God and both assumed the Lord to be as moderate in His religious views as they were themselves.'

What can be said of the Kirk in 1790 might also be said of the writer of 1936 who saw the Church of Scotland as testament to a freedom-loving and law-abiding people, a remark which might be taken to mean that the Church had become a mirror image not of the kingdom of God but of bourgeois society. By then there had been a century of evidence that Divine law and the laws of *laissez-faire* capitalism were much the same.

Although its outcome would not have satisfied Knox or Melville, Scotland was profoundly changed by the Reformation. In the climate of orderly self-regulation mediated by an unknowable Providence, science and the arts flourished as much as trade and industry. Fifty years after the union of the English and Scottish parliaments (1707) internal and overseas trade in cattle, linen and tobacco was laying the financial basis for Scotland's industrial revolution. Now linked by a common crown, a common parliament, by trade in goods, technology and ideas, and by religions different in denomination but singularly favourable to commerce, England and the Lowlands of Scotland advanced into the Age of Improvement in the same happy partnership in which, increasingly, they advanced into European and colonial wars.

The generosity which the leaders of the Kirk applied to themselves was not extended quite so amply to the common people, and not at all on the evangelical frontiers. For those who did not profit from business activity the Kirk provided an efficient education system (for children were not born innocent, but ignorant of Godliness) and a strict code of moral conduct based on scripture. These were weapons against Satan and those of his agents who corrupted the word of God by mingling it with 'the errors and traditions of men'. They were also weapons against social disorder and rebelliousness, for they armed the State with Divine vengeance.

Catholicism remained the religion of much of the north-west Highlands. In some areas the old Church was dismantled without the substitution of the new, and a religious vacuum was created. Where Presbyterianism did take hold it was a less virulent form than the southern clergy preached, and without the violent sectarianism. Even by the end of the eighteenth century a visitor found to his astonishment that 'protestants and Papists, so often pronounced to be eternally inimical, live here in charity and brotherhood'. David Stewart, another visitor, found that the Highlanders' religion was 'peaceable and unobtrusive': 'He never arms himself with quotation to carry on offensive operations. There is no inducement for him to strut about in the garb of piety, in order to attract respect, as his conduct insures it. Not being perplexed by doubt he wants no-one to concentrate his faith.'

No doubt not all Highlanders were quite so spiritually fulfilled as Stewart thought, but there is abundant evidence of a level of tolerance that was unknown in the south, and a persistent refusal on the part of the Highlanders to accept the notion that religion was synonymous with boredom and misery. In this they swam against the tide but not always against the original precepts of Presbyterianism, nor against everyone in the south.

To the cruel language and the jeremiads of the Kirk, Robert Burns opposed a humanism rooted in the popular traditions of Scotland, both of the Highlands and the Lowlands. Burns and some of the traditions have survived Presbyterianism, but the poet himself was an example of the two worlds the Scots inhabited after the establishment of the Kirk. He was a 'natural' man *and* a Calvinist, but never both at the same time. 'He oscillated,' said Edwin Muir, 'like many Scotsmen, between staidness and wildness: he clamped himself down, and broke out, and clamped himself down again.'

This was not greatly at odds with some of the theoretical underpinnings of the Church. Just as Calvinism could sustain a belief in the virtues of free economic enterprise, so it could accommodate the idea of unimpeded choice in other worldly matters. The Moderator of the General Assembly of the Church had said in 1743 that 'It would be much better if fornication gave less scandall and there was less jealousy of wives and mistresses.' Knox just might have agreed. He was himself not so hostile to the life of the body as is commonly supposed, or as many of his followers represented him to be.[5] Even his puritanical successors seem to have fought a losing battle with the physical senses—if not always with their own, then with those of their parishioners. The south and east of Scotland

5 There was much in scripture, and in John Knox's version of it, to say that women should be forever humble. It was a woman, Knox said, who brought about the fall of man, so 'there is no boldness that ought to be permitted unto her, but she ought to be in humility . . .' 'Thou art the port and gate of the Devil,' he said. Still, he married twice and always seemed to prefer women to men.

had a peculiarly high rate of illegitimacy in the eighteenth and nineteenth centuries—a much higher rate than in the Highlands where for so long the Kirk had lamented its lack of influence.

In the Highlands the potential for a liberal stream of Calvinism diminished as more material threats to Highland society grew. Samuel Johnson noted the change during his visit in 1773:

> There was, perhaps, never any change of national manners so quick, so great, and so general, as that which operated in the Highlands by the last conquest, and the subsequent laws. We came thither too late to see what we expected, a people of peculiar appearance, and a system of antiquated life. The clans retain little now of their original character: their ferocity of temper is softened, their military ardour is extinguished, their dignity of independence is depressed, their contempt of government is subdued, and their reverence for their chiefs abated. Of what they had before the late conquest of their country, there remain only their language and their poverty.

The late conquest was of course the defeat of the Jacobite forces at Culloden in 1745. The British campaign had been inspired by strategic considerations: it was intolerable that a region of Britain, however wild and barren, should be a stronghold of French and Jacobite ambitions. By the time Johnson wrote, however, it was apparent that the military assault had been but a prelude to the destruction of Highland society by legislative means. The Highlanders were disarmed, and the military and judicial powers of the chiefs over their clans were abolished. Highland dress was outlawed—a seemingly gratuitous act which in fact ran deep into the basic ordering of clan society. Highland men now complained of the 'unmanly' dress they were obliged to wear. The *Disarming Act* was repealed in 1782, and

Highlanders were soon fighting in the plaid for British causes on European battlefields; but by then the rout of Highland society had gathered an ineluctable momentum.

At the centre of the process were the chiefs themselves. From the early eighteenth century they had been drawn into the commercial world of Britain and western Europe. As the southern economy expanded, the trade in Highland cattle increased. The chiefs invested the returns in other parts of the empire. They became as familiar with French and English as they were with Gaelic—'the consequence', an acerbic commentator wrote, 'of a tinsel refinement which, finding its claim to gentility doubtful, thinks it establishes it by repudiating the language of the humbler class . . .' The chiefs became known in the salons of London and Edinburgh.

Robert Somers, who saw the Highlands and Islands during the famine of the 1840s, said the effect of southern society on the lairds had been 'the same as when a hawker of the backwoods spreads out his toys, and trinkets, and firewater before a tribe of Indians'.

But the chiefs' land in the Highlands would not pay their bills. The old Celtic tenures reflected the military and political expediencies which governed clan society. They did not yield an income. Increasingly the Highland chiefs saw the need to draw rent from the land. Their new commercial world demanded the modernisation of their estates. Yet to do so would invite revolt from their tacksmen and their people.

Put simply, the incorporation of the Highlands and Islands into British capitalism *demanded* the destruction of Highland society, and in so doing it *demanded* an act of treachery by the lairds against their people. The destruction of Highland society was thus both an act of invasion and an act of collusion. So long as they remained patriarchs whose political and military power rested on the support of the clan, the lairds, for the most part, held. When those powers were abolished they gave way.

After Culloden the Highlands were colonised economically. Southern landlordism replaced the clan system. The people were cleared from their ancestral estates and placed on allotments (crofts) which were generally cut out of the most unprofitable coastal land. Thus were born in the last half of the eighteenth century the Scottish crofters. The plots frequently being too small to return a subsistence, or even to pay the new rents, the clansfolk were obliged to work in a wages system for a chief who had become little more than a conventional landlord. As often as not the crofters received no wages, but simply discharged services in lieu of rent. For the majority of them that service was in the kelp industry.

From the mid-eighteenth century the western coast and the islands became a major supplier of kelp to southern glass, linen and soap manufacturers. The high alkali content of kelp was useful to soap makers and the linen industry used it in bleach: glass makers used the salts as a flux. When imports of Spanish barilla were cut off during the 1790s the price of kelp rose sharply and Highland landlords with coastal country took advantage of the windfall. The price was maintained in the first two decades of the new century by a tariff on both barilla and salt. In the summer months the seaweed was gathered by men, women and children standing knee-deep in the Atlantic. It was then dried and calcined between layers of burning peat—'a very warm and troublesome task'. In good years the finished product brought up to twenty pounds a tonne in London or Glasgow. In the early years of the nineteenth century Lord MacDonald was reputedly earning £20,000 a year from the kelp on his Hebridean estates.

The crofter obliged to gather kelp in summer suffered from more than arduous and unhealthy work. In a climate offering only a few months each year to harvest, store and repair, the introduction of kelping placed an impossible burden on both the people and the economy. For the crofter,

> . . . the contradictory and incompatible labours of securing fuel from the peat mosses, of shipping off kelp, of cutting and securing hay and corn, of building folds for cattle, of attending cattle markets, and repairing house thatch, march dykes, and what are called inclosures—throng all at once . . . in the months of September and October when the Atlantic pours his incessant storms and torrents upon his head. He despairs of overtaking the innumerable demands upon his industry, and sinks into stupour and neglect, in which the horrors of winter always find him.

Kelping made the crofter miserable in every sense. So long as he was obliged to gather kelp all talk of agricultural improvement was fatuous.

In the inlands the people were replaced by southern sheep—the blackface and the cheviot, known to the Highlanders as *Na Caoraich Mora*, big sheep. The Gaelic tacksmen were largely replaced by southerners skilled in management and breeding, and dedicated to extracting the greatest possible financial return from the land. The Highlands and Islands became the sheepwalks of British capitalism, and the hunting grounds for gentlemen capitalists 'whose patrimony earns them 3 per cent per annum' and who laboured only in pursuit of grouse and deer, Robert Somers said.

Along Highland roads southern travellers now came to see the grandeur and the remnants of an age that had passed. Explorers and naturalists such as Thomas Pennant and Sir Joseph Banks (who found the Isle of Staffa as remarkable as anything he had seen on his recent circumnavigation of the globe) soon gave way to condescending observers like Johnson.[6] These 'little men without ancestry', as the Highlanders were prone to call them, indulged a patronising and morbid curiosity in the 'natives', filled their romantic imaginations with the wildness of the scenery or the beastliness of the weather, and soon had books ready for the eager southern public. Not infrequently they observed the same things as completely different. After the outbreak of war with France in 1793 they went in even greater droves. Europe had lost its charm. They traipsed about the mountains and glens, gazed with wonder at the burns and lochs, had themselves rowed from island to island; and they gave to it all such old English names as fastnesses—'unexplored fastnesses', 'wild romantic fastnesses', 'secret fastnesses'. Such scenes stimulated the fashionable proclivities for awe and melancholia. The Highlanders hated them with varying degrees of politeness. Charles MacDonald, an educated gentleman of Skye who had extended hospitality to the insufferably supercilious Dr John MacCulloch, thought his guest 'one of the greatest ***** unhanged'. Another Skyeman, Keith Macalister of Strathaird, said the doctor went a long way towards explaining 'the aversion which the people show to that class of Sassenach intruders who enter the country pre-determined to make a book, and who, in lack of matter more attractive, or of honesty, intelligence, and observation, cram the pages of their "memorable books" with tavern

6 Like so many of his successors, Samuel Johnson could not refrain from using the word barbarous, one suspects because he knew that was what his audience wanted to hear. For instance, Gaelic was 'the rude speech of a barbarous people who had few thoughts to express, and were content, as they conceived grossly, to be grossly understood'.

adventures, taking care to season them with the necessary portion of exaggeration and falsehood'.[7]

The travellers saw a people who had been culturally and materially impoverished struggling to survive, and they decided very often that the Highlanders and Islanders were a curiously ineffectual race by comparison with their own. It was the common response of the coloniser to the colonised. Few of the people who actually saw the Highlands saw so acutely and so ironically as Karl Marx did from London: 'The aborigines had been thrown upon the seashore,' he wrote, 'and attempted to live by fishing. They became amphibious and . . . lived half on land and half on water, and after all did not half live upon both.'

Other informed observers noticed a change in the religious temper of the Highlanders. In the wake of their dispossession they took up the message of the Calvinists: that they suffered because they were sinful, and that they should not attempt to free themselves of a burden which God had placed upon them. They bowed to the spiritual batterings of the catechists and the missionaries of the SSPCK. They came into the mission.

---

7 Thomas Browne agreed. He numbered among the steady stream of tourists who 'as the negro says, take walk to make book': 'a plodding antiquary', 'an impudent Stone Doctor', 'a silly view hunter', 'a crazy sentimentalist', 'the Cockney literati'. All of them returned with the same 'mawkish rhodomontade of drivelling deliration'.

CHAPTER TWO

IMPROVING THE RACE

We have seen that no savage nation ever emerged from barbarism by its own unaided exertions . . . the natural tendency of tribes in such a condition is to grow worse instead of better.

W. COOKE TAYLOR, *THE NATURAL HISTORY OF SOCIETY*, LONDON, 1840

We were pleased humanely, to order a new arrangement of this country. That the interior should be possessed by Cheviot Shepherds and the people brought down to the coast and placed there in lotts under the size of three arable acres, sufficient for the maintenance of an industrious family, but pinched enough to cause them to turn their attention to fishing. I presume to say that the proprietors humanely ordered this arrangement, because, it surely was a most benevolent action, to put these barbarous hordes into a position where they could better associate together, apply to industry, educate their children, and advance in civilization.

PATRICK SELLAR, FACTOR OF THE SUTHERLAND ESTATE TO LORD AND LADY STAFFORD, 1815

Now we have many chimneys, and yet our tenderlings complain of rheums, catarrhs and poses. Then we had none but reredosses, and our heads did never ake.

IMPROVED HIGHLANDER, *c.*1800

Nowhere in the Highlands of Scotland was the process of social and economic collapse better illustrated than on the Isle of Skye. The heart of Highland myth and legend, Skye became a rural slum in the first half of the nineteenth century—a 'nursery of mendicants' the *Westminster Review* said in 1841—and the people left. Now there are only traces of a once intensive occupation. At Elgol in Sleat, the remains of a cottage sit under a cliff on the very lip of Loch Scavaig. Elsewhere there are clumps of trees which once surrounded houses, broken down walls, solitary chimneys. They brought chimneys to Skye in the eighteenth century, guided by such works as James Anderson's 'Practical Treatise . . .' on the subject with 'full directions for removing smoke from houses'. The idea was to improve the black houses and their inhabitants.

There can hardly have been a more incongruous setting for a people's misery. Every impression on Skye seems fleeting, except perhaps the sense of timelessness the land, the sea and the sky evoke. Like the rest of the Hebrides, Skye has hundreds of tangible reminders of its ancient heritage. The countryside is dotted with the duns, tumuli and standing stones of early Celtic and Norse occupation, all as incongruous in a nineteenth-century Presbyterian community as the pagan superstitions which remained. On Skye the weather changes fast and frequently, from the benign to black drenching storms which swell trickling burns to torrents in an instant. The island enjoys the 'perpetual ventilation' of generally warm but very wet winds. For half a year, Johnson said, 'a dry day is hardly known, except when the showers are suspended by a tempest'. It seemed to a nineteenth-century judge on the Highland circuit, Lord Cockburn, that the tempest had said to Skye, 'Thou art my brother,' and, the judge continued, '. . . Everything we behold attests their cordiality.'

The mightiest and most frequent storms are in the Cuillins, the range of hyperstein cones which run east–west across the island and almost divide it in two. The Cuillins are both beautiful and menacing, the more so because of their sudden storms and the tricks played by light and water on the hyperstein—a phenomenon which reminded one visitor of the affinity diamonds have to charcoal. From the foot of the Cuillins one step seems to change the shape and the juxtaposition of the peaks, just as a scudding cloud, rain, or a burst of sunshine changes their colour. The peaks 'shoot themselves forth in every variety of fantastic figure and appearance, each struggling with its neighbour, and each possessing every imaginable characteristic of native rudeness and grandeur'. To the southerner, the Cuillins, like the Highland glens, were the romantic home of vanquished tribes, and a century of art and literature portrayed them in their 'natural' setting for the excitement of civilised audiences.

When C. Leasingham Smith, a gentleman who rambled in Scotland in 1835, saw the bewitching Loch Coruisk hidden in the centre of the Cuillins, he was 'lost in astonishment' and found himself 'unable to contemplate without an appalling thrill such a desolation of sterility'. For Walter Scott and his illustrator, J. M. W. Turner, the loch and the Cuillins were monuments to the cult of the picturesque on which they had been raised: they defined the primal, a 'permanent record of the cataclysmic events that shaped the early history of the earth'. With a vision like this it was hard to see the rest of the world as it really was.

For the less intrepid, the sight of the Cuillins in contrast to the gentle hills and changing colours of the heather might have been enough to remind them that they were ephemera—had they not been Sassenachs and unafflicted by doubt. For the most part Skye is low hills, peat bogs and mosses, heather and bracken: 'Some grass,' Dr Johnson said, 'and some happier spots of earth are capable of tillage.'

Traditionally there were three great estates on Skye—those of MacKinnon, MacLeod and MacDonald. Having bought up most of the MacKinnon land, by the end of the eighteenth century MacDonald's was by far the most extensive. He was also the proprietor of the Outer Hebridean island of North Uist. A newcomer, Macalister, acquired the remainder of MacKinnon's estate in 1789—this was Strathaird, about 8,100 hectares, joining MacLeod's Bracadale land virtually in the centre of the Cuillins. In the first half of the nineteenth century substantial parts of Skye were acquired by outsiders, but MacDonald and MacLeod remained the dominant landholders. Legendary enemies, much given to burning each other's clansfolk in churches or smoking them to death in caves, by the end of the eighteenth century their military zeal had been diverted to the cause of empire and their domestic energy to the pursuit of profit and distinction in London.

The decline in the realm of MacLeod was rapid and somewhat pathetic. Owners for several centuries of a considerable portion of Skye and Harris and other islands in the Outer Hebrides, and Glenelg on the mainland, by the late nineteenth century the Lord of the Isles was a quaint postcard figure and sometime big-game hunter. His castle is now a museum of lost provincial and empire glories.

In 1772 General Norman MacLeod inherited debts which absorbed the entire rental of his father's estate and he was obliged to sell large parts of it. Harris and St Kilda in the Outer Hebrides, Waternish, Glendale and Orbost in Skye, were all lost. Norman's father had squandered his money in the south, leading a social life which befitted his lordly status in the island but not his rentals there—a common pattern among Highland chiefs. The money they derived from kelp and increased rents was not returned to their estates. The interests of their people were 'bartered for the merest baubles' in the London salons, Robert Somers said in 1848. Their exoticness in the south was highly valued: 'Highlanders are what he will best like to see,' Walter Scott told MacLeod when inviting him to attend the King's visit to Edinburgh in 1822.

Norman MacLeod of MacLeod took a great deal more interest in Britain's military affairs in India than he did in his estates and when he died his son, John Norman, was obliged to sell still more—Glenelg, for £100,000, in 1811. Still, his domain ran to about 100 to 130 square kilometres. He was married to the daughter of a London banker, and his sister wed an invaluable commercial friend, Sir John Pringle. His son was at Harrow. He had a resolute and conscientious factor on the Dunvegan estate: in 1811, Charles Robertson, MacLeod's 'most obedient and much obliged humble servant', wrote to him in London seeking directions to deal with the housekeeper who was feigning pregnancy in order to marry the miller's grandson, and to ask if he wished him to 'throw down the cottages about the castle so I may inform the possessors to provide for themselves'.[1]

John Norman MacLeod was instructed by financial necessity and his London bank. He talked less and less of his social obligations to his tenants and more and more of

1 Mr Robertson may well have been Skye's Patrick Sellar. Sellar was the factor on the Sutherland Estate of Lord and Lady Stafford. He put the cheviots in the interior and the people on the coast, on lots of less than three acres (1.2 hectares): 'sufficient for the maintenance of an industrious family, but pinched enough to cause them to turn their attention to the fishing'. Three thousand Gaelic families were replaced by 29 imported ones—mainly English—who were to administer 131,000 sheep on 321,000 hectares 'humanely' appropriated. The huts and villages were razed by British soldiers as they went through. Sismondi said it showed British law to be more tyrannical than the boot of Prussia.

maximising his income and status in the wider world. A southern friend said of him: 'He is a particularly clever and sound-headed man, with a very unusual turn for business of every kind and a great liking for it, and he both speaks and writes above par.' With such skills and such patronage in the sophisticated world MacLeod thought he should enter the House of Commons, but even after declaring an irresistible policy of 'protecting the pastoral and agricultural interests of the country' he was unable to wrest the seat of Invernessshire from either Sir Charles Grant or his illustrious son, Lord Glenelg, and had to settle for an unfashionable London borough. Late in his life he wrote to Sir Robert Peel, reminding him that he was one of the few Highland chiefs still without a baronetcy or a higher title.

MacLeod of Dunvegan was an improver. With the money he made from the sale of lands he built roads and harbours and started a fishing village. He was public spirited, but in much the same way as Patrick Sellar was public spirited. Beginning in 1811 he increased his rents, and with the aid of his imported factor, Robertson, converted his *runrig*[2] holdings in the interior into sheepwalks and placed his tenants on crofts near the shoreline where they provided cheap labour for kelping. MacLeod thus integrated his estate with British capitalism. That, in the final analysis, was the motive for improvement in the Highlands. In the short term the return for MacLeod was considerable: but when he died (still untitled) in 1835, his son Norman inherited not just financial debts but the human debris created by improvement.

Tacks (leases) on the MacLeod estate were given for 19 years, for which period the tacksman maintained possession

---

2 The Celtic custom, combining feudalism and tribal communalism, of annually distributing the laird's land among the households.

so long as he paid his rent regularly, performed such services as the laird demanded, observed county regulations, and kept a good neighbourhood. Tacksmen who failed to meet these requirements could be replaced, and increasingly they were. As MacLeod was advised in 1810, there were plenty of farmers willing to take the place of any tacksman who chose to emigrate in protest at his increased rents.

The tacksman traditionally performed another function in the clan community. For all his privileges and rank, the tacksman was of the same culture as the tenants and cottars. He was above them but of them, a fact which seemed more important when men from outside usurped his role. There was 'a great difference', John Lanne Buchanan said, 'between that mild treatment which is shown to sub-tenants and even *scallags*,[3] by the old lessees, descended of ancient and honourable families, and the outrageous rapacity of those necessitous strangers who have obtained leases from the absent proprietors, who treat the natives as if they were a conquered and inferior race of mortals'. The tacksmen of the late eighteenth and early nineteenth century were in the changing economic order, an ascendant class and therefore an Anglophile class. Often Gaelic tacksmen took on the habits and the language of the English. Frequently they emigrated. That betrayal was profoundly important to the future of the Highlanders and Islanders. For not only did they become wage earners and mendicants at the moment their masters became bourgeois and genteel, they also became culturally isolated, and therefore the more likely to be thrown in with the Irish as a pitiable and obsolete *race*.

The animals of the Celts were put in the same category. The Hebrideans had a great love for their beasts:

---

3 The lowest rank in Highland society—people without land.

'Like the Germans of Tacitus their pride consists in the numbers of their flocks and herds: these are their only riches, and in these they place their chief delight.' It seemed to the writer that it was not so much for their milk and meat as for their 'fine symmetry' that their owners valued them. But too often they shared the same roof with the rational inmates!

In 1812 the two great landlords formed the Isle of Skye Farming Club to encourage the improvement of black cattle, sheep and draught horses. It was the sheep which stood in most need of improvement. The native sheep (Jacob's or Norwegian sheep were their common names) had probably been introduced by the Norse. They were small, the smallest in Europe, with coarse multi-coloured wool. 'The quantity of the wool which the fleece yields,' declared an improver, 'is equally contemptible with the weight of the carcase.' 'The animal is sickly and puny and frequently carries four or even six horns,' said James MacDonald. John Walker had no doubts when he saw them: 'This small race ought to be, and will be, in general, dismissed.' These abominations were soon replaced by the faces of progress, attached to the Linton (known universally as the blackface) from the Lowlands, 'the boldest, most hardy and active of all the sheep kind', which were three times as heavy, three times as valuable and, fed on heather, three times as tasty as Jacob's sheep. The elegant cheviot of superior wool but less resistance to bad weather also arrived in Skye in the early nineteenth century.

It appears to have taken just a decade for imported sheep to conquer Skye. At about the same time, 1810, as Sir John Sinclair introduced them to Caithness they were introduced to Skye, probably by a MacLeod tacksman, Ewan McMillan. By the 1820s they were the dominant breeds.

Jacob's sheep were not the only local species to be vanquished. 'In every point of view an ineligible and worthless breed,' the Hebridean pig was 'gradually to be extirpated'. At least in this the Hebrideans would have concurred. They loathed the pig and extended their contempt to those who ate its flesh—'sow-eater' was thus an epithet for Sassenachs and Irishmen. They were not so hostile to their horses. But the improvers thought these were too numerous, poorly fed, inefficiently used and chronically 'infarcted and plugged up'. Until such time as the breed could be improved, carts introduced, and asses imported, the Hebrideans were to be taught the southern recipes for glysters. The black cattle at least were worthy beasts and their flesh was the only source of cash, but they were unhoused and underfed in winter, their manure was not gathered and they stood, along with the rest of Hebridean husbandry, in need of greatly improved management.

'The instruments of agriculture in the Hebrides are of a very early and unimproved age of the world,' wrote the Professor of Natural History at Edinburgh University. He found them ingenious nonetheless. The *caschrom* (crooked foot or crooked spade), which Dr Johnson thought incommodious and certain to be 'improved', John Walker found 'exceedingly well adapted' to the cultivation of rocky ground. Indeed without the caschrom—a sort of one-man stump-jump plough—much of the Hebrides was uncultivable. If there was another unique domestic implement in the Hebrides it was the *quern*, which ground the people's oats and barley until mills began to be constructed. On Barra the recently Protestantised laird MacNeil, having constructed a mill, employed a man to gather the querns from every hut and throw them into the sea.

*

Improvers never understood the complexity of the society they sought to change. Peat cutting in the Hebrides, for instance, was a simple process, using the simplest of implements for a simple necessity. But like grinding meal with a quern, or ploughing with a caschrom, it was a social act as well. Peat cutting was a ritual of co-operation and enjoyment. It bound the members of the society together and was part of its poetry. Improvers saw with improvers' eyes. A very early example of the species, Edmund Burt, was cutting the first roads in the Highlands in the 1720s when he inquired of a Highlander why he walked backwards in front of his horse when ploughing. The Highlander first asked him 'most civilly' if there were places where the people walked forwards, and then pointed out to Burt that it was the best way to see partly submerged rocks in time to avoid them with the ploughshare.

Early in the 1820s the taxes on salt and barilla were abolished. The lairds, having organised their estates around the industry, were almost as forlorn as the kelpers. Poverty in Skye now became endemic and famine a regular occurrence. Bad weather alone highlighted the precariousness of the position. A minister described the scene on the island in 1832:

> The weather has been very bad for some time past, and today it is terribly so. The poor creatures cannot stand for a moment on the shores to collect shellfish. The sea is running mountain high, and the spray is carrying far inland, so that fishing or shell gathering is out of the question.

In poor seasons the people were reduced to starvation diets and the lairds were soon obliged to import meal to keep them alive. The irony was that they had been reduced to poverty by the policies of improvement, a doctrine which purported to enhance the people's dignity and self-reliance.

In 1791 Skye's population was 12,195: in 1821 it had reached 22,453. On Skye and elsewhere in the Hebrides a rapid growth of population occurred at the same time as a substantial decrease in food production for general use. Once the land had been withdrawn from the population in favour of sheep and cattle the majority became dependent on a combination of wages, potatoes and shellfish, or charity and shellfish. The reasons for the population increase are complex and paradoxical. Contemporary commentators were agreed that the main cause was 'early and improvidential marriage'. The cause of 'early and improvidential marriage' was rarely explained except in terms of the moral and intellectual levels of the people. In fact it was for the most part a consequence of the coincidental introduction of the crofting system and potatoes as a staple crop. Individual rather than communal tenancy of the land under the crofting system left families free to divide their small plots into even smaller ones; and potatoes, needing far less land for a subsistence crop than cereals, conspired in the process. The crofts became no more than tiny potato plots. Kelping and roadworks provided wages (however variable) with which to buy food in the event of a shortfall. Combined with milk and occasional fish the crofters' food supply was sufficiently assured to encourage early marriage, and sufficiently nutritious to keep their children alive.[4]

The figures for Skye did not match the staggering rate

4 Some contemporary commentators claimed that inoculation played a significant role in the dramatic population increase. As early as 1764 a Mr MacCaskill ('a well-qualified surgeon') inoculated 287 people on Skye and subsequent campaigns were readily accepted by the crofters. John Walker found that island children were particularly susceptible to smallpox without inoculation, but Skye people often claimed that this disease and others like tuberculosis only became a problem after regular social intercourse was established with the south.

of increase in Glasgow and other manufacturing towns to the south which had attracted both destitute Highlanders and Irish, but there were basic similarities in their predicaments. Both populations contained high proportions of immigrants: Skye did not have the other Celtic outcasts, the Irish, but the congestion there was partly due to forced migration from the Highlands and the problems of both populations were substantially ones of cultural upheaval. The Superintendent of Police in Glasgow told the British Association in 1840 of a population of 'miserable creatures' inhabiting the centre of the city 'from whence they nightly issue to disseminate disease and to pour upon the town every species of crime and abomination'. In Skye authorities also talked of 'miserable creatures', complained of petty crime among the lower classes in a society where it had been virtually unknown, and deplored the corruption of traditional values and the diseases and bad habits introduced by 'a variety of vagrants, such as gipsies, rag-men, vendors of crockery, tin and smiths, egg-doctors and old clothes men'.

The roads the improvers built into the Highlands and Islands carried cultural as well as economic trade. Like the people of Glasgow, the people of Skye had been detribalised and made wage slaves and scavengers. As in Glasgow, the ever increasing population in Skye competed for an ever decreasing share of the social wealth.

So long as work was available the lairds and the Kirk were agreed that work was what the people needed. 'Devotion and industry go hand in hand,' John Girvin told the landholders, factors and tenantry in 1803. 'If in concert with the gentlemen [the SSPCK] would introduce some kind of work amongst them, and teach the people to labour, they would soon become practical Christians as well as professed protestants,' said Sir Patrick Lindsay.

MacLeod, for one, agreed that the earth obeyed no idle hand and put his people to work. But it saved neither the Christians nor the Church from penury. 'We have no fixed Poor's funds in this parish,' the Reverend William Bethune complained to MacLeod in 1809, 'except what arises from the fines of delinquents who are convicted of Fornication.'

From the fines of fornicators and other criminals, parish collections and the occasional windfall such as that which followed the death of Captain MacLeod in 1805, the Kirk on Skye dispensed regular assistance to the blind, the lame, the widowed, the decrepit and the destitute: the 'very great objects' like 'Catherine MacKinnon of John Taylor's house who is palsified from her infancy', or 'Norman MacLeod's daughter at Glencolbert who is lame and bedrid from her infancy'. Irregular assistance was made to those in sudden need or those who earnt it by performing social services: for 'Donald Stewart to bury Nighean Ghobain' (the blacksmith's daughter), for ferrying the poor's meal, for coffin, shoe and candle making. Thus the Church on Skye carried out John Knox's injunction to aid the 'impotent poor' and 'your poor brethren, the labourers and manurers of the ground', so that they might feel 'some benefit of Jesus Christ now preached to them'.

The people of Skye 'repaired in crowds' each Sunday to feel the benefit of Jesus Christ: to confess that their thoughts had been evil and vain, and their members the instruments of unrighteousness to sin, and they begged for mercy. The General Assembly found they had a 'profound respect for religious institutions and . . . an ardent thirst for religious knowledge': 'After the sacrament in one particular parish, there may be seen the beautiful and touching spectacle of from forty to fifty boats setting sail at once, to bear homewards the pious multitudes, who from the remotest boundaries of its vast extent have been devoutly in attendance at the service of communion.'

In his book, *Circuit Journeys*, Lord Cockburn wrote that he 'never saw a more respectable congregation' than that on Skye.

> There were about 350 present, all except Corry's (MacKinnon's) party in the humblest rank. The men had almost all strong blue fisherman's jackets. The women, with only one exception, so far as I could observe, had all on red tartan cloaks or shawls and clean mutches of snowy whiteness, with borders of many plies. I can't comprehend how such purity can come out of such smoky hovels.

And no-one could question the charitability of these people. When, in the winter of 1837, bad weather destroyed the peats on Skye, lots were drawn among the cottars to see whose houses would be used for fuel, and further lots decided who would take care of the families thus deprived of shelter.

For the Kirk, however, the need to catechise remained. The lesson of Ireland was plain: in the parts 'where the Protestants prevail, in these, and in these only, order and tranquillity prevail'. Protestantism was the only salvation for the savages. One J. C. Colquhoun pointed to Scotland's lower crime rate and attributed it to the Presbyterian Church, for 'peace and industry are co-extensive with Protestantism, and are overthrown by popery'.

From time to time the Kirk declared a Day of National Humiliation as a sort of general repentance. In normal times each parish was issued with codes of behaviour, and 'forms of process' to be adopted by parish elders when dealing with misdemeanours. The forms could be brutal: denial of a crime required 'taking his blessed name in [one's] mouth and swearing by him who is the great judge, punisher and avenger', as if one would choke if one lied. They were also extraordinarily pedantic: there was a detailed procedure to be followed 'if a scandal of uncleanness be committed where neither party resided, as if persons having their fixed residence in one parish, do commit uncleanness in another parish, or perhaps in the fields or in the time of fairs and markets'.

Zealots in the south dreamt of Arcadian licence which the people of Skye were not enjoying. The people of Skye, the ministers reported, were 'with few exceptions . . . sober and correct'. In the first half of the nineteenth century a basic flaw in Presbyterian political economy appeared. For increasingly in the parishes of the Hebrides the number of 'impotent poor' exceeded the capacity of fornicators and criminals to pay. Now, the congregations were not disabled or decrepit and in this way deserving of help; nor were they crafty beggars and thus, in view of Presbyterian moral philosophy, undeserving. They were able and they worked. Yet they were poor and impotent.

In 1805 a fiddler and catechist from Skye, Donald Munro, was converted to evangelism. Within a few years Munro's prayer meetings on Skye had people talking of an 'uncommon awakening' and a state of religious frenzy 'attended with distress and trembling of the body'. The leaders of the evangelical movement were known as 'the men', and they stirred the crofters not just with visions of their own salvation but with appalling images of the damnation awaiting the landlords, factors and sheep farmers who oppressed the poor. The lairds were displeased with the rebellion. MacLeod believed that these lay preachers taught doctrines that were 'injurious' to his people. Some of his fellow proprietors refused the people sites to build churches, so the people worshipped wherever they could find a spot sheltered from the weather and safe from the harassment of the laird. From the state of religious harmony so often remarked by observers, the Highlands and Islands, particularly Skye and Lewis, became noted for religious unreason and rancour.

The origins of the struggle were primarily economic. The revivalists' strength lay in the destitution of the people. The crofters eagerly sought a religious panacea to their problems, welcomed the attacks on their lairds who had become landlords (to keep 'strange women' it was sometimes said) and were readily convinced that the Established Church was in league with their oppressors and the devil. The revivalists' campaign was aided by their use of the Gaelic and the grounding of their doctrines in the recent history of the Highlands and Islands. From this a tide of fanaticism grew which culminated in the creation of the Free Church of Scotland in 1843. On Skye its leader was Maighstir Ruaridh, the Reverend Roderick MacLeod, who for years filled his church in the parish of Bracadale by preaching his own brand of Gaelic fundamentalism to congregations imbued with a deep sense of their betrayal and a ready acceptance of supernatural solutions.

The Established Church had tended to smooth over the rift between the laird and his tenants. It had bound them 'in formal if not spiritual union', one commentator wrote. But while the creation of the Free Church in 1843 was a demonstration of the people's rebellion against the lairds, it also drove another wedge between the people and their Gaelic culture. The Free Church had found a footing in the traditions and history of the Highlanders and Islanders, but in the end it represented the ideology of a people cut off from their past. It was the ideology of the dispossessed.

The people saw no economic benefit in the Protestant formula of hard work and piety. Those who wished to improve themselves grew impatient. MacLeod was told to plant an English village on his estate and set the people to work productively. Plant villages, plant maize, plant willows, plant flax, plant Englishmen. The lairds were barraged with suggestions from outside. The Highlanders were beyond help, MacLeod was told in 1812, so long as they continued to see nothing but the black hut:

> Chimney-less, ceiling-less and floor-less—having nothing of a house but its confinement, and everything of a dunghill but its solidity—to be contented for food with Potatoes—and with Cloaths for himself while his wife has few and his children none . . . without any sense of the advantages to be procured from exertion, or any comparison within his reach to excite it—so long must he be the Personage he at present exhibits himself, and so long must the country remain destitute of the best means of improvement.

The people of Skye, it was thought, could only profit from English example. English practices, 'tending so much to public good and private interest', would cure Gaelic sloth. It was not to be the public good or the sloth which prevailed, however. It was private interest—for the lairds could not maximise the return on their lands by creating agricultural communities.

Education, too, was something of a failure when measured against the great advances in the south. In 1811, J. MacDonald, the author of the *General View of Agriculture*, was appalled at the illiteracy in the Hebrides, for without education, without an awareness of the advantages of being a Briton, the natives were 'liable to the seduction of every artful imposter'.

The lack of schooling traditions, the great size of the

parishes and the difficulty of travel within them, and the Gaelic language barrier, thwarted the attempts of both the parochial schools and the SSPCK to bring 'useful knowledge' to the Highlands and Islands. In addition, it is doubtful whether the intensity of work in the people's lives was compatible with learning.

Theirs was an oral culture, conveying knowledge and tradition by story-telling and song, and religion—in established or revivalist form—by preaching and psalm singing. Parts of the Bible had been translated into Gaelic in the late seventeenth century and a Gaelic edition was published in 1801: but it must have been of limited use on Skye where, in 1824, of the 75 per cent of the families who spoke only Gaelic almost half had no member who could read, and 65 per cent of the population were without bibles anyway. To augment the work of the SSPCK and the parochial system, and to give it some religious spine, the Gaelic societies of Edinburgh, Glasgow and Inverness began moving into the Highlands and Islands after 1811. By 1824, 40 per cent of schools in the region were theirs. The name should not be taken to suggest an interest in the regeneration or preservation of traditional culture—their schools aimed simply at moral reformation, and the destruction of tradition was a primary aim.

For the educated and the Anglophile there appeared in the north-west Highlands and Islands in the first years of the nineteenth century, the *Inverness Courier*. Inverness was the centre of the new gentility in the Highlands and the *Courier* radiated that warm glow which the improved have in an unimproved society. The moral orthodoxy of the age was expressed in praise for the gentlemen of the district, especially if they were ministers or judges; and in warnings of the punishments, such as transportation to Botany Bay, which awaited those who transgressed the code. The court reports were a grim guide to the brutality of the society, and in their language there was more than an echo of Knox and Melville at their most savage. 'After your execution,' Alexander Gillon was told, 'you shall be hung in chains until the fowls of the air pick the flesh off your body, and your bones bleach and whiten in the winds of heaven, thereby to afford a constant warning of the fatal consequences which almost always attend the indulgence of the passions.' Elspeth Hayes was to be 'incarcerated in the tolbooth at Elgin for the space of one year, and to stand in the pillory thereafter with a label upon her breast denoting her to be a Notorious Thief, and at the expiry of her sentence to be banished from Scotland for life'. The tolbooth at Elgin also accommodated women convicted of concealing their pregnancies. Murder for the *Courier* was heinous and executions just and salutary. Other tragedies also had their proper descriptions: suicide was always a melancholy event; accidental death, which was increasingly the result of fire, was invariably an indication of sloth and carelessness, characteristics of the common people that had to be extirpated. The *Courier* might politely suggest that the practice of flogging prostitutes through the streets of Inverness was degrading and 'inefficacious': but such sentiments were not at all at odds with the moral tone of improvement which had become virtually synonymous with the sensibilities of the well-satisfied beneficiaries of the *status quo* in the Highlands.

The *Courier* also reflected the inroads of the empire. Dr Solomon's Abstergent Lotion and Middlewood's Royal Abyssinian Flower Soap were now available for Highland skins. Foreign intelligence came with these exotic products for the edification of Scots Britons. Reports on the progress of improvement in the Highlands were buried under news from the European war fronts. The *Courier* compared Napoleon with Macbeth. There was no better illustration of the new temper of Scottish gentlemen than in the little port on Skye, Portree, after the British victory at Vimiero in 1808: 'Great guns were fired, tables with excellent liquor placed on the terrace by order of Lord MacDonald, and the vessels in the harbour, to the number of nearly sixty, hoisted their flags.'

The *Inverness Courier* brought the empire in and took the Highlanders out into the imperial wonders. It widened the world in Invernessshire. At the same time it encased it in myth. The literate saw the world outside through the *Courier*. For the poor and illiterate, the world remained largely closed; unless, if they had sixpence, they took in Bagshaw's Grand Collection of fantastic animals ('all well secured so that even the most timorous may approach them') which was touring the Highlands around 1810. There in 'Two Commodious Caravans' could be seen (together with some 'most admirable monkies'):

> The OUNCE or HUNTING TIGER a curious animal from Seringapatum, where a number of them were collected and were the only favourites of the Tyrant Tippoo, kept by him for hunting Antelopes. A surprising animal from the woods of Abyssinia, the great YAHOO ORANGOUTANG, or, WILD MAN . . . when full grown near seven feet high; he always walks upright and sits in a chair. This surprising animal for strength and sagacity astonishes every beholder. THE RAVENOUS AND UNTAMEABLE WOLF COTTA-MUNDY, from the River Nile . . . a great enemy to the crocodile and the snakes of Egypt.

There was also a harmless beast, though wisely secured: 'A WONDERFUL KANGAROO from New South Wales which will take most astonishing leaps of from twenty to thirty feet.'

CHAPTER THREE

REMOVING THE RACE

How amiable does the design appear of withdrawing the poor and humble from the miseries incident to their situation, amidst the cold selfishness of an advanced period of society, and transport them to a new country where the same odious distractions do not meet them, but where they will all find themselves equal, in being dependent only on nature and their own exertions for their support and enjoyment.

THE EARL OF SELKIRK, *OBSERVATIONS ON THE PRESENT STATE OF THE HIGHLANDS*, 1805

We do not like emigration; it is to the social what bleeding is to the physical.

FRASER'S MAGAZINE, 1838

Sometime in the last few years of the eighteenth century on the Isle of Skye an 'Advertisement' appeared in which 'several of the Gentlemen farmers . . . having taken into their most serious consideration the dismal circumstances which have lately been imposed upon them by the Exhorbitant Land Rent so as to put it absolutely out of their power with all their Industry and application to live in any Sufferable Ease, or any degree comparable to what their predecessors did', announced their intention to leave. They would raise funds to buy 100,000 acres (40,400 hectares) in North Carolina, and they invited 'artificers of all sorts to go with them'. In 1811 MacLeod of Dunvegan was considering raising an armed party to prevent the planned departure of his tenants. His factor wrote to him that in 'the most ungrateful act that can be conceived' the tacksman in Rhu Dunan was leaving for America by chartered boat and 'all the small tenants' in that parish were intending to leave with him. 'This is a serious matter,' the factor advised, 'and you are to consider what is to be done, whether you are to take steps to prevent this ferment in time, or let it go on, and if it does, there is no saying where it may stop.' But after taking open boats to Tobermory on the island of Mull to the south, the Skye folk sailed to America. They had 'leagued together', the factor said; they had told him that he had been sent 'to distress the oppressed'. He told MacLeod that he sincerely wished that all the laird's 'Enemies would lie committed at the bottom of the sea' and that his family would enjoy good fortune 'as long as the rock stands'. The ingrate who had gone was MacCaskill, a descendant of an ancient and honourable family, the traditional tacksmen of Rhu Dunan. MacCaskill was the defender of MacLeod lands against the seaborne invasions of the MacDonalds of Clanranald. The tacksman had deserted his master, because his master had deserted him.

Emigration was anathema to the lairds. So long as the kelp industry flourished, the tenants of Skye were expected to remain and work hard and gratefully. Emigration outraged the idea of improvement in the Highlands. How could the estates be improved if the people were not there? How could the people be improved? The Highland Society of Scotland, formed in 1784 by 'noblemen and gentlemen of the first rank and character' (who by 1803 numbered just 781), had two planks to its platform: the encouragement of fisheries and manufactures, and the maintenance of a workforce by the prevention of emigration. Emigration offended every notion of commerce and propriety.

But the Highlanders were going. Unwilling if not unable to pay the new rents, resentful of deceitful lairds and imported factors and increasingly aware that America offered the opportunity to regain the independence which went with the possession of land, tacksmen led their tenants across the Atlantic in droves. The Highlanders became convinced that it would be easier to maintain their way of life in America than it was in the locations and occupations their lairds had found for them in Scotland.

About 20,000 Highlanders arrived in America between 1763 and 1775. After the War of Independence, loyalist Scots moved north from the United States to establish settlements in Canada. Thousands of Highlanders were attracted to it. By the turn of the century, North Carolina and large parts of north-west Canada had become outposts of Highland and Island civilisation, albeit with some extraordinary modifications.[1] It seemed by the end of the eighteenth century that there was no-one in the Highlands who did not have kin in America—and therefore, through correspondence, an impression of the place.

Highland culture was inevitably modified by the transplantation. In a new environment old habits of mind attached to new objects. The process had been obvious for some time among the Highlanders in their relations with Britain. They had become 'habitually attached' to the British monarch. Their attitude puzzled the American republicans: it was 'one of the most singular things in history', that the people of Scotland at home and in the New World should have been so loyal to George III, and

1 It was said that the black servants of Highland settlers in the American colonies frequently acquired the Gaelic, and on hearing them speak it for the first time, new arrivals were prone to exclaim, 'A Dhia! Are we all going to turn black like that?'

so hostile to the Americans who had 'in no wise ever harmed them or crossed their path'.

There *was* something 'singular' about their behaviour in the war: about the Royal Highland Emigrant Regiment, for instance, which, having fought the French in Quebec, proceeded south to do battle with the 'unnatural rebellion' of the Americans. Just as there was something 'singular' about the Highland regiments in Europe and the empire for the next hundred years. Countless people on every continent in the nineteenth century died at the end of Scottish guns. Sometimes the Highland soldiers were motivated in the colonies by a desire to protect privilege already acquired, sometimes by offers of grants of land in return for their military support. Often it seemed as if they believed that while recent history had been against them it was manifestly on the side of the British. There was a psychological component as well: what appeared in battle as unqualified loyalty to Britain was at the same time a demonstration of the Highlanders' superiority, and it kept alive—in bastardised form—the spirit of the clans.

On Skye in the late eighteenth century enlistment in Britain's wars was a way of life, and one much encouraged by the lairds. To demonstrate his loyalty to London, MacDonald raised the Regiment of the Isles in 1799. It was estimated that from the beginning of the American war to the end of the Napoleonic wars Skye produced 10,000 foot soldiers, 600 commissioned officers under the rank of colonel and about 70 above it. For the men of Skye the decision to enlist was for the most part no more than to prefer a relatively well-paid risk in uniform to civil impoverishment. Some changed their minds: the Inverness papers regularly carried notices calling for the apprehension of deserters.

Until the end of the Napoleonic wars the army was a

brake on overcrowding and poverty in the Highlands, and probably a significant stimulus to the Highland economy. Yet by encouraging enlistment in Britain's cause the lairds encouraged the emigration they so desperately wanted to curtail. Thousands stayed in North America where the British army had taken them. Nova Scotia, Cape Breton and Prince Edward Island became Gaelic speaking communities.

In the maritime provinces of Canada the Highlanders adapted to the sea, the bleak climate and the wild country to a degree which was probably beyond what might have been expected of urban or agricultural Lowlanders. Deprived of the land on which their livelihood and culture had depended in the Old World, they placed an almost fanatical value on it in the New. They were not particularly good farmers, partly because they knew little of agricultural techniques, but also because of the mentality which Joseph Howe noticed among his Nova Scotian neighbours in 1830—'the extravagant desire they cherish to purchase large quantities of land'. 'They will toil night and day,' he said, 'spend as little as possible, and live upon the commonest fare until a sum of money is saved, either sufficient to buy an adjoining tract, or to pay the fees required to get a grant from the crown.' Land continued to be associated with rank and influence and independence: it lay at the root of this transplanted culture as it had in the Highlands and Islands before the clearances.

Because they settled as almost intact communities sharing common traditions and experience, and relatively immune to the inroads of the English language, Gaelic culture survived in the north-west of Canada to an extent unmatched anywhere else in the New World. The ceilidh was transplanted, traditional songs and stories, habits of work, drinking and religion, and the Gaelic language were sustained well into the twentieth century. Their sensitivities and deep rooted prejudices, their intense pride and craggy individualism, their propensity for intemperate drinking and violence, thrift and industry, and their devotion to the Church, all survived in the new community. And so did the memory of the emigration.

So long as it suited them the lairds and the improvers made much of the natives' attachment to their homeland. When, in 1803, Thomas Douglas, Fifth Earl of Selkirk, was driven by his distaste for British capitalism and its destruction of Gaelic culture to settle 800 Skye folk on Prince Edward Island, the improvers objected vigorously. Who was going to drain the marshes at home, 'inclose fields, remove stones and other obstructions'? asked MacLeod's friend, Robert Brown. Who was going to combine with capital? Who was going to gather the kelp? In 1811 MacLeod offered to raise another regiment on Skye. It was partly to prove his patriotism, but presumably also to help contain his tenants who were so flagrantly breaking their filial bonds by threatening to leave.

Underneath the cant of British capitalism there lay the reality of emigration and the broken spiritual bonds. A settler in Cape Breton, John MacDonald of Lochaber, put it simply: 'Coming for the first time to stay in this place has blinded my eyes with tears . . . I left my country. I left my heritage. My spirits remained behind . . . The cause of my brooding is that I wasn't allowed to stay there forever.' A number of commentators saw the emigration as an act of spiritual suicide brought on by the British invasion and the clearances. Writing in 1774, 'A Highlander' said it was as if the Highlands and Islands were possessed by a 'fatal spirit' which would, if it were not checked, depopulate the entire region. It seemed to him that the people had a collective death wish. In England, William Cobbett was of the same mind about emigration after he had spent a year in America. Leaving one's country was 'violently hostile to all our notions of fidelity', he wrote in 1819. 'To quit at once, and forever, all the associations arising from objects familiar to us from our infancy, is very much like quitting the world,' he said.

Those views could only hold, however, while life was possible in one's birthplace. By 1829 Cobbett was convinced that the life of the English labouring classes had sunk to such appalling depths they all should leave, and he wrote guides to emigration to help them quit the Old World. In the Highlands in the same decade life also became very much worse. Soldiers flooded back to their own communities or the Lowlands to find no work in either place. In the Lowlands the Irish were forcing the Highlanders out of the labour market. In the Highlands the road, harbour and canal building projects were completed, and with the abolition of the tax on Spanish barilla the kelp industry failed. The lairds began to realise that their tenants were of no use to them: worse, they were a burden.

And so when she visited Skye in 1840 Catherine Sinclair discovered that 'every family' on the island had someone in or going to Australia. She was probably right. The three great proprietors of Skye had made a common effort to rid their estates of surplus population. Whereas the MacLeod of 1811 had forcibly restrained his tenants from leaving, the MacLeod of 1840 had for some years been encouraging his tenants to go.

Cobbett had said only America was worth a thought to the intending emigrant. America was free and independent. As Cobbett remarked, it grew green 'pease': Canada imported green pease. New South Wales he said was even worse than Canada. There the number of official executions was only exceeded by those which bushrangers, one's servants, and 'murdering natives' committed. It was too far away to readily return when one discovered one's mistake. Indeed, said William Cobbett, 'if any man, not actually tired of his life, can prefer emigrating to a country like this to emigrating to the United States, he is wholly unworthy of my attention.' In the *Edinburgh Review* he was echoed by Sydney Smith, who declared New South Wales a sink of wickedness, and compared it to a marsh which, until it was drained, was not fit for habitation.

Despite this New South Wales had become the focus of emigration from the Highlands in the 1830s. There were new opportunities there for unpropertied people—for common labourers and 'artisans of very ordinary quality', as an 1831 Colonial Office advertisement said. In Australia, Highlanders were told, they could earn twice the wages they earnt in Britain, and buy beef and mutton at a penny a pound—beef and mutton had become almost unheard of in the crofters' diet. America remained a much shorter and a cheaper journey, but now a bounty was offered to emigrants to Australia—£12 to be paid to the ship's master for each emigrant landed safely on Australian shores. On Skye, the proprietors and the gentlemen co-operated with the emigration agents. The Reverend MacKinnon of Strathaird sent out three of his sons by way of example. Other gentlemen did the same. In their wake a series of emigrant ships bearing poor tenants sailed between 1837 and 1839.

Now in the southern journals emigration was described as an unpleasant but necessary bleeding of the social body. Harriet Beecher Stowe spoke for those who had convinced themselves it was all part of a great movement, the necessary consequence of civilisation's march. Everywhere the proponents of emigration echoed the words of the Earl of Selkirk, the man they had once reviled.

Emigration was suddenly a *desideratum* designed and blessed by Providence. If only the people could see it. At Borve on Harris Lord Dunmore offered his old tenants new plots at home, and the young free passages to Canada; but they would not go. The factor claimed they had been killing and maiming sheep. Reluctantly the laird brought in a military force and they were cleared.

Not all Highlanders were convinced that the clearances were tantamount to expatriation. Even in the crofting communities the cultural attachments were deep. Too many of them were hindered by 'the *amor patriae* so strongly implanted in the breast of every Highlander', the Reverend MacKinnon reported in the *Statistical Account* of 1845.

The answer for Highlanders paralysed by the love of their country was to have them take it with them. The 1837 immigrants were blessed on their arrival by the Reverend Archibald MacGilvray: 'May [you] perpetuate the language and the customs of [your] fathers and the same poetic feelings which inspired them in the hills and vales of Caledonia . . . still, beneath Australian skies, be couched in the same nervous language and poetic imagery.' And the peripatetic Presbyterian from New South Wales, the Reverend John Dunmore Lang, had visions of tens of thousands of destitute Highlanders making 'the hills and vales of Australia resound with the wild note of the pibroch and the language of the ancient Gael'.

For the Highland gentlemen promoting emigration as an answer to destitution, the idea of a transplanted kingdom of the Celt became a theme. 'Shall we not, like Rachel, weep for our children when they are not?' Certainly, but, 'In a little while the unchristened streams of the distant land, the unfamiliar hills of the other shores, will bear their names and return their melodies.' These settlers were seeds of Gaeldom, they would grow as the Highlands withered: '*We* shall look in vain for the men we loved, but they will be at rest in the abundance of a new world, in the dayspring of new fortunes to the Celtic race.' Emigration was the death *and* the resurrection: Australia was the promised land—Heaven—a place where Gaels could go to rest. There were visions of patriarchs overseeing shepherds and shepherds overseeing flocks.

The idea of heaven was undoubtedly as strong in the minds of the emigrants as the idea of Gaeldom. Those who travelled on the *Midlothian* from Snizort in 1837 were told by the minister attending them, the Reverend William MacIntyre, that they were going forth to extend, not the domain and the customs of the Celt, but the kingdom of Zion. And at Sydney, before they set forth for the hills and vales of the Clarence and Manning rivers in northern New South Wales they were told that they went there to raise the altar of God as Providence had decreed. It was probably the first church service held in Gaelic south of the equator, and it was 'indescribably affecting', the *Sydney Gazette* said.

It was thus rather suddenly that emigration became providential for the Highlanders. Of course they might have anticipated Providence, rather than waiting for the blessing to descend; like William Matheson and Roderick MacDonald of Harris, who found their way to Australia via the Inverness court in 1842 for stealing nine and four sheep respectively. But most trusted to Providence and, within a decade, Providence had revealed itself so manifestly that virtually everyone in Britain from Lord Rothschild to the lowliest scallag on Skye was convinced that emigration was providential. Even the squatters in distant Australia were convinced.

In 1840 MacLeod surveyed his tenants. He found them as pitiful as the rents they were returning him. He found that some were 'required', and some were 'useful', but most were 'incumbrances' of one kind or another. Anne MacLeod and Widow MacLeod were 'two poor people, unfit for anything'. A more complex though by no means uncommon case, with his family of nine, Neil Campbell was 'an useful man being a carpenter and boat-builder, yet . . . an incumbrance having paid but £5 for 20 years, and that pittance only by work; is fit subject for emigration'. Like those of his tenants, MacLeod's motives were mixed. He expressed pity for a 'wretched object, scrofulous, bedridden and miserably poor'; and pragmatic concern for his financial interests, whether in the instance of the worthy but useless Neil Campbell, or in that of the irredeemable Christy Cameron, 'a half-witted body of no use'. Among the 'sickly', the 'pitiable' and the 'embiciles' [*sic*], there lived people of excellent character, industry and physical strength, but only a few were of use to him. The chief of the clan had become the Protector of a mission, for as he said: 'As for the other People I have no use, nor can I get any remunerating employment for them, and though I have marked the greater number as having "no lands", yet to keep them from starvation I am obliged to give a quantity of land to each family.' That land was for potatoes which, by 1840, constituted between three-quarters and seven-eighths of the diet of the Highlanders and Islanders.

In 1846 the food failed. MacLeod addressed his people:

> Your usual food has failed, and reduced you to buyers in markets where you were wont to sell . . . The awful possibility of starvation has approached too nearly to be disregarded; yet we must not despair, nor permit ourselves to think no remedy at hand. God, for his own reasons, perhaps to punish, possibly forseeing that from evil good may come, has visited us with an affliction, which, while we should bear with resignation and stout hearts [*sic*]. Every man is subject to the law of mortality and must 'earn his bread by the sweat of his brow'.

No fragment from the Bible was used so constantly as this in the debate over the famine. In the language of improvement it was a stock phrase. But MacLeod was almost certainly moved by another injunction–'Dwell in the land and verily thou shalt be fed.' And so long as he retained a notion of his patriarchal duty he was conscious that if he provided 'not for his own, and especially not for his own house, he hath denied the faith, and is worse than an infidel'.

MacLeod swore that he would spare no exertions to relieve the distress of his people, 'not by gratis relief to the strong and healthy, but by affording employment, and enabling every person to feed his family by his own independent labour'. The government was doing everything in its power. The people must pull together. Soon the fields would 'smile again in abundance'. MacLeod was going to make his country work again!

A year or so later MacLeod's sister, Emily, wrote that the people on the estates, 'from being the most contented . . . on earth . . . are rapidly becoming a set of rebellious discontented Chartists', who only needed a leader to 'do desperate acts'. The people were indeed desperate. The patch of potato ground MacLeod granted them in return for rent they could not pay refused to yield an adequate supply of potatoes. The basis of their precarious nineteenth-century economy had been removed. As an 1850 inquiry found, 'in proportion as the potato had entered into the subsistence of the people were they prostrated by the calamity'. Now their fragile existence fell to pieces. The 'divers almost useless tasks' they had been employed in, 'under pretence of learning them to be better workers', were now useless. They had generally been done in lieu of rent: they brought in no food, and increasingly the people grew too weak to perform them anyway. For years the people had supplemented their diet with shellfish gathered from the Atlantic beaches. Without 'farinaceous food' the task became too arduous. Many men no longer sought seasonal work in Inverness or Glasgow because they feared their families would starve before money was returned; many who did seek it died in urban hovels of the fever and smallpox. The Reverends MacPherson and MacKinnon now found whole families prostrate from hunger in their houses. MacLeod himself found only 16 people 'comfortable' on one of his farms, the other 114 being between 'needy' and 'starving'. And the food supply diminished to the extent that the people were unable to relieve one another. 'Our people get more merciless and hard taking hold for himself and not caring for his fellow creatures,' a minister told MacLeod.

MacLeod despaired. They would not eat what he put in front of them—Indian corn. He did not know why, but they were most violently prejudiced against everything but oatmeal. He was providing all the meal but he was receiving no rent. His people had lost not only self-respect but 'even a sense of gratitude for past favours'. Forty men had come to him and said that if he did not give them meal then he should give them coffins; 'Yet these very people I have supported these last two months and they owe me an average of five pounds each . . . the whole burden being thrown on me I cannot stand it.'

MacLeod was more generous than many of the Highland proprietors—though, as a local minister told him, his acts were not so charitable as just, given that the soil had been taken from the tenants. Like his fellow lairds, MacLeod had laid the basis of a charitable economy when he gave the land over to sheep and moved the people to the shoreline. He had removed their independent livelihood, and now found himself obliged to feed them.

Relief was coming. In London, Edinburgh and Glasgow the consciences of the Church, and of bankers and merchants were kindled. The British Relief Association, which enjoyed the patronage of Baron Lionel de Rothschild, among others, raised substantial funds and despatched people to relieve the plight of both Ireland and the Highlands. In Edinburgh and Glasgow committees for the relief of destitution in the Highlands and Islands were established.

The abiding concern was the *danger* of charity. In the first year of relief, 1847, aid was given only to those who had entirely exhausted their resources. As the Edinburgh Committee reported:

> In a state of society where the people are habitually accustomed to the lowest scale of subsistence, and to whom the comforts and the habits of patient continuous labour of the ordinary labouring class are equally unknown, the result of this system of relief must palpably be, that all classes would prefer a bare subsistence earned with so little exertion, to the higher wages of remunerative employment.

So the committee increased the amount of work exacted in return for relief: a 10½-hour day from an able-bodied man earned him about three kilograms of meal, and a sliding scale determined the amount of work required of the less able. Where relief was given to a family, attendance at school for the young children was compulsory.

For a nation in which *laissez-faire* was an article of faith the famine in the Highlands, not to mention Ireland, could not have come at a more inconvenient time. The Assistant-Secretary of the Treasury, Sir Charles Treveylan, was the man charged with solving the problem without offending the principle. To the Highlands and Islands he sent the same official he had sent to Ireland, Sir Edward Pine Coffin. In spite of his discouraging name, Sir Edward did his best to get the mills grinding and the meal distributed, even to the point of blasphemously suggesting that the government should consider regulating prices. Treveylan was not impressed.

Like price control, unearned relief was nearly unthinkable. It sent a shudder through the bones of British benefactors: 'omnipotent for evil it is almost impotent for good', said the Episcopalian bishop of Argyllshire. Captain E. Gardiner Fishbourne, the Resident Inspector for the Relief Committee on Skye, was convinced that charitable aid was hiding the people not only from the stiffening lessons of the market place, but from 'the hand of the Allwise Disposer'; and, consequently, from the lesson in prudence that the famine—the chastisement—contained. For the likes of the Resident Inspector the famine should have been an agent of improvement teaching the benefits of industry and thrift. At all costs famine relief should do no more than keep the people grateful to their masters and fearful of God.

The poor of Skye—and in 1849 one-third of the population was on relief—neither improved nor rebelled. There were expressions of anger and some observers spoke fearfully of a revolution, but the Skye folk seemed more inclined to stoic endurance than any contemplation of reprisals. For this response there can be no doubt that both the Free and the Established churches were largely responsible. The Church was active enough in the administration of relief, and no-one expressed more sympathy for the plight of the destitute than the local ministers of Skye. No-one was more able to. But the Church contributed to the passivity of the people in fundamental ways. For the Established Church the famine was, as the lairds themselves were prone to suggesting, a manifestation of God's unknowable will. For adherents of the Free Church the famine was a visitation brought on largely by the lairds and a corrupt and acquiescent Kirk. However, there was, as well, always a suggestion that the people were paying for their own sins. This was how Norman Ferguson, who appears to have been a layman of the Free Church on Skye, interpreted the famine when he wrote to Lady MacLeod. The people of Skye were under a severe judgement he told her, 'wickedness abounding and poverty which tells us that the same Lord who chastised Israel of old ["III and IV chapter of Isaiah", he reminded her] will not soon raise his hand of our Nation'.

The benefactors despaired at the helplessness of their charges and grew angry at their indolence. 'If only they could be taught to help themselves,' Miss MacLeod was told, 'that would be the best help we could give them.' In the minds of such people the poor became 'children', and 'creatures'—'poor creatures'. They were in need equally of comforting and admonishing. 'I exhausted myself in a strong scolding and was restored again by perhaps improperly giving them 3/- to reach the Road,' a Rossshire farmer told an agent of the relief committee after a group of Skyemen descended on his farm seeking work.

The continuation of the famine, despite carefully considered attempts at relieving it, produced new theories of its cause. The *Quarterly Review* joined a southern throng who declared that alcohol was the problem. A distiller at Carbost replied that he had never seen a more sober people, but the *Review* was convinced that the relief had led to 'a diminishing frugality as shewn by the increased consumption of alcohol . . .' They did not explain how the destitute might be more frugal with a bowl of gruel and a handful of shellfish a day, or how they might increase their exertions on such a diet—if the numbers seen wandering the mainland or living wretchedly in the cities of the Lowlands were not evidence of their exertion. The *Quarterly Review* insisted: the people of Skye were better known for their 'relaxful exertions' than for productive ones.

The creed which claimed that the Highlanders and Islanders were irredeemably indolent and genetically incapable of helping themselves grew fast in the south. It was fed on the one hand by a problem which would not go away, and on the other by a new fashion for theories of race.

In the *Dublin University Magazine* of 1840 the view was expressed that the Irish who had been driven from Ulster to Mayo, Leitrim and Sligo had been so brutalised by their exposure to 'hunger and ignorance', that they were now 'remarkable for their open projecting mouths, with prominent teeth and exposed gums, their advancing cheek bones, and depressed noses, bearing barbarism on their very front'. The proto-Darwinist view perhaps did not run to these lengths with the Highlanders and Islanders, but as their society sank deeper into the slough the Walter Scott portrait of the wild but essentially noble race was transformed into one much closer to the English view of the Irish. The *Westminster Review* in 1841 acknowledged the ennobling presence of the Norse in the history of the Highlands and Islands 'but the greater and predominant portion was a band of Irish, whose fate has been singularly uniform with that of the parent stock, and has produced like fruits'. The Highlanders and Islanders were now characterised by 'a soddened and inveterate indolence and a listless imperviousness to improvement'. The opinion of the *Westminster Review* is worth quoting at length:

> Their attachment to the spot of their birth is a mere barbarous love of inaction. All who know their habits must have remarked that they are singularly blind to the effect of fine scenery. When they *are* prevailed on to move, they will at

> once, and without compunction, abandon their wild hill sides, where, with all their wretchedness, they breathe the healthy air of heaven, and huddle together in the filthiest districts of the large towns, where they quickly assume the worst characteristics of a population among whom misery, disease and crime, seem struggling for pre-eminence. If we find no solution for all this in political events, there is but one method of accounting for it, and that is by presuming a generic difference in inherent physical and moral qualifications, which will keep the Celtic race always behind the Saxon.

Thus were the Celts undeserving of the Highlands and Islands, much less of their relief.

These sentiments soon found their way into the popular press, and presumably into the popular imagination in the south. By 1860 scientists and laymen alike had placed the Celts towards the nether end of the scale of civilisation, although superior to Hottentots, Aborigines and Papuans. 'The earliest Celtic and Germanic skulls,' R. G. Latham said in his *Ethnological Aphorisms*, 'all unite in exhibiting a prominent supraciliary development, and a flattening of the frontal bones, so as to form a low type of cranial conformation, exhibiting somewhat an approximation to the negro races.' By contrast, early Saxon skulls he had observed were 'fully equal in point of grade of development to the Greek or Caucasian skulls idealized by Blumenach as the summit of everything which could be predicated of virtue, intelligence and beauty'. The Reverend Dr Anderson of St Andrews, who believed that the earth was 7,300 years old, qualified the 'accustomed' regard of the Celts as 'low' only by the observation that the very earliest of them were much 'lower', and that even these barbarians were not 'unendowed with unperishing souls like ourselves'. By the 1880s even the Duke of a Highland shire was convinced that the isolation of the Celts had assured their demise by 'Teutonic blood and Teutonic institutions'. It was a 'triumph of clear and definite ideas over men in whom all ideas were as yet indefinite and obscure'.

The Highlanders and Islanders thus bore the brunt not only of cultural and physical deprivation, which was in the main the result of the English colonisation of their lands, but inevitably also of an English imperial ideology which cast them as a race, if not at the bottom of humankind, then certainly as an archaic excrescence in British civilisation. The absurdity of the racial analysis must have been plain at least to the lairds and gentlemen in Scotland, supposedly the epitome of Celtic stock (or were they Norse?), whose cranial conformations seemed to have had no bearing on their station in British or colonial society. But the Highland poor now enjoyed not even the status of an English textile worker or miner; but rather that of other subjects of British colonial expansion, from the Irish to the Australian Aborigines. The Irish, of course, were considered to have been rendered so much worse by centuries behind the 'shutters of the papacy', though opinion in London was scarcely more favourable to the excessively pious reformed church in Scotland.[2]

The Highlanders and Islanders were dying, but not dying out—at least not at a satisfactory rate. They were no longer of use in industry, they would not improve. Charity was no solution. They were a burden and blight.

Robert Somers, who toured the Highlands and Islands during the famine, was one who believed the attempts at

2 With astounding historical myopia the *Quarterly Review* could write in 1851 that the triumph of Calvinism in the north derived from the character of the Highlanders themselves. 'Want of sun and want of animal spirits go naturally together and it is not unnatural . . . that the man of dull spirits should think the lively something less than frivolous.' Just 80 years earlier Johnson had attributed to the Highland climate and landscape the Highlanders' 'red-bloodedness'.

improvement had been largely disingenuous, and the famine itself an inevitable result of the cynical policies followed by the lairds and their advisers. Somers had no doubt that 'The croft system was . . . a temporary expedient to facilitate the clearances, and to afford a refuge to the outcasts till an opportunity should arise of transporting them to their allotted homes in Australian and Canadian wildernesses. From that day to this the idea of emigration has never been relinquished by the Highland lairds.'

Sir Charles Treveylan was told of lairds who year by year had been '. . . withdrawing land from the occupation of the people, and from tillage, and adding to the number of those who have not a legitimate dependence upon it, thus increasing the disproportion which exists between the amount of food produced and the amount of the population, and at the same time encouraging the dependence of the latter upon the potato, as a means of subsistence, until they can be got rid of by emigration or otherwise.'

Not all lairds were quite so cynical. Some combined munificence with wisdom and endeavoured 'to adapt the condition of the people to their altered circumstances'. These people, Treveylan's adviser believed, were 'the hope of the Highlands', but the famine years somehow blurred the distinctions between the lairds. On Skye, MacLeod, in many ways an example of the munificent category of proprietors, was soon appealing for help to remove his tenants with as much rigour as Lord MacDonald had employed; and Robert Somers had pilloried MacDonald for his cynical self-interest.

In 1853, Karl Marx reported that the figures of the Colonial Land Emigration Office showed that nearly four-fifths of emigration in the preceding six years had been 'Celts' from Ireland and the Highlands and Islands of Scotland—people whom both Marx and his foe, Ricardo, believed were of 'classes and races too weak to master the new conditions of life' and who must inevitably give way. Marx was of no more comfort to a Celt—or to a philanthropist—than the spokesmen for *laissez-faire*. It was clear to Marx that capitalism's internal laws spelt the end for the Celts. 'Society,' he said, 'is undergoing a silent revolution which must be submitted to, and which takes no more notice of the human existence it breaks down than an earthquake regards a house it subverts.' No other Victorian could have put it more boldly.

But Marx at least understood that assisted and forced emigration was a consequence of private economic interest, and of the doctrine that national wealth was measured not by the living standard of the majority but by rents and profits. The notion of peaceful industrious villages peopled by fat and happy Highlanders, every one a horticulturist, was at best an amiable self-indulgence. In the end it did not matter who produced the wealth, or how many people it took, so long as the wealth was produced. To use Marx's words, it was 'the increase of productive power which demands a diminution of population, and drives away the surplus by famine or emigration'.

Comfort, however, could be found if one could substitute for the realities of capitalism a blissful reconciliation of charitable Christianity and self-interest. The Highland Emigration Society, which desired 'to make Hope, and not Fear', the mainspring of Skye emigration, was capable of this logical procedure: 'Instead of living on our alms, they will give valuable equivalents to our manufactures; and, above all, they will exchange a life of demoralizing dependence for one which will abound with the rewards of industry and enterprise.'

The idea of emigration which had emerged among improvers in the 1830s was reborn in the famine with the mark of Providence even more dramatically upon it. It was plainly Providence because it could be shown to solve more than one problem at a time. Emigration was both the surgeon's knife and the improver's spade, a combination of roles no mortal could fill. Emigration would turn the wilderness of Australia 'into smiling acres of industrious happy men', while enriching Britain and removing 'the canker from its core'. Emigration left society 'twice blessed', the *Quarterly Review* said: 'It blesses those whom it directly relieves, and it blesses, by its consequential effect, those whom it leaves behind.' When gold was discovered in Australia in 1851 and the woolgrowers were left without a labour force, the design seemed all the more marvellous—so wise was the Almighty that he had created a new calamity in order to alleviate an old one. It was plain for any English woollen manufacturer to see.

The problem was to get the paupers of Skye to believe it. In some areas it was reported that they were delighted at the prospect, perhaps because Lord MacDonald's intention was plainer than MacLeod's. The MacLeod country people, Miss MacLeod was told, 'have some idea of injustice connected with Emigration, as if it were a plan to deprive them of some rights that poor people they cannot define'. MacLeod had possibly made the mistake of allowing the people on his estates to harbour the idea of residual rights for too long.

But it seems to have partly been their perception of Australia which made the people of MacLeod country so reluctant to go. 'No remonstrance will prevail,' Norman Ferguson said in a letter in which he wrote of 'what appears to be the end of matters in Skye'. Reports from New South Wales had drifted back from the boatloads of 1837 and they 'did not at all give a favourable account of the place, they gave an alarming account of their position among the

Natives, and the mixed people of all Nations . . .' Wives and servants had been stolen. The place was 'unruly' and the 'convicts etc . . . desperately wicked'. It was the same in the parish of Bracadale where the starving cottars had heard that the natives of Australia took people away and they were 'never heard of or seen again'.

If they had been told of some of the letters in the *Inverness Courier* their fears would have multiplied. An 'intelligent and well-educated young man' from the shire wrote that after a few months in New South Wales his life was a misery. Heat, flies, ants, mosquitoes which brought him out in boils; fleas, bugs, centipedes, tarantulas, great red and black ants (it was not safe to sit upon the grass), snakes, particularly the deaf adder ('a child was bitten a few weeks since, it died in horrid convulsions, and was a mass of putrefaction a few minutes afterwards'), stinking maggot-ridden cemeteries, 'the worst colds and coughs' he could remember, sea breezes which dropped the temperature from 39° C to 7° C in under an hour, an absence of any trees 'deserving the name', and his inability to find steady employment should have been enough to drive him barmy or back to the Highlands. But California was worse—there, the only people making money were digging graves—so he said he would stay put and signed himself 'Australian'.

These sorts of reports must have become enlarged in the imaginations of the illiterate cottars of Skye. 'I sleep every night with a pair of pistols under my pillow, my father's big sword hung up by the bed head, and also an American bowie-knife under my pillow,' wrote another emigrant.

In some places people were removed to the ships by force. The outer isles of Barra and Uist had suffered terribly in the famine, a Free Church minister recalling that many of his flock were afraid 'when going to rest at night that they would faint to death before morning'. But they resisted the attempts of the new proprietor, Colonel Gordon, to remove them. Modern memory on Barra and Uist recalls Gordon's party of police chasing Islanders over the hills, manacling them and loading them onto ships harboured in Lochboisdale. In his *History of the Highland Clearances*, Alexander MacKenzie asked if the Highlands and Islands were to be 'converted into a hunting desert, and the aborigines banished and murdered', and delivered a thunderous jeremiad against the new rulers:

> You Christian rulers, Christian electors and representatives, permit not Christianity to blush and hide her face with shame before heathenism and idolatry any longer. I speak with reverence when I say, permit not Mahomet Ali to deride our Saviour with the conduct of His followers—allow not demons to exclaim in the face of heaven, 'What can you expect of us, when Christians, thy chosen people, are guilty of such deeds of inhumanity to their own species?'

But there were not many then who believed the process could be reversed or even that forcing them to go was not a Christian act.

To smooth the passage religion served better than anything else. In 1852 the Reverend Dr MacLeod of Glasgow, who had long promoted the emigration idea, addressed the passengers on the *Georgiana* in Gaelic. It 'was not possible to describe the effect of his speech', a Glasgow paper reported. MacLeod told the passengers that they were obeying a familiar command to 'go thee to the promised land'. Their migration was predestined.

But the parting was no less tearful for that. Gaelic psalms and the Shorter Catechism distributed, their mission explained, and their souls fired, 'the 23 Psalm was sung amidst much sobbing, and under very deep impressions. There was not one dry eye to be seen; even those who did not understand the language evinced the greatest sympathy.' It was a cold heart, said the *Glasgow Constitutionalist*, which did not wish that 'God may be pleased to bring them in safety to their place of destination and prosper them in their undertaking'.

Women in particular suffered severe privations on the voyage. They rarely spoke English, which compounded their problems. Cobbett, who seems to have always found it hard to take British women seriously, was nevertheless right to say that their modesty made them particularly poor sailors. It all too frequently restrained them from 'relieving themselves by going to the usual place for the purpose, which place is, and must be upon the deck, and within sight of all . . .' The consequences he believed were very serious and sometimes fatal. That sort of modesty was deeply ingrained in the Calvinist women of the Highlands and Islands and made the trip more uncomfortable and dangerous in a number of ways. When a doctor visited a ship anchored at the Cape in 1837 and saw among the Highlanders on board a scene of unparalleled 'squalor, discomfort and wretchedness', he noted that the women suffered and even died in silence rather than discuss their symptoms through a male interpreter. He recommended female interpreters, among other suggestions which included a piper and a fiddler on every ship for both entertainment and health. If these imaginative suggestions were difficult to fulfil, Sir Charles Treveylan was advised of more pedestrian advances. The 'Lowland accomplishments of knife, fork and spoon' might be taught on the trip, and the passengers might be initiated into 'the mysteries of combs and brushes'.

There were other ways of making life a little easier on

a voyage which always threatened annihilation and often delivered it. Gaelic bibles and psalm books and Gaelic speaking ministers as catechists were provided to replenish the faith, give comfort and see that idle sin did not bring on a fatal storm or a personal tragedy, such as the one which struck John MacKinnon: 'Oh . . . throwing out my two boys into the deep sea it will never go out of my heart.' They were two out of 53 children who died on that voyage. Others were better fated and passengers wrote home simply wonderstruck by their experience. Alexander Cameron, a fiddler to MacCaskill, wrote of his voyage on the *Georgiana* in 1852:

> If I was near you, I would tell you many a thing I had seen coming, but it was the flying fish the greatest wonder that I saw, they was so numerous about the ship for 4 or 5 weeks, they would jump up about the ship, they would fly 200 or 300 yards before they would hold, they are about the size of a big herring the smallest of them—3 or 4 of them jump on board although the ship was very high—I see shirks near the Cape, but we don't call at the Cape.

Donald Cameron wrote that although his wife and children were 'delicate all the way', he was only 'spewing about three hours', and all were 'spared till this day'.

The emigrants who survived the voyage—the men at least—often felt that they had in fact been blessed. Alexander Cameron took a job near Geelong with a Scottish settler who had the unthinkable number of 18,000 sheep. Although he heard that his employer was one of the richest men in the colony, and a magistrate, 'although he hath that, he don't think so much of himself as —— does, nor any other of his kind in Sky [*sic*]'. Australian egalitarianism took hold very quickly. But Cameron wrote as if still in a dream. 'I cannot hold hear [*sic*] the half of what I wish to tell.' He *could* tell that he seldom saw in Skye any mutton 'so good as the worthest we get here', and although 'Mary and Anne Matheson is afraid of them', he hadn't seen any of the natives. He was happy: 'Many a night I will be minding old lang sighn, play the fiddle in such a private place, none to hear but the fowls of the wood. I remain yours truly till death, Alex Cameron, your old Fiddler.'

It was the same with Donald Cameron who lamented only the lack of 'gaelic characters'. And John MacKinnon, who had suffered such a tragedy en route, wrote that he had already cleared £20 sterling after paying for his 'room and firebox' in Collingwood. He urged his countrymen in Roag on Skye to join him. They had the impression they 'would be in danger . . . day and night, but it is not true. I saw some of the *natives* going bare naked but they will hurt no person and the people here are as kind and free as ever I saw.' There was only one regret: 'There is no peats here.'

It may have been a combination of this good fortune together with the zealous attention to their souls on the voyage which produced a galling problem for their benefactors. The Reverend Henry MacKenzie hoped that ministers and catechists on board might transfer 'with the colonists the elements of the highest civilization, faith in the revelation of Christ, and the principle of mutual goodwill'. But Sir Charles Treveylan had written with more than a trace of irritation to Miss MacLeod that while they were 'profuse in their expressions of gratitude to God he wanted to see some proof of the reality of this feeling by the performance of the most ordinary duties to man'. The emigrants were paying their debts to God and not to those who put up the money for their fares.

When the pastoral workforce of Australia departed for the gold fields, Australian woolgrowers discovered undreamt of qualities of industry among the Aborigines. The buyers of Australian wool similarly discovered that the Highlanders' ancestral characteristics could be turned to account. Mr Bonamy Price, an English woollen manufacturer, now thought that the Highlanders were 'peculiarly fitted for supplying the wants of Australia'.

> Their virtues and their failings alike qualify them for the task. They are familiar with the care of sheep. The great strength of the bonds of the family and race disposes them, as their brother Celts of Ireland, to emigrate in masses, whilst their indolent temper, and their aversion to long sustained labour, would make the pastoral life of Australia precisely suited to their taste, and render them comparatively insensible to the temptations of an exciting but toilsome search for gold.

So, while Alexander Cameron counted his blessings under a tree in the Australian bush, Mr Price counted his in Yorkshire; and he wondered if 'a religious mind' might not 'discern in it the benevolent action of Divine Providence'.

CHAPTER FOUR

HIGHLANDERS AT LARGE — THE KURNAI AT HOME

The most stirring sight which the sportsman can witness is the first view of a new pastoral district; and to the lover of the picturesque perhaps this is the most beautiful scene that Australia can afford . . . Plains and open forest, untrodden by the foot of the white man, and, as far as the eye can reach, covered with grass so luxuriant that it brushes the horseman in his saddle: flocks of kangaroos quietly grazing as yet untaught to fear the enemy that is invading; the emu playfully crossing and recrossing his route; the quail rising at every step, lagoons literally swarming with wildfowl. Then mark the change that follows upon discovery. Intelligence of the new country reaches the settled districts and countless flocks and herds are poured into the land of promise. To some the regions bring wealth, while Anglo Saxon energy at last triumphs over every obstacle. But nature, as if offended, withdraws half her beauty from the land.

A SETTLER ON THE MONARO c.1839

As much as I was able to observe, there is nothing in the nature in which they live which they have not yet discovered.

LUDWIG LEICHHARDT ON THE ABORIGINES, 1843

The Highland emigrants of the 1850s arrived in a society altogether different to the one their countrymen had found in the 1830s. Gold had been no more than a rumour then. It was the peak of the pastoral age and the great fortunes were being made from sheep—John Macarthur's 'extremely economical' merinos, bred to grow fine wool in Australian conditions. The sheepmen had everything in their favour. As the woolgrowing countries of Europe began to consume more wool than they grew, the Australian share of the expanding British market increased dramatically. The seasons were good. Good land in the interior was there for the taking. And there were 20,000 convicts assigned as free labour under a system which some people began to say was akin to slavery.

The frontier expanded to accommodate the sheep. From his run on the Murrumbidgee River at Gundagai, W. A. Brodribb saw 100,000 of them pass in three months in 1836-37. They were on their way to Port Phillip which had been recently opened up by squatters from Van Diemen's Land (Tasmania) and publicised after the explorations of Thomas Mitchell. The sheep moved and the law followed. The limits of location set by Governor Darling to contain settlement had long been ignored. When an act to regulate squatting was passed in 1836, there were men already grazing sheep as far south as Wagga. Now grazing on Crown Land would cost £10 a year, and settlers would be required to submit to the rule of law, in so far as it could be effectively administered by Crown Lands Commissioners.

For those who wished to go beyond the boundaries credit was freely available from the Sydney banks, and sheep could be bought from successful pastoralists with surplus stock. 'New chums' with the right credentials frequently became agents on the frontier for men of substance. With useful connections, some shrewd, tough and ambitious men arrived in Port Jackson with £50 and when they died left principalities behind them. There were Etonians on the frontier who hunted dingoes with bugles and hounds: and there were former convicts who began their careers as 'gully rakers'[1] and ended their lives much wealthier—albeit always less respectable—than the men who had been their masters.

Having travelled so far new emigrants took time to decide on their best chance. The population of New South Wales was 'in a state of constant migration', Alexander Harris (*The Emigrant Mechanic*) observed. It was almost as true of Sydney as it was of the inland. Labourers 'tended not to create working class living areas, but followed seasonal work and chanced their arm at a variety of jobs. In a pre-industrial society the mass of people sought, if not fortunes, then the maximum return on labour which, in the 1830s, was in increasing demand.'

However, ultimately this mobility was geographical rather than social. In New South Wales land had rapidly become the key to influence. If by the 1830s the merchant classes of Sydney were beginning to make some social and political progress, the great mass of the population were not. They did not much care. Religion told some of them that all were born in sin and to accept the powers that be: material success and, perhaps, *freedom* from religion, led others to the same conclusion—or to a more cynical belief

1 Gully rakers gathered stray cleanskin stock and put their own brand on them.

that the powers that be were of more consequence to the powerful than they were to ordinary people.

Politics in New South Wales was the province of a divided elite. A Tory gentry whose wealth was based on land and who had fought viciously with successive governors to rule the roost in New South Wales were now locked in battle with Whiggish merchants, clerics and financially disinterested improvers who saw a more democratic future for the colony. As the decade progressed the debate centred on transportation.

Quite apart from the considerations of its value as a punishment, a deterrent, or a means of reforming British criminals, transportation had been the basis of the colony's prosperity. But as well as a source of labour it was a source of moral infamy. Improvers said New South Wales had sunk to the lowest depths of depravity because of it. The Vicar-General said there had been no pestilence like it since the Deluge. The Presbyterian Reverend John Dunmore Lang said it made New South Wales 'the dunghill of the Empire'. Even a gentleman like James Macarthur, who had profited greatly from the system and ultimately supported it, had to concede that transportation contaminated society. To be a gentleman on a dunghill was a mixed blessing.

Transportation was one of those vexed questions which begged an answer from Providence. By the late 1830s the Reverend John Dunmore Lang believed that he had divined the answer.

Lang was the great exponent of Scottish emigration to New South Wales. Born in Greenock, Scotland, in 1799 and educated at Glasgow University, he emigrated to Australia in 1822 to become the first Presbyterian minister in Sydney. He was possessed of a vituperative code of Christianity and a tongue to match and with them he assailed the civil authorities as readily as he slandered his fellow clergy. A political radical, he campaigned for the separation of the colonies, republicanism, and a national system of education. Lang was raised an evangelical and maintained until his death a belief in the absolute authority of scripture and the morbid millenarianism which characterised the founders of the Free Church: but he was no more capable of reconciling his personal visions with *them* than he was with those whom he believed to be backsliders in the established church. Nothing shines through the writings of J. D. Lang so much as his egotism. He was always half a humbug.

In the 1830s Lang's prime purpose was to cleanse Australian society by the substitution of Protestant—particularly Scottish—emigration for transportation. In pursuit of this objective he made a number of trips to Britain (indeed the frequency of his arrivals and departures must have done something to dispel fears of the voyage among prospective emigrants). In 1830 Lang arranged with the Colonial Office for the emigration of 140 Scottish tradesmen and their families. In the course of the next decade he persuaded 4,000 Highlanders to migrate to Australia. Highlanders were uniquely impervious to the corrupting influences of convicts and Catholics, and the best antidote to the moral plague that transportation spread. Their language itself would place them 'beyond the reach of contamination'. Lang's plan was to establish 'a reputable tenantry' in Australia from these 'very superior' migrants who, no longer needed in their own country, were desperately needed in Australia.[2]

---

2 When the *Midlothian* arrived in Sydney in 1837 with a cargo of these 'very superior' migrants bound for a settlement at the junction of the Hunter and Maitland rivers, the *Sydney Gazette* expressed doubts about the vaunted Highlanders. Their families were too large, it said; they had inflated notions both of themselves and of their prospects, and they asked for exorbitant wages.

Recognising that Highland families alone could not combat immorality and the popery which fed it, and painfully aware that God led a diminutive life in the inland of Australia, Lang also recruited ministers. In Britain in 1836–37 he gathered 25 of them—12 Presbyterians and 13 Lutherans. They would work in the Australian wilderness: some among the white settlers, some among the Aborigines. It was 'an undeniable fact that two such flocks as black men and merino sheep cannot be attended by the same shepherd', Lang said.

In New South Wales beyond the ranges where God did not exist, a Protestant Highlander was extending the empire in the ancient way. By 1837 Captain Lachlan Macalister was one of the colony's men of substance. He must have felt that he at least had paid his way. He was born in 1797, the son of Duncan and Janet Macalister who had recently arrived in Skye from Campbelltown, Argyleshire, to live on the 7,300-hectare estate the family had purchased from the traditional owners, the MacKinnons. The Macalisters had taken with them numerous families and settled them on crofts of about one to one and a half hectares, or employed them catching fish in stone traps on the shores of Loch Slapin. The circuit judge, Lord Cockburn, saw the families there in 1841, in five miserable hovels: one person had drowned and his body was awaiting burial in some place beyond the churchyard.

Lachlan Macalister arrived in New South Wales in 1817 as an ensign in the 48th Regiment. In 1824 he received an 810-hectare grant of land a few kilometres north of where Goulburn was soon to grow. Macalister had a great appetite for land and for most of his life he was able to satisfy it. But in 1838 his reputation was built on more than the acquisition of land. A decade before he had been made Resident Magistrate of the district and officer in charge of the mounted police on the Goulburn Plains. The country was infested with bushrangers and Aborigines. We know nothing of Macalister's successes with the latter who were accused of killing sheep and shepherds and, in 1827, of eating both, but he was a terror to Bold Jack Donohue and his colleagues, spending months in pursuit of them: 'Mr Macalister has not descended from the Highlands since I have been at Camden,' Mrs John Macarthur told her son.

In 1831 Macalister was wounded in a battle with the bushrangers at Shooters Hill in the Great Dividing Range. He survived, but one of the bushrangers was killed and eight others were captured and later executed at Bathurst. When the depredators had been quelled, Macalister's friends presented him with a piece of plate, for it was to him, they said, that they largely owed their tranquillity and the security of their property.

The growth of Macalister's para-military reputation was matched by the extension of his land and flocks. By 1838 he was living on a substantial station called Clifton, close to John Macarthur's Camden. The 810-hectare grant near Goulburn had grown to more than 6,500 hectares and now adjoined the Taralga property of his friends James and William Macarthur. Macalister called it Strathaird after the family estate on Skye. His daughter had married the son of Thomas Livingstone Mitchell, the New South Wales Surveyor-General and celebrated explorer of Australia Felix. Lachlan Macalister had done very well and he was looking further afield.

A gallows and gibbet were erected in Goulburn even before it was declared a township, and it is said that when Governor Bourke visited it in 1833 he demanded that two skeletons hanging in chains be taken down. Goulburn grew up with a garrison that had been posted there in advance of settlement. The free inhabitants coexisted in the 1830s with a gang of 70 men in irons. The settlers enjoyed the advantage of free labour from assigned convicts and learnt to live with the infamy with which the system invested their community. Once a month a magistrate, a constable and a scourger (the most notorious was 'Black Francis', the Goulburn Castigator) toured the district administering justice to the convicts on the basis of their masters' complaints. The lash was used as liberally for drunkenness as it was for 'illusing sheep'—John Harrington received 50 strokes for each offence. Between 1829 and 1834 David Cameron suffered 200 lashes and 86 days on the treadmill. The Quaker, James Backhouse, who passed through in 1836, spoke of convicts receiving up to 800 lashes in 18 months. They presented 'strong marks of depravity, and not a few have defectively formed heads', he said, and thought this might explain, to some extent, their continued turpitude. Some convicts who could neither reform nor bear the punishments chose to live beyond the law in the bush, raiding huts in the outlying districts. Some must have lived much better as bushrangers, but it was not a vocation pastoral society would tolerate. When they caught a bushranger named Whitton in 1840, they tried him in Sydney and brought him on a cart with his hangman to the Goulburn gallows, and they hoped that the lesson would not be lost on the large crowd of 'inhabitants of all grades' who witnessed the execution. Despite this (some might say because of it), and despite the fact that the hospital was 'pretty fully occupied by stockmen and others of the lower order; victims of immorality . . . in sequestered parts of the colony, frequented by Aborigines . . .', by 1839 Goulburn had become, Lachlan Macalister's kinsman said, 'a township of some respectability'. The pastoralists now looked further afield.

To the south-east of Goulburn lay Maneroo, or Monaroo, or Manero or a dozen other names. The area had been named Brisbane Downs by its English discoverers in 1823 after the Governor of New South Wales. Eventually the Brisbane Downs became known as the Monaro, the Aboriginal name for it. The name might have meant 'like a woman's breasts', but as W. K. Hancock says, we can be no surer that the first Europeans understood the Aborigines' meaning any better than they were able to reproduce their pronunciation. Backhouse described it thus:

> The plains of this district, succeed each other, for upwards of 200 miles. They are upon Granite, Mica, Slate and Quartz, with here and there, Limestone and Basalt. The parts overlaying the Granite are generally free from trees, and they form extensive downs. The intervening hills are more or less covered with wood. Snow falls frequently in winter, but it seldom lies many hours; hoar frosts are also prevalent, and they sometimes occur in summer. The country is watered by rivers, generally forming chains of ponds except in rainy weather.

The Monaro is bound in the east by the sea, and in the south and west by the Australian Alps. By the end of the 1830s it was populated by about 1,500 whites (overwhelmingly comprised of single men) and an unknown number of Aborigines (the census of 1841 did not bother to count them even in the category of pagans and Mohammedans) already decimated by syphilis, smallpox, influenza and alcohol: 'They seeped into sheep and cattle stations . . . And there they rotted,' W. K. Hancock said.

In 1837 Farquhar MacKenzie, the son of an old Highland soldier and the partner in New South Wales of another, was up on the Monaro in a bark hut.[3] There were a couple of thousand sheep outside, together with the 'whole of the possum tribe' and native dogs 'howling most dolefully'. MacKenzie lived on more than sheep and possums; there were mountain ducks weighing up to two kilograms, and if he cared to visit other squatters on the Murrumbidgee they could catch him freshwater cod. MacKenzie seems to have liked the Australian landscape and its animals, at least where they provided for him and his sheep. He adorned his journal with primitive brightly coloured drawings of his surroundings and the two-kilogram duck. He was struck by the peculiarities of the 'platibus', and tried to shoot it. Every gentleman with a passing interest in science tried to shoot a platypus. It was to Australia what the llama was to Paraguay.

Being at the bottom of the world had magical effects. The barometer was said to rise before bad weather and fall before good. In 1828 the *Quarterly Review* reported that change 'in the physical constitution of all kinds of animals on transplantation to Australia is astonishing'. Prostitutes who had been barren in Europe bore children in Australia and, the *Review* said, women who had long ceased bearing children were suddenly prolific again. Barron Field spoke of 'birds without wings, as large as deer, their bodies covered with hair instead of feathers; beasts with the beaks of birds . . .' The swans were black, 'the eagles white, the cod fish is found in rivers and perch in the sea, the valleys are cold and the mountain tops warm, the trees shed their

3 He was born in Rossshire in 1811, the son of Captain Kenneth MacKenzie and a nephew of Sir Hector and General John MacKenzie. Farquhar arrived in Sydney in 1836, met Captain William Murchison who was an old friend of the family, formed a pastoral partnership with him and set off for new country. It was a very common pattern. He later married Murchison's daughter who bore him 10 children—another common pattern. Most of their lives were spent at King Parrot Creek near Melbourne.

bark annually instead of their leaves', wrote a new settler in 1837. He had surely read Field. There was a hot wind from the north which caused illness in people and made parrots drop from trees. The whole place was 'as if dropt from another planet'.

The uniqueness of Australian animals of course did not encourage their preservation—quite the reverse. When Australian animals were not being slaughtered for commercial purposes or for food, they were slaughtered for fun—casually despatched with the gun or a stirrup iron (one did not even have to dismount!). It was as if in the European mind their peculiarities deprived them of the right to exist. They were almost a sacrilege—they had not been on the ark. South America was distinguished by the size and ferocity of its human and animal inhabitants. It was much the same in Africa and India, and even New Zealand had 'ferocious Zealanders'. But in Australia animal life was uniformly timid and peculiar. What was noble about an emu? Or an Aborigine?

Despite himself Farquhar MacKenzie was a doubter. It was not that he did not consider daily religious reflections of the 'utmost importance', but even his terrible loneliness failed to create much more than a casual religious mind. MacKenzie thought that it was 'folly to cloud the present with discoloured anticipations of the future, to render ourselves miserable during the only time we are sure of our existence'. There was too much pleasure in the world for him to consistently seek heaven or worry about hell. The sight of the 'Aurora Borealis (if it may be so called in the Southern Hemisphere)', more brilliant than the Northern Lights, did not make him tremble at the thought of its Designer. The natural beauty that surrounded him only reminded him that humans spoiled. In winter on the Monaro the nights were long and often intensely cold: the Monaro has blizzards, and frosts which leave a weird cobwebbed world of white long after the sun has risen through the mist. Yet MacKenzie wrote of days when he had been 'rather more in the humour of Castle than hut-building—I lay down on a hill side whence the Snowy Mountains were distinctly visible, covered with snow nearly to the base, whilst the air was so balmy that I could enjoy sitting out as much as in a summer day at home'.

But loneliness brought on a great depression in MacKenzie. His journal filled with gloomy poems: 'O solitary life I lead, less happy than the flocks I feed.' His thoughts grew morbid. Even when spring came, the new grasses shot and the mimosa bloomed, he was only reminded that his newborn lambs would 'have to expect more bitter than sweet'; that it was a 'world of care' they faced. Sometimes it seems MacKenzie wanted to leave the world—he wrote out poems 'On the Prospect of Death'.

Stockmen were his most frequent company. Stockmen were the factotums of white civilisation in Australia, in a sense the flux in the transition from black to white occupation of the interior. MacKenzie enjoyed their occasional visits to his hut, if only because no-one else came. They rode up on their 'poor looking, ewe-necked horses', sporting their formidable whips and spurs.

> His talk is of Rum, Tobacco, Cattle, Horses, Brands, Increases, and Stockyards—always interlaced with an abundance of oaths and imprecations—and he is generally known by a bye name such as . . . 'Dick drive hard', and so forth. He prides himself upon knowing all the Ranges, Creeks, Gullies and Swamps for 100 miles around, the situation and distances of different places and where particular cattle and horses are to be found.

In the end it was not the company of stockmen MacKenzie craved. It was the company of refined men. Men who read and reflected like himself. Men who had travelled and who were, for preference, Scots. Men like the much-travelled Archibald MacLeod, late of Bernisdale, Skye, now of Gundaroo on the Yass River near Lake George, whom he visited in 1837. When he thought about it, Farquhar MacKenzie found that travel had a profound lesson: it was that Divine Providence was distributed with marvellous equity. The Scots for instance had been granted certain blessings and certain encumbrances. Their country was

> . . . highly civilized, the necessaries and luxuries of life abundant, noxious reptiles and beasts of prey almost unknown, and the crops seldom fail.
>
> On the other hand, the climate is wet and cold, vice and misery prevalent, the necessaries of life unequally distributed, and disease and sickness brought on by luxury, dissipation, hard work, and hard fare if not by the climate . . .

With the Aborigines it was the same but different:

> The Australian Savage (the lowest in the scale of civilization) excells us in activity, the chase, in the use of his weapons and in the capability of enduring privations—he is the freest of mankind and would not exchange his savage independence for our luxuries—his climate is one of the finest in the world—he can hunt without fear of game laws or Man traps and is not pestered with duns and tax gatherers. He is not annoyed by failures in his crops or flocks and herds, and has no rents to pay or fears of eviction.
>
> On the other hand he suffers much from cold and starvation and is sensual, cruel, revengeful, and enjoys none of the higher pleasures of the mind, or comforts of civilization . . .

It was only civilisation that MacKenzie lacked. All MacKenzie needed to enjoy his life was some Scots with whom to share it.

The Monaro does not come to an abrupt halt. It does not run into a mountain wall. The Australian Alps are not the Andes, and the Snowy River is no Orinoco; but the Alps are rugged and travel through them is difficult and laborious. No-one on their northern side, however, can ever have believed that reaching the southern side was anything but a tiresome task which would be completed when necessity demanded it. By 1839 the necessity was there: there were reports coming into Sydney from the countryside that stock were dying in hundreds from thirst and starvation and that if the rain did not come soon there would be a 'famine'. J. D. Lang echoed the evangelicals of Skye. He said sin was the cause of it. The Governor declared a day of fasting and humiliation. But everyone coped with it in his own way.

Droughts drove the men on the frontier deeper into the interior. Nothing could contain restless, hungry, lonely men in their temporary huts on the Monaro. Their lives were as unencumbered as they were unrecorded. As Governor Gipps said in 1840: 'As well might it be attempted to confine the Arabs of the Desert within a circle drawn on their own sands as to confine the herds of New South Wales within any given limits, and if it were possible to confine them there, the herds must starve and perish as surely as the Arabs.' The continent was being explored by a tribe of nomads.

To Europeans on the Monaro the land beyond the ranges was godless, nameless and unknown. It was a fastness. But there were probably 2,000–3,000 people living there in 1840, members of the Kurnai tribes. Kurnai means 'the men'. The land they inhabited was known by the Aborigines on the Monaro as *Cabone Benel*—the south land. It was remarkable for its diversity, and in a continent notably lacking in water, for the number of its lakes and rivers. Geographically it was virtually self-contained. It was hemmed in by mountains to the north and thickly forested hills to the west. The sea bounds it in the south. The ranges run down to the sea, straddling rivers which, although not Amazonian, swell with frightening speed after rains and regularly flood the lowlands. Higher up, in the summer, they glint brilliantly blue in the ravines. The ranges sink into gentle lightly wooded hills and broad flats before the lakes in which the rivers end. South of the lakes scrubby tea-tree flats, once alive with dingoes and native cats, end in the sand dunes of the Ninety Mile Beach, or in mangroves at Corner Inlet.

The Kurnai, as Alfred William Howitt observed them, comprised five tribes. In the south-west, as far as Wilson's Promontory, lived the Brataualung; to the east, on the narrow strip of land between lakes and sea, the Tatungalung; to their north the Briakalung; east of them on the rivers that feed the lakes, the Brabralung: and further east on the lower reaches of the Snowy River the Krauatungalung. Beyond them, in wild wet country, lived a tribe of outcasts, descendants of refugees from tribal justice or individual vengeance and 'organized . . . as far as they could do so, on the old accustomed lines'. They were called the Biduelli. Higher up in the mountains lived the Yaitmathang, deadly enemies it seems of some of the Kurnai tribes. The Krauatungalung, however, almost certainly had more intercourse with the Yaitmathang of the high plains than they did with the Brataualung of the Ninety Mile Beach and Corner Inlet. We don't know the extent of contact between the Kurnai tribes. It is quite possible that they did not even speak the same language, although there is no doubt that they had a large number of basic words in common, as all the tribes of the Australian mainland had.

There were two branches of the Yaitmathang, the Theddora and the Kandangora. Each year they met with other mountain tribes to feast on swarms of newly hatched Bogong moths. The Kurnai feasted on fish.

Both Kurnai and Yaitmathang were divided into smaller groups bearing the name of the country they lived on. Often the names of these subdivisions described some distinguishing practice of the people—those who carried fire, for instance. The subdivisions were in turn divided into smaller units down to the basic unit of society in Aboriginal Australia: 'a small group of kindred, frequently an old man, his sons, married or unmarried, with their respective wives and children'.

Even by the end of the nineteenth century anthropologists recognised that the Australian Aborigines had occupied the continent for a period in excess not only of the Celtic occupation of Britain, but of the 4,000 years or so since Adam. Alfred William Howitt, surveyor, explorer and anthropologist, told his readers in 1904 that they must try to comprehend 'a very long period of at least prehistoric time' in thinking about Aboriginal society.[4] In 1840 this was not conceivable. Now we know that Kurnai culture in 1840 had not changed much in at least 6,500 years. There is evidence of occupation at least 18,000 years before that,

4 Howitt's *The Native Tribes of South Eastern Australia*, which was compiled in the last decades of the nineteenth century, remains by far the most comprehensive survey of the Kurnai tribes. Although the observations of missionaries and the memories of surviving Aborigines may have not been the most reliable sources, the study which Howitt made from them is the best available to us until more archaeological and anthropological work is undertaken.

and unless the Kurnai differed substantially from the rest of the Australian tribes the span is likely to be twice that figure. The Kurnai had probably once hunted the diprotodon and the giant kangaroo.

In 1840 they lived on fish and small game which teemed in their environment. The plains swarmed with emus and kangaroos, the scrubland with possums, bandicoots, wombats and other small marsupials, reptiles, birds, grubs and insects: the lakes, rivers, estuaries and swamps abounded with ducks, swans and water fowl of all descriptions which could be harvested for both their eggs and their flesh. They took abundant shellfish from the rocks, and caught flounder, flathead, mullet, bream and gurnard at night from canoes in which they lit small fires to attract the fish. Before the invading sheep and cattle destroyed it there was also a constant vegetable supply.

They were hunter-gatherers, although that is not to say their society was the same as, for instance, the Kalahari Bushmen's, or even that of other Aboriginal tribes of Australia. Each society adapted to varying physical conditions. The Kurnai, in fact, may have been significantly different. Their society was not truly totemic—totems were only incidental to marriage rules, for instance, the procedures being governed by locality. The sexual division of labour and ritual may have been less rigid than elsewhere in Australia. Their creation myths had differences. As they did not trade with the tribes to the north and west their material culture possibly had grown apart. And it is possible that there was a genetic difference.

But all hunter-gatherer societies are alike in generally providing amply for their members—although it may be too much to say, as some anthropologists have, that they were the first affluent societies. The Kurnai with access to the lakes, inlets and estuaries (it is possible that all groups within the Kurnai nation had access to them for varying periods at different times of the year) took fish with nets, spears, probably hook and line and possibly stone fish traps. In the late summer they drew eels from under the tussocks along the river banks. Occasionally whales beached themselves and large sections of the clan came together for the feast. Each year hundreds of thousands of mutton birds visited the islands offshore: the Kurnai harvested the eggs and chicks. They made canoes from great slabs of bark cut high up on the trunks of trees. To catch waterbirds they 'moved along under the water, leaving nothing but their nostrils visible above the surface ... As opportunity afforded they seized them by the legs, drew them quickly under water, and held them until they were drowned.' Possums, pademelons and parrots were readily clubbed to death, larger marsupials were speared or brought down with boomerangs and *kunnins*.[5] The women gathered yams and grubs with digging sticks. Digging sticks also made useful weapons. From the reeds and the bark of melaleuca the women made baskets and bags.

It was a culture of wood, stone, skin and bone. Spears were sometimes tipped with quartzite, sometimes with bone from possums and kangaroos. But wood had the greatest advantages. It was light and pliable. Multi-purpose implements could be made from it which reduced the weight to be carried by a travelling people. Wood was in abundance. As fire drills and as fuel it served them well. Bark and branches made their shelter. (They did not need chimneys because they lit their fires outside.) They clothed themselves in possum and kangaroo skins. These animals were the most variable resources, providing materials for shelter, weaponry and clothing as well as food.

5 A wooden instrument which in battle served as both a spear and a shield.

The Kurnai, like many other tribes in the resource-rich riverine and maritime areas of Australia, travelled neither far nor wide. The extent of each group's locality was largely determined by the extent of its resources. But even the almost sedentary groups did not till the ground: they grew no crops. They culled the life about them—bled it as they needed. To create fresh growth they regularly fired the bush: this also kept the forest litter to a minimum and so removed the danger of summer wildfires. Aborigines farmed the land with fire.

The Kurnai did not give thanks to an Almighty for these favours, although they did look up to the crow: the crow had given them fire and their language and remained their protector. The natural world, they believed, had been made by *Bunjil* and his name was synonymous with knowledge. His son, Mungun-ngaua, was the Kurnai ancestor who taught them all they knew before ascending to the sky, where, it seems, he remained and rarely exercised omnipotence. Knowledge of Mungan-ngaua was intended for males only and was passed on to novices at initiation ceremonies called *jeraeil*. But somehow the women learned the secret and Mungan-ngaua sent a great fire—the Aurora Australis—and

> Men went mad with fear, and speared each other, fathers killing their children, husbands and wives, and brethren each other. The sea rushed over the land and nearly all mankind was drowned. Those who survived became the *muk-kurnai*. Some turned into reptiles, birds, fishes and *Tundun* [the son of Mungan-ngaua] and his wife became porpoises.

It was then that Mungan-ngaua left the earth and ascended to the sky, where his power appears to have been manifest only in the Aurora and the crow. His teaching was carried on by the men with special qualifications whose names were prefixed 'Bunjil'.[6]

The initiation ceremony was more than a time for knocking out the teeth of initiates. It was a grand entertainment for the clan. Heroic and humorous tales were told. Amusing but salutary pantomimes were performed. Howitt marvelled at their dancing and mime skills and their 'harmonious' and 'expressive' language. There was music; similar perhaps to that which an eccentric Polish explorer named John Lhotsky had heard on the Monaro.

> Their strain was in 2–4 time, which they marked by beating crochets, and in moments of greater excitement, quavers . . . the music and the words . . . for majestic and deep melancholy, would not dishonour a Beethoven or a Handel. The tones weakened by degrees, the tones died away, and grand silence and aethereal clearness filled the Plain and all the wilderness.

But the intention of the jeraeil was primarily that of cutting off a boy from his past. 'His connection with his mother as her child is broken off, and becomes henceforth attached to the men,' Howitt observed. The practice might suggest a male monopoly of power in Kurnai society. It is likely that, as in other parts of Australia, the women were objects of barter and at the centre of most of the internecine squabbles. In some tribes women were the prime commodity and the major object of trade, while at the same time they provided the bulk of the subsistence food and cared for the

---

6 All this, like the translation 'our father' for Mungan-ngaua, so closely parallels biblical teaching one suspects that Howitt's informants had been influenced by the mission. But Howitt was certain they were speaking as initiates: 'I must guard myself,' he said, 'from being thought to imply any primitive revelation of a monotheistic nature.' But it was common on the Australian frontier for Aborigines to retail 'whitefellow talk'—it was what whitefellows wanted to hear, and of course the Aborigines themselves found it increasingly difficult to separate what was white legend from what was their own.

children. But the Kurnai women were by no means slaves of the men. Whether through a separate cultural life or because they were party to the central creation myth, the women seem to have participated in nearly all aspects of Kurnai society. When a man was subjected to an ordeal by weapons for causing a death his wife stood by him, helping him to turn aside the missiles and breaking them as they fell. At these ceremonies the women of the tribe sat in front of the men 'beating their skin rugs in measured time'. The women of the aggrieved party led the men towards the accused, beating their rugs as they went. The men crouched behind them. If a general fight broke out the women joined it with their digging sticks which they used 'much as a man would do a quarter staff'.[7]

It was the Kurnai marriage rules which seem to have ensured the most remarkably decisive role for women. The Kurnai were organised on the basis of localities. There was no marriage within a locality and certain other divisions were also out of bounds. Each tribe, it appears, lived in reproductive isolation from the other. The old people of the tribe, 'especially the old women, carefully kept in memory all the marriages, descents, and resultant relationships'. From this knowledge, Howitt said, the rights of marriage were laid down to exogamous principles. In practice, he said, men 'could acquire a wife in one way only, namely, by running off with her secretly, and with her own consent'. In courtship women had the whip hand. Should an unmarried man have a marriageable sister and a friend

7 Across the ranges on the Ovens River, George Faithfull ran into a similar unity among the blacks sometime after 300 of them had fallen on his overlanding party and killed eight of his men. There was a six-hour battle in which, he said, 'it was remarkable that the children, and many of the women likewise, had so little fear that they boldly ran forward, even under our horses' legs, picked up the spears, and carried them back to the warrior men'.

in a permitted division who was similarly placed, he might arrange an exchange—provided the desired woman agreed; for 'the choice of a husband rested altogether with the women'. There were numerous ways to arrange an elopement, and from Howitt's account most of them involved a protracted brawl at some stage.

> If it happened that there were marriageable girls, but that the marriageable young men did not take the initiative, the women set it going by killing *Yiirung* (emu-wren) [the man's *thundung* or totem], that is, one of the 'men's brothers', and casually letting the men see it. Then the men became very angry because one of their brothers had been killed. The young men who might be suitors got sticks, the girls took their digging sticks, and a fight commenced between them, at which many blows were struck, heads were broken and blood flowed. Even the married men and women joined in the fight. The following day the young men killed a *Djiitgun* (superb warbler), that is a 'woman's sister', and in consequence caused another fight, perhaps worse than the former. After a time, the wounds and bruises having healed, one of the eligible young men and one of the girls meeting, and being inclined towards each other, he looking at her would say *'Djiitgun'* to which, if she responded to the understood meaning of the term so used, she would reply *'Yiirung*; what does the *Yiirung* eat?' He in reply says, 'He eats so and so', mentioning kangaroo, possum, or some other game. This constitutes an offer and its acceptance, and the couple then on a favourable occasion elope.

In a much easier but perhaps less practical approach the Kurnai man might call in the services of a *Bunjil-yenjin*, a wise man or magician, to sing the woman a spell which would induce her to elope. The spell might go: 'Why did the young man cut off his beard long ago? The maiden sleeps in the camp.' It was then necessary to induce sleep in the girl's parents so that she might be stolen away. On awakening the parents also cast a spell, perhaps on the legs of the abductor to slow him down—or they too would call in a *Bunjil-yenjin.*

The girl meanwhile had possibly been subjected to the sexual rights the suitor's fellow initiates had to her. Thereafter, in Kurnai society, no sexual licence existed, except when the Aurora occurred—on such occasions wives were exchanged for the day. When caught, the couple were thoroughly beaten. They then ran away again: if they were Brataualung it might be to Snake Island in Corner Inlet which was a sort of Gretna Green for that clan. Howitt, who had a talent for investing anthropology with the ring of English domesticity, wrote of such an elopement: 'Finally the affair blew over and they settled down among the married people, who indeed had themselves gone through the same experience.'

> The explanation of this extraordinary state of matrimonial affairs is to be found in the deadlock brought about by the widespread system of the Kurnai relationships, the universal abhorrence of sister marriage, and the practice of exogamy in the local groups only. The prohibition, thus arising out of the prohibited degrees and from locality, rendered it next to impossible for a man to find a woman who was not so related to him that she was forbidden to him as a wife.

Elopement was the only course and the office of the *Bunjil-yenjin* arose 'to give sanction to the practice'.

Although the Kurnai did not believe in God or Satan or any of their agents, their world was nevertheless full of magic. Among a number of notions the Kurnai shared with Calvinists was the belief that no death was an accident. However, where the Calvinists put death down to God's will, the Kurnai believed it was the result of magic worked by some hostile human party and had to be avenged. There was therefore always a good deal of plotting, raiding and posturing.

The Reverend John Bulmer, a missionary who listened sympathetically to the remnants of the Kurnai tribes, was certain that quite independently of their Christian instruction the blacks believed in the separation of body and soul. The soul was inclined to leave during sleep which made it vulnerable to the sleeper's enemies—they could call it up and tell it what they intended to do with the body it had deserted. Bulmer thought this sorcery probably worked sometimes when the victim dreamt of his antagonists' plans and died of fright.

Belief in sorcery was common among Australian Aborigines. It was practised against the white invaders with, it seems, only limited success. More significantly, sorcery appears to have always been a major cause of internecine warfare. When Aborigines began to die, seemingly unaccountably, after contact with Europeans, internecine warfare increased proportionately.

In Kurnai society the spiritual and physical were separate but equally active and equally knowable. Kidney fat is a case in point. The kidney fat of an enemy was held to be the most potent of all substances for magic. It was therefore the greatest prize in battle. Howitt's informants related tales of the fat being taken from men, roasted or smoked and rubbed on the victors' weapons to make them more deadly, or being wrapped up and carried to make the hunters more effective. Howitt was told of a Kurnai man with a scar to show for having lost his kidney fat. But there is a suggestion that a psychological weapon was as much at work here as a physical one. It was said among the Kurnai that sometimes men died after dreaming that their fat had been taken. It seems likely that the practice was confined to the upland tribes, in which case the Kurnai's main enemy might have been his fear and what sorcery and his dreams made of it. There is generally a barbarian in the hills.

Among other practices allegedly revolting to Europeans, cannibalism on a modest scale was probably part of Kurnai culture, and there is little doubt that they practised infanticide. Infanticide was common among the Australian Aborigines as a means of controlling the population and maintaining resources. Their diet and the custom of suckling children for three or four years is supposed to have kept the fertility rate low, but it is estimated, nonetheless, that in some tribes up to 30 per cent of newborn children were killed at birth. If one child was born too soon after another, threatened the well-being of the older child, made it impossible for the mother to fulfil her food gathering duties, or was deformed, it was likely to be killed.

Cannibalism appears to have been largely ceremonial and selective. Howitt was told by a Yaitmathang man that he had eaten some lowland blacks and found them less salty than whitefellows. It was a similar tale to that of the Presbyterian minister on the Monaro who was told by an Aborigine, who licked his lips as he spoke, that 12-year-old boy was 'cabon budgery patter like it emu'. Cannibalism lived in the minds of the Europeans like the kidney fat thief lived in the minds of the Kurnai. Aborigines were no doubt aware of it and liked to see whites roll their eyes in horror.

The Kurnai probably did not understand the physiological nature of paternity. They knew nothing of physiology at all. Their medicine men pretended to suck the evil out of the stomachs of sick people. They placed pellets in the excreta of enemies to make them sick. But the Kurnai were not prone to fatal illness and had never known an epidemic.

When a Kurnai died his relatives wrapped the body

in a possum-skin rug and enclosed it in a sheet of bark. For days they lay with their heads on the corpse. They shrieked and wailed and gashed themselves with stones until their bodies and heads streamed with blood. Sometimes the body was carried about for several years by the relatives. Finally it was buried or placed in the trunk of a hollow tree. On occasions a hand (the *bret*) was taken and dried and worn around the neck where it was said to warn of an enemy's approach.

There was nothing in the natural world of the Kurnai that was not animated by myth. Olive Pink wrote of the phenomenon in Central Australia:

> The whole country through which we passed was apparently only mulga scrub, a few gum trees, a low or high range here and there, or some open plains, yet it is made a scene of much activity by aboriginal history embodied in myths, such as the journeys of 'dream-time' people travelling in various directions, whose roads we bisected or rode parallel with, or who were 'sitting down', that is, camping permanently and performing ceremonies, or 'finishing' and going into the ground . . . So vivid are the tales that the investigator has the feeling of an inhabited area with much activity around: people hurrying hither and thither, or living normal lives like blackfellows did only a few generations ago.

The Kurnai landscape buzzed with myth. *Narguns*, evil things with breasts like a woman's, lived in holes and caves and dragged travellers in to their deaths. *Yabungs* were relatively friendly: they lived in trees and made a noise like a gunshot. And *Mraats*, the ghosts of the dead, haunted the living.

The Kurnai would have satisfied neither Hobbes nor Rousseau, for they lived neither in perfect harmony with nature nor in perfect terror of it. They understood it well enough, however, to enjoy a society which fed them well and was, in D. J. Mulvaney's terms, 'leisured, enriched by spiritual contact, moral bonding, obligations which ensured social welfare and individual identification with the clan estate'. They enjoyed, in other words, if not the physical comforts, then those fundamental characteristics of a good society which the Scottish Highlanders had lost when their ties with the land were broken.

Just as the great silences which worried Europeans in the Australian bush veiled life they could not see, the greased and decorated bodies of the Aborigines obscured white perceptions of humanity. If the squatters gathered on the fringe of the Monaro had had clearer vision they would soon have seen that while the Kurnai did not live in a state of grace they lived much better than most of their countrymen in the Highlands or the slums of Glasgow. But they were no more likely to see this than they were to notice an affinity with them.

The Kurnai recognised *them* when they came. They thought the white man was a *Mraat*, a ghost of one of their own dead. They thought he had 'sinew eye' or 'lightning eye' and a look with it would kill them. So they ran off crying, 'Don't look! Don't look! He will kill you!'

CALVINISTS AND CANNIBALS

In a moment of illumination, in a confused ecstasy of awe, terror, relief and self congratulation such as it is almost impossible to imagine now, Knox recognized that he had received the incredible asssurance.

EDWIN MUIR ON JOHN KNOX IN A GALLEY SHIP

A ship is a prison with the chance of drowning.

SAMUEL JOHNSON

They prefer the land unbroken and free from the earliest curse pronounced against the first banished and first created man. The only kindness we could do for them, would be to let them and their wide range of territory alone: to act otherwise and profess good-will is but hypocrisy. We cannot occupy the land without producing a change, fully as great for the aborigines as that which took place on man's fall and expulsion from Eden. They have hitherto lived utterly ignorant of the necessity for wearing fig-leaves, or the utility of ploughs; and in this blissful state of ignorance they would, no doubt, prefer to remain. We bring upon them the punishments due to original sin, even before they know the shame of nakedness.

SIR THOMAS MITCHELL, 1850

Angus McMillan was a Highlander whose life spanned the years in which the British completed the colonisation of both his homeland and Australia. Like so many other Highlanders, he emigrated, and prospered, and died in a province substantially of his own creation. Like his Calvinist countrymen he found ways to serve the empire as he served God—by serving himself. Like Alexander MacKenzie on the Canadian frontier, he blazed trails in the wilderness, albeit easier ones than MacKenzie's. Like so many of his fellow Skyemen he fought wars in the interests of empire, God and self, without ever wearing a uniform. Like so many Highlanders he came from the smallest of universes yet treated the world as his personal frontier. He was a loyal British Highlander, nothing if not a man of his time.

He may not have been aware of it, but his name derived from the ancient Celtic church: in Gaelic it means 'the tonsured one', or perhaps, 'son of the devotee of the tonsured one'. In the nineteenth century of course such things mattered less to a man. 'There can be little doubt,' the Scottish scholar Ian Grimble says, 'that the clan descends from some dynast of the early church in Dalriada.' To cut a very long story short, the McMillans traditionally occupied the lands about Lochaber in the central Highlands as 'hereditary servants' of the MacIntoshes. At the time of Culloden the McMillan chief refused to fight for the prince, though it is said that he substantially aided him. The McMillans inhabited Cameron country, so it was a Cameron who cleared them at the beginning of the nineteenth century.

It was from somewhere in this country, presumably, that the McMillan family went to Skye at the turn of the century. Ewen McMillan was an educated Protestant of limited but relatively secure means. He was an improved

Highlander. The first record of his tenancy on the MacLeod estates of Skye occurs in 1803 when his name appears in the minutes of a meeting regarding the need for a Customs House: the absence of such a facility was a serious impediment to the growing wool trade of Skye and an encouragement, the woolgrowing tacksmen said, to 'the pernicious effects of emigration'. Ewen McMillan was then a 'tacksman of Glenbrittle'. For 20 years or so after the Customs House meeting his name appears sporadically in the records of the MacLeod estates, usually in connection with the breeding of sheep and the business of selling them. It is believed that he brought the first improved breeds of sheep to Skye—no-one on Skye seems to know whether they were cheviot or blackface. Although he was without much land and probably enjoyed less status than those tacksmen with a traditional tie to the soil of Skye, Ewen McMillan was undoubtedly a gentleman farmer. He was also a Presbyterian.

He married Marion MacLeod, who seems to have been well connected on the island. She bore at least 14 children, one of whom was Angus, born on 14 August 1810. The birthplace, Glenbrittle, in the parish of Minginish, is hemmed in dramatically by the Cuillins. At the end of the glen lies Loch Brittle. The parish had been described matter-of-factly by an SSPCK missionary in 1741: '15 miles long, hath 1630 catechisable persons, 13 Waters, two preaching Places, many Lochs but no Papists.' One hundred years later the overcrowded crofters of Glenbrittle were scratching shellfish from among the useless kelp in the loch.

For all intents and purposes, the McMillans were lay missionaries, Protestant agents of improvement. Sometime in the 1820s they left Skye for the Outer Hebridean isle of Barra, whose traditional owner, MacNeil, had recently converted to Protestantism and embarked on a modest programme of improvement.[1]

Barra was not, as the *Encyclopaedia Britannica* had described it towards the end of the eighteenth century, 'a rock ½ mile long and inhabited only by geese'. It was a reasonably fertile island, nearly 20 kilometres long, 5 to 10 kilometres wide and inhabited largely by Catholics. The Barra folk have always held that their island derived its name from St Barr. The churches bore his name and so did an annual holiday. The Reverend Alexander Nicolson, the Presbyterian minister in the McMillans' time, cast a condescending eye on the proceedings of the papists:

> On that day (25th of September) all the Roman Catholic population convenes in their chapel in the forenoon to hear mass, from whence they set off to Killbar, each man riding a small pony, with his wife or favourite lass mounted behind him; who, after riding thrice round the sacred edifice return to the place from whence they set out. The females provide, before-hand, quantities of wild field carrots for this occasion, with which they treat their partners.

Presumably the Reverend Nicolson could witness these rites with some equanimity so long as he reckoned Catholicism to be passing. But neither the conversion of the chief nor the introduction of Protestants altered the faith of the natives. Barra and South Uist, 10 kilometres to the north, remain Catholic communities.

Barra was as well endowed by nature as any other parish in the Highlands and Islands. Fish was both a commodity

1 It is possible that Ewen McMillan had substituted for MacCaskill at Rhu Dunan while the traditional tacksman tried his luck in America. When MacCaskill returned McMillan may have been obliged to seek new pastures for his family. Barra provided an ideal opening for him.

and a staple, and the Barra men were remarkably adept fishermen. Cockles could be gathered by the horse-load from the beaches. In certain seasons aquatic birds were caught in hundreds from the rock face. There were, if the land had been equitably distributed, sufficient patches of good soil to feed the people with their staples, potatoes and barley. In the low hills there was good pasture for sheep and cattle. If there was a major scarcity it was timber—there was hardly a tree on Barra.

Although John MacCulloch said they were as cut off from its use as they were from tokay, there is no doubt the people of Barra were also especially fond of whisky. Alexander Nicolson lamented their habit:

> The natives have little or no idea of cleanliness or comfort. They have seldom much furniture to boast of; sometimes not a chair to sit upon, a bed to sleep on, or bed clothes to cover them from the severity of the night air; yet these people resort to the dram house as often as they can spare a shilling for that purpose.

They were addicted to tobacco too; but, according to MacCulloch, it was snuff they craved. This at least put them above savages, civilised man being 'distinguished from the savage by the number of his wants and gratifications'. They took their snuff in housing of the bleakest kind. MacCulloch thought it 'probable that Ovid lived in a sort of Barra house during that philosophical retirement of which he so bitterly complains'.

In the south of Barra lay Castlebay, 'a village ornamented with dried skate', and to MacCulloch's sensitive nose, 'having a most ancient and fish-like smell'. In the bay stood the particularly ancient seat of the MacNeil, Kissmuil Castle. MacNeil's kingdom may have been puny but it was said that when he had eaten in Kissmuil he announced, 'Now the world may eat.'

Increasingly impoverished by the same economic processes which afflicted the people of the Highlands and Islands generally, and further disadvantaged by their isolation, the people of Barra, both MacCulloch and Nicolson observed, seemed remarkably contented. MacCulloch's visit allowed him 'the opportunity of imagining how life is passed in a remote island, without society or neighbours, and where people are born and die without ever troubling themselves to enquire whether the world contains any other countries than Vatersay and Barra'. It may have been that isolation which produced among people who lived in a 'truly deplorable' state, a spirit of co-operation which Nicolson found noteworthy.

The Protestant MacNeil, while maintaining such semblances of vassalage as suited his pocket and his ego, established a Presbyterian community in the centre of the island at Eoligarry. A church and manse were built, a farm house and a mill established. The surrounding land was drained and enclosed. And Protestants, about 350 of them by 1831, were imported to supervise the farming and the kelp industry. It was hoped they would set an example of industriousness and sobriety to the natives and lead them from their pagan, popish ways. The social setting was bound to encourage in a Protestant youth a sense of superiority at the very least: it may even have given him a clue to the nature of the elect.

It was inevitable that a family like the McMillans should lose some members to the colonies. It was not that they were the most in need of the opportunities, but that they had skills, means and sufficient worldliness to comprehend them. The impoverished tended to remain until the last minute.

For those who could comprehend it there was no shortage of information about the colonies. It came to Scotland through men like John Dunmore Lang and his friend in Glasgow, the Reverend Dr MacLeod, as well as through the British Colonial Office. In 1837 it came in a report of the Scottish Surveyor-General in New South Wales, Major Thomas Mitchell, who had recently explored new country 'more extensive than Great Britain and equally rich in soil'. If the length of the journey, the convict system and the reports of fierce natives were disincentives, to compensate there was land and the presence of the Highlanders who had gone before. The emigration proceeded in a wave. As one Highlander established himself in New South Wales he created opportunities for the emigration of several more and, just as importantly, created confidence among his countrymen. Thus Highlanders flocked to the ports in the late 1830s, bearing letters of introduction to Highlanders in Australia.

Early in 1838, eight months after Sir Robert Peel had entranced his audience in Glasgow, and less than two months after J. D. Lang had preached there on the virtues of Scots Britons, a representative type arrived in the city seeking a passage to New South Wales. Angus McMillan was 28; short, thick-set, granite-jawed and grim. On the day of his arrival he might have read in the *Greenock Advertiser* that there had been an earthquake in Kingston and an insurrection in Trinidad; that two Protestants had been murdered by Catholics in Sligo; and of the revelation that the Meetawallers had been robbing and poisoning travellers in Patua and Sarun for years. If he read the *Glasgow Herald*, he might have noticed the story of the survivor of a shipwreck in Torres Strait who lay down to sleep with his companions on an island off the New Guinea coast only to be 'suddenly awakened by the violence of a native who had in his hand a knife . . . He advanced,' the survivor said, 'as I thought to cut my throat, but I struggled hard for my life, and I had the best of it.' Later the same man watched the natives eat the eyes and cheeks of his friends. It was a story worth remembering.

Had McMillan read the newspapers he might have been glad that of all the choices the empire offered a Highlander, and a Highlander offered the empire, he had chosen New South Wales. But he was not happy about going anywhere.

It appears that no-one has ever known precisely why McMillan left Barra. Clearly there were plenty of economic incentives—enough, anyway, to send at least four of his brothers to the colonies. There can be no doubt that among the Presbyterian community of Barra, as on Skye, emigration was a daily fact of life. But his departure was not an economic inevitability. His journal suggests two possible causes: a ruction with one of his brothers, and a failed affair with a woman he refers to only once, 'My dear Miss Margaret'. This solitary reference, compounded by subsequent folklore, has generated a popular view that 'Miss Margaret' was the reason for his going. Whatever the particular cause, his sorrow was such as to make him feel that his was a special, isolated suffering and that no communion with passengers could help—only communion with God.

McMillan's 'Journal of a Cruise from Greenock to New Holland' reveals a good deal about both himself and the Calvinist Scot in general. (It is as well because he left very little else.) The journal may also say something about the effects of migration on Australian colonists. Despite the fact that he is sanctimonious, intolerant and churlish, his thoughts evoke pity for a young man battling great sorrows and fears. 'This day I set sail from dear Island of Barra far from all I valueth . . .', he begins, and his sense of loss grows deeper as the voyage drags on. For a long while there is a struggle between his proud and cantankerous public face and his private desperation. In the end McMillan is a survivor.

McMillan left Barra on 5 September 1837. He travelled to Glasgow via the western Highlands port of Oban. Here he met a gentleman who tried to cheer him, but, said Angus, 'he had no cure for the deep wounds of my tortured heart'. Perhaps it was some compensation that the gentleman then paid his expenses to Glasgow. After some difficulty he secured a berth in the cabin of the captain of the barque *Minerva*. It cost him £55, which was a fair price under the circumstances. A cabin on a similar chartered ship, the *Brilliant*, which was about to sail, cost £73. And 'going in the hold I would never dream of', McMillan said, even at a price of only £21. On the ninth he put his things on board, including a copy of J. D. Lang's *History of New South Wales*. He went to church 'in the fore and afternoon but the Clergymen I heard were strangers'. He put some New Testaments on the Uist boat for his sisters, the Reverend Nicolson at the Barra manse and 'my dear Miss Margaret'. He wrote on the back of his journal some incongruous homilies: 'May I never want a friend for a friend in need is a friend indeed'; 'Remember a man should keep his friendship in constant repair'; 'The Academy of Fine Arts is the most celebrated school for painting in the world'. And he signed his name in a variety of styles.

Angus McMillan did not like his companions. The steerage passengers were vulgar and ungodly and behaved quite contrary to the advice of people with some understanding of the workings of the Almighty's mind; people like the editors of a guide to emigration published the following year who included not just some thoughts of Coleridge's on the benefits of being English, but warnings against all sorts of apostasy, especially the voluntary extinction of reason with alcohol, and suggestions that all behaviour likely to kindle the anger of God be abandoned or at least suspended for the term of the voyage. Nothing was more likely to bring on a tempest than blasphemy or self-indulgence, yet the steerage passengers on the *Minerva* 'enjoyed themselves in dancing on the decks' before the ship was out of the Bay of Greenock. 'They should occupy their time to better advantage,' McMillan said, and prayed that the Almighty would give them a prosperous voyage.

With the exception of Allen MacCaskill, a friend who had also embarked in Glasgow, the 15 'gentle' passengers were no better than those in steerage. Angus was 'sadly disappointed' by them, and he was still rancorous long after his seasickness had passed. The worst of them he thought were two German clergymen recruited by John Dunmore Lang. One of them, he said, 'talks very bad English', and it irritated McMillan to hear him preach sermons. It offended the ears of a patriotic Highlander: the German should give 'a general sermon to his own countrymen', he said. It was not just that as a Briton he found Germans offensive. McMillan was accustomed to hearing the word of God in Gaelic. When he asked a Skyeman on board to read and give a prayer it became apparent how important the language was to his religion:

> I was quite delighted to hear worship in my mother tongue. It brought to my recollection the last day I heard my beloved friend Mr McCrae pour out his whole heart to the fountain of grace and truth. Oh may I ever remember the 5th of September 1837. May the heartfelt word of God heard that day sink deep into my heart and make me always look to him that sticks closer than a brother.

The Gaelic prayer was no doubt also appreciated by the numerous passengers who spoke no other language. But the

German went on his odious way. Later in the voyage he offended grievously: 'He was whistling on the poop after sermon which is a very uncommon sound to a Scotch highlander's ear. I remarked at the time he was the first clergyman I heard guilty of such a thing.'

McMillan was also sensitive to his natural surroundings. He observed the birds, especially a small land bird 'called in galic [*sic*] "clucharan"', and a dove which he hoped would not be 'killed by any of the wild sailors'. He studied an albatross a sailor caught, and, of course, the flying fish—every emigrant wrote home about the flying fish. They were 'about the size of a herring', McMillan said. 'Their wings are shaped like a bat, they sometimes fly 100 yards. Indeed it is not uncommon for them to fly on board deep loaded ships.' Indeed they did, and he found they tasted like the mullet. He made close observations of the weather, recorded the ship's progress carefully, and watched the stars. He lamented the gradual disappearance of the Great Bear from the night sky.

The emigrant was caught between home and the unknown. Every thought took him back to Barra. A blanket of his lost over the side reminded him of his mother and sisters who had made it. As he sailed under a vertical sun he thought of the cool breezes of Barra. On 'the hottest day I ever felt' he approached the equator; crossing it on 30 October he noted that now the sun was between him and home. The heat forced him to part with his homemade clothes and dress in cottons. This too saddened him, though his friend, MacCaskill, pleased him by wearing his Highland garb—'it becomes him', said McMillan. Time also measured his homesickness. He noted the passing of each week separating him from Scotland. Being 'very fond of reading the gailic [*sic*]' he tried this as a comfort, but without much success.

There was nothing on board to comfort him. The ship was excruciatingly slow; every other vessel overtook them. The provisions were poor; the salt beef did not agree with his stomach, and on at least one occasion the 'gallant captain' dispensed 'bad biscuit'. He called the *Minerva* a 'floating prison'. As the voyage dragged on his loathing for the other 'prisoners' ripened. He described the dinner table he had to suffer every night. There was a 'regular English bolter' and his 'trifling' wife. A Greenock sea-captain who had 'a very cannibal appearance' and an appetite to match: he seldom took anything 'but salt beef and pork with biscuits well-seasoned with mustard and vinegar'. Somehow this barbarian was married to a sister of the Reverend Dr Lang. McMillan continued to despise the 'fat and greasy' Germans, and he had no more time for 'a certain Mrs —— [who] had fried pork liver and a boiled salt herring on the same plate which she masticated together with great relish'. They were all fools and gluttons and dipsomaniacs, and he watched them very closely. He noted an English woman among them who was 'coextensive with her husband in turning the little finger for I have seen her quaff 5 glasses of wine with a tumbler of strong beer before 3 o'clock'. Such behaviour made him cry out for 'the highland lady that would hardly put her rosy lip to the glass'. He could not stand these people who were 'too fond of the good things of this life'. For three days after he put his spleen about them on paper he had heartburn.

The captain, a Mr Furlong, whose cabin McMillan shared, was a tolerable gentleman—at least until he ordered a sheep to be killed on the Sabbath. McMillan refused to eat the mutton. He attacked the captain and all those who would not join his boycott of the beast. 'Do *you* slaughter sheep in Germany on the Sabbath?' he asked the German clergyman. 'Do you call it *slaughter*?' asked the German in reply. 'Yes,' said McMillan. The German confessed to the crime. It would not happen in Scotland, McMillan told him. The German walked away. McMillan's opponents threw 1 Cor. 10: 27 at him: 'If any of them that believe not bid ye go to a feast, and ye be disposed to go, whatever is set before you, eat, asking no question for conscience sake.' McMillan parried with verse 28: 'This is offered in sacrifice unto idols, eat not for his sake that shewed it . . .', and he declared to himself, 'I have the word of God on my side.' Only his Highland friend and a man named Taylor supported him. McMillan thought it was a disgrace to Britain. In fact it shook his faith in the union; he had never dreamed that 'a Scotch highlander is quite different from an Englishman with regard to eating and drinking . . .' The captain told him he would not be holding to such opinions in 40 years' time.

In exile from his fellow passengers, McMillan laboured alone with his troubles, his sorrows and dreads. His writing suggests that it was more than the cool breezes of Barra that he longed for. But only once did he put the other subject of his thoughts in his journal. Six weeks out of Greenock he wrote:

> I must own my weakness on thinking of dear —— that loved me while I lived near her . . . I hope she will preserve my memory while in a foreign clime and under the heat of a tropical sun. Oh may she live and be happy in enjoyment of health and freedom and those blessings which providence has bestowed on her.

However, to his thoughts of ——, like his thoughts of his brother John, there was only one solution—'God's will be done'. Perhaps they would meet somewhere else. After all, 'this life is only a scene of vanity, which soon passeth away and affords no solid satisfaction but in the consciousness of doing well, and in the hope of another life'.

Propelled by Providence at little more than six knots, the *Minerva* floated on; it floated on the edge of the abyss and only Angus McMillan knew it. Only God could shield him from his sorrows and only God could save them all from death. When a woman died he could not bear the spectacle of her body being dropped over the side—it was 'a fearful consideration . . . [to be] confined to the deep. Oh may I ever remember the 29th September and think of him who has the boundless ocean in the palm of his hand.' Yet the sailors could be so stupid as to risk offending him by baking loaves on the Sabbath.

As his anxieties grew more profound McMillan's prayers grew more frequent. He took it to the Lord in verse, assuring Him that he knew that He was his only shield against calumny and his only hope against death.

Oh teach me Lord to leave the world
When thou shalt give command
Joyful as when with sails unfurled
The sailor leaves the land
Oh teach me to embark in hope
On the long voyage of death
When called to leave my [?]
And yield my fainting breath.

Each expression of misery, or bitterness or fear was tempered by an assertion of faith and a plea for strength. Angus McMillan was working out a contract with the Almighty: when passengers began dying of a contagious fever and he began to suffer from a headache he finalised it.

McMillan was easily reminded of his mortality, and therefore of the safe pastures he had left. The fever was clearly God's punishment of the wicked. When a victim died McMillan preached himself a sermon about the fools who were 'postponing repentance'. He for one was not going to leave it until he was on his death bed before he came to terms with his Maker. He wrote out some resolutions and submitted them to the Almighty.

He resolved to devote his life to God's glory, which meant in effect that he was declaring himself an agent of Providence. In future 'Only his holy word be my guide and staff through the helping of his spirit which will make my path easy and burden light.' He asked the Lord to underwrite this resolution; 'Being sensible that I am unable to do anything without God's help I do humbly entreat him by his grace to enable me to keep these resolutions so far as they are agreeable to his will.' He resolved also to do 'whatever I think to be most to God's glory and my own good'; to never lose one moment of time but to improve it the most profitable way; to live with all his might; to 'never . . . do anything which I should be afraid to do if it were the last hour of my life'; and 'never hence forward to act as if I were in any way my own but entirely and altogether God's and agreeable to his will'. More specifically he would in future speak no evil of anyone 'without good call', or act out of revenge or irrational anger; he would trace any evil action of his to its origin and fight it; he would be faithful to his trusts; he would strive to 'a higher exercise of grace' than he had the week before. In future Angus McMillan would be 'sweet, benevolent, peaceable, quiet, contented, generous, humble, meek, obliging, diligent, industrious, charitable even of aliens [the Germans could take heart], moderate and forgiving'. He would never be deterred by misfortune or adversity. He would always 'examine whether I have done my duty and resolve to do it: and let it be just as Providence orders it. I will be as far as I can be concerned about nothing but my duty and my sins.'

McMillan sensed too much danger in the world to live without his set of scriptural rules. As Phillip Greven has said in *The Protestant Temperament* of the followers of the evangelical brand of American puritanism: 'Threatened continually by enemies from both within and without, they found reassurance in following the will of God, knowing that their own wills had been conquered and had been surrendered altogether.' In a style reminiscent of Cromwell after a victory, McMillan submitted to God's will. And in so far as this gave him a purpose and a method in life, an assurance that he was of the elect, God kept his side of the bargain.

The resolutions were a profoundly practical solution to McMillan's problems. If it took some time for his headache to abate, the fever, nonetheless, bypassed him. Far more importantly, he had steeled himself against his homesickness. Although he shed tears at finding in his luggage two letters from his brother on the same day, he wrote on 18 November that the ship was 'now almost the same longitude as the west highlands of Scotland for I must now give up calling them home'. This followed from another of his resolutions, 'never to allow the least measure of fretting'. It was as if McMillan had been dying of homesickness, and it was this which drove him to his pact with God, this which toughened him for the colonies. 'I have got my hand to the plough,' he said, 'I must not look back.'

On 13 December he noted that they were sailing within nine or ten degrees of the ice and that the weather which would be regarded as temperate in Scotland was cold for the Antipodes. On the fourteenth his headache was improved 'but it still aches'. The next day he was sorry to hear there were more passengers with the fever and some were dangerously ill. He thanked 'the giver of all good' for the passing of his headache. The journal ended, a week later, a month away from Port Jackson.

Angus McMillan sailed 'upside down', beneath a country which natural historians had generally agreed was 'suspended in time'. 'Compared with other countries, Australia furnishes the conception of a country in an imperfect state of formation,' the *Westminster Review* reported in 1841: 'The whole animal race differs from that of other countries, and appears to connect the present with a former world.' As the Scottish Highlanders had found that their human status was debased by their being cast as arcane and archaic in a colonising age, in Australia the natives had met with people for whom the distinction between animals and humanity was blurred. The press of Edinburgh, London and Sydney concurred on one point about the Antipodes; that man there was in 'his lowest known state'.

John Dunmore Lang resisted the idea. He called it the 'damnable doctrine' of the squatters, that the Aborigines of Australia were scarcely better than monkeys. Lang believed that the blacks were 'part of that great family of nations which was known to the ancients under the generic name of Sythians, and which derived both its name and its origin from Cush, or Cuth, the eldest son of Ham, the son of Noah'. He had no time for the notion that God had pronounced a curse upon them. He reminded colonists that they must once have been the greatest navigators in the world, and colonised an area in the southern hemisphere far greater than the Roman Empire. He quoted the evidence of the explorers, Mitchell and Leichhardt and his own missionaries—people whose contact with them had been more disinterested than the squatters'—who said the Aborigines were an admirable race, at least before they were contaminated by contact with Europeans; 'hospitable and not at all devoid of kind feelings', Leichhardt said.

But when McMillan reached Sydney, everything he saw was likely to have supported the harshest judgement. For Aboriginal society had been destroyed at Port Jackson and the remnants lived about the town in a state more degraded than even the inhabitants of the worst hovels on Skye and Barra. In the country they were vanishing. The Reverend Mr Schmidt, one of the German missionaries McMillan loathed so much, was soon reporting from his mission that the squatters around Moreton Bay had sunk so low as to resort to the 'infernal Italian practice of poisoning', as Lang described it. Schmidt accused them of poisoning upwards of 50 blacks.

There were some in Britain, like Henry Mayhew in London or Robert Somers in the Highlands, who noticed a relationship between a people's habits and the material condition of their culture; and who reminded Britons of the barbarism in their own society. But there was much less interest of an anthropological or any other kind in the poor of London, Liverpool or Skye than there was in the peoples who had recently fallen under the British flag in more distant places.[2]

---

2 Among the poor of London Mayhew noticed behaviour reminiscent of 'a menagerie at feeding time':

> At one moment a lad would imitate the bray of a jackass, and immediately the whole one hundred and fifty would fall to braying. Then some gagged urchin would crow like a cock, whereupon the place would echo again with a hundred and fifty cock crows. Then, as a black-boy entered the room, one of the young vagabonds would shout out 'swe-ee-op'. This would be received with peals of laughter, and followed by a general repetition of the same cry. Next a hundred and fifty catcalls of the shrillest possible description would almost split the ears. This would be succeeded by 'Strike up, you catgut scrapers' . . .

It was all rather like a corroboree, or a rain dance or the ritual accompanying a cannibalistic feast.

The popular press was full of the habits of the Hottentot, or perhaps something even more exotic—some abomination in Africa that Richard Burton had risked his life to witness, for instance. August bodies, like the Royal Geographical Society, were also interested in Burton's reports as they were in sober scientific accounts of New South Wales from Paul Strzelecki. Christian explorers in the wilds of the empire were forever trying to stir the consciences and the pockets of readers of the *Record* of the Home and Foreign Missionary Society, with tales of appalling heathenism. The native races of the world were a subject of universal interest in Britain, even when they were not rebelling.

'The great objects which usually influence savage life are self-gratification and self-preservation . . .', the *Quarterly Review* said in 1824. It stood to reason that savages could be measured by degrees, and the first of these was the degree to which a society regulated the instincts of its members. This was not just a matter of government, of course. As the unnamed author of the *Circumnavigation of the Globe* pointed out in 1836, it was common to see monarchical processions amid ceremonies of human sacrifice and idolatry in the lofty forests of the Pacific Islands. This was 'half civilization'. The inhabitants of a 'lofty forest' were more likely to have attained this status than the scavengers of 'barren wastes', presumably because Adam was created in a garden and not a desert. Those who had ceased to live in the garden, and did not cultivate—the hunter-gatherers—were history's outcasts.[3] Their inferiority was historically demonstrated, and they were condemned to

3 By 1848 the Catholic journal, the *Rambler*, was able to state that Adam was a black man created somewhere near the Caspian Sea: '. . . the analogy of nature proves . . . that the transition is from black to white in most animals, but not conversely'.

something even worse than the classic sons of Ham, the negroes.

A belief in a superior being was also an indication of the level of civilisation. For the most part those who believed in a false God were judged to be superior to those who believed in no God at all. But the godless sometimes enjoyed the appellation 'children' as opposed to barbarian—if they survived long enough to hear it said of them.

Secular and religious interests agreed on the validity of several criteria—women, for instance. In savage life it was well known that women were 'condemned to drudgery, and to bear . . . the violent and brutal conduct of their husbands'. Here was an echo of the visitor to the Highlands who said that by their 'natural contempt for the fair sex', the Highland men showed themselves to be 'mere savages, but one degree above brutes'. The condition of women in any society, the *Quarterly Review* believed, was 'that great line of distinction which will usually illustrate the extremes and intermediate stages of refinement and barbarism'.

From this position it was a short and natural jump to establish the ideals for men and women. It was well known in England that indolence was not ideal for a man, and that drudgery was anathema to women. The ideal for a man was, among other things, physical prowess, and for a woman, femininity; '. . . a persuasive gentleness of demeanour, a winning delicacy and . . . a beauty of figure and countenance joined to a softness of voice peculiarly pleasing . . . a quiet submissiveness . . .' The writer was not describing his wife, but the qualities Indian squaws sometimes displayed, despite their husbands.[4]

But the male defined the level of civilisation. Some

4 The last of the Beothics, Shaa-naan-dithit, 'possessed classical regularity of form. Her face bore a striking similarity to that of Napoleon . . .' Her father's features were 'strictly Roman', *Fraser's Magazine* said in March 1836.

civilised Britons thought the colonies were 'in much the same social condition as Britain was when discovered by the Romans'. There was the same constant warring between the tribes, 'the same unappeasable spirit of retaliation'. It was the attributes of the male which decided who qualified as stable unimproved Britons. The Maoris did. The Maoris were 'a finely developed, highly spirited but completely savage race': like the American Indians their males were 'ferocious', 'revengeful', 'irascible'—all superior qualities to the 'effiminancy and mildness' of the Tahitian men. In physique it was possible for savages to approach the Romans and Greeks. Should they combine this with fierceness it was even possible that they would be granted a treaty. But the mode and the rules of warfare they observed were another consideration: a Kaffir for instance was 'a fine animal . . . tall, well-knit, clean-limbed and graceful', but he exhibited a natural cunning which would not have become a Greek. His claim to classicity was stymied.

By 1837 the nobler savages of the world were already dying in a classical manner. The style of frontier death later standardised in Hollywood was employed by Robert Montgomery Bird in *Nick of the Woods*, published in the mid-1830s. In this the heroes fired with 'fatal effect upon the rash warriors, two of them fell dead on the spot, while the third and foremost, uttering a final whoop of defiance, and making an effort to throw the hatchet he held in his hand, suddenly staggered and fell in like manner to the earth'. People were reading about it in Glasgow when Angus McMillan passed through.

Scientific inquirers into the native races made great use of phrenology, seeing the mind's construction in the skull. No-one was more adept at proving the superiority of the Caucasian cranium (in the final analysis, the prime function of phrenology) than Sir Richard Burton. His remarks on the inhabitants of the Lake Districts of Central Equatorial Africa are worth quoting at length:

> The cranium is of the long-narrow shape, and the parietal portions are so crushed in the regions of acquisitiveness, ideality, and constructiveness, that, by the side of the Africans, the Arab's flat skull appears well filled out, and the Indian's a 'bullet-head'. As in the Egyptian, the line rises from benevolence, which is low, by an upward elongation to firmness and self-esteem; these organs are well developed, whilst the rest of the arch, supposed to contain the moral sentiments, wants roundness and height. Not unfrequently the forehead converges to a central protuberosity, where phrenologists locate eventuality, like the convex boss of a shield, and the surrounding organs fall away from it. The cranium from behind often appears of cauliflower shape, the coronal region is ignobly flat, the occiput—the breaching of the gun—weakly droops, and the bony processes, where cautiousness is supposed to reside, protrude like knobs.

Phrenology was not just an example of Victorian arrogance: it epitomised the way in which the language of colonisation obscured its real impulses. Ratbaggery became received wisdom. Phrenology was a new language for Providence.

The study of anthropophagy (cannibalism) was also fashionable. Good students could even discern different levels of savagery among 'the Cannibals that each others eate . . .' The worst of course was the anthropophagist, the 'habitual cannibal', the one with 'an enormous desire for human flesh' with whom the missionaries of the Church of Scotland were contending in the New Hebrides. These truly appalling people ate their fellows for no better reason than 'sensual animal gratification'. There was a theory that human flesh was addictive. Less depraved savages ate sparingly and with discretion, to satisfy a superstition rather than a craving.

Or perhaps in a moment of excitement: savages could forget themselves too.[5]

Most reports of cannibalism were at least second-hand. The few eye-witness accounts to reach Britain tended to follow a pattern. The poor observer watched with such horror that he could not but describe the banquets in the most minute detail and at the end he had to coyly decline the offer of a limb, or worse, eat a portion to save his own life. The *Quarterly Review* grew tired of the tales and began to doubt their authenticity. It doubted whether cannibalism was widely practised: 'We are slow to believe that any people—at least any above the most abject condition of the savage—are in the habit of using human flesh as a luxury—"dog no eat dog", as the negro says.' Mr Alexander Dalrymple, the Admiralty's hydrographer, had travelled all over the world and had never seen one 'tittle of evidence on the question of man-eating that would be received in a court of justice'. These were opinions expressed well before Burton penetrated central west Africa and sent back reports and specimens to London. But there is no doubt that a good many accounts in the press and journals were geared to a blood-hungry market at home, perhaps, as Burton himself recognised to some extent, not adequately catered for by public hangings. The idea of cannibalism would have existed without the reality. Since the Spanish conquest of South America at least, it had been a justification for conquest of native tribes—physical and spiritual.[6]

5 It was probably in a moment of excitement rather than by force of habit or addiction that two Scotsmen bit off each other's noses in Glasgow in September 1837. The judge described their conduct as 'ferocious and unmanly'. The *Glasgow Herald* referred to both of them as cannibals.

6 It is more than remotely possible that Europeans at least subconsciously encouraged cannibalism in the tribes they contacted. In the case of Burton's visit to Dahomey his hosts were performing not only his fantasies but those of the British nation in general, and Algernon Charles Swinburne in particular.

There were missionaries who said, with a fair degree of justification, that the native survivors of European imperialism owed their lives to the Christian belief of the men who protected them that all mankind was one. And there were scientific men arguing that the societies of central Africa were no more barbaric in many respects than their own. Some resisted the popular belief 'that the Negro forms . . . the connecting link between man and brute creation'. That was an idea used to justify slavery, J. C. Hall said. His own research showed no essential differences between Simians and 'even . . . human idiots'. But even sceptics like Hall, and men who loathed much in their own society, like Burton, could not escape the conclusion that the Caucasian skull had the most room for civilisation. By the time Burton described the peoples of central Africa to the English none of them would have noticed the assumptions underpinning his analysis. The children of these folk were 'distinguished by that grotesque prettiness which we admire in the young of the lower animals. The general aspect in old age, when the limbs have shrivelled, and the muscles have relaxed, especially amongst the women is hideously ape like.'

From these varied criteria something like a 'scale of civilisation' had emerged as early as the 1840s—men like Burton only added names to the bottom rung of the ladder. At the top of the savages were the American Indians, with their belief in 'the existence, the omnipotence, and the unity of God, and a future state of reward or punishment'; their classical beauty; the fierceness of the warriors; the femininity of the women and their superior mode of government—the English saw traces of democracy. Not far behind the Indians, and the outstanding savages of the British Empire, were the Maoris of New Zealand, despite their cannibalism. The Zulus rated highly, as did the

Kaffirs who had 'very respectably shaped noses'. Towards the lower end lay the sleepy Hottentot, 'the most improvident, lazy animal on the face of the earth', Alfred Cole said. 'The Hottentot never seems to be touched by his intercourse with the European. His civilization such as it is, drops off him, as soon as a change of circumstances makes it possible or agreeable.' By comparison with the Hottentot, Cole said, 'the negro is a polished being'. There were those whom the garment of civilisation simply would not fit. The Hottentot was one example, but there were even lower beings: 'Compared to a Bushman, the Hottentot is a gentleman, an Adonis, a philosopher.' It was to the Bushmen of South Africa that the Australian Aborigines were most often compared.

In 1828, in a review of Cunningham's *Two Years in New South Wales*, the *Quarterly Review* expressed the popular opinion of the colony: the Aborigine is 'among the lowest, if not the very lowest, in the scale of human beings'. For Bennett, in 1836, they were 'many degrees below even the worst of the Zealanders'. Bennett numbered them among 'the most hideous of all the living creatures of humanity'. They failed every test of humanity. Even their warfare was of the unmanly, stealthy kind. And they ate women; or so a Mr Sievewright said in this classical description of a human banquet in western Victoria.

> ... with as much indifference as I could assume, I stretched myself upon a tree and narrowly watched the proceeding ... Horror stricken and utterly disgruntled, while obliged to preserve the equanimity of demeanour upon which I imagined the development of this tragedy to depend, I witnessed the most fearful scene of ferocious cannibalism. The bowels and viscera having been disengaged from the body were at first portioned out; but from the impatience of some of the women to get at the liver, a general scramble took place for it, and

> it was snatched in pieces, and, without the slightest process of cooking, was devoured with eagerness and avidity—a keen feverish expression of impatience for more, from which scene a memory too tenacious upon this subject will not allow me to escape.

Mr Sievewright went on to describe limbs being 'wrenched and twisted' from their joints, blood being 'eagerly collected in handfuls' from the chest cavity, 'the teeth employed to dissever the reeking tendons when they would not immediately yield to their impatience'. Having suffered this nightmare, the poor European was given a foot which he felt obliged to accept. He put it in his handkerchief and 'joyfully availed myself of the opportunity to retire'. Mr Sievewright's civilisation was intact—the savages had just proved it.[7]

However, if nine out of ten commentators and colonists thought that the Australian Aborigines were not much above 'almost brutal stupidity', there was a significant body of opinion disputing with them. Horatio Hale and Charles Pickering were both members of the United States Exploring Expedition which visited Australia in 1840. Hale's ethnographical observations led him to the conclusion that the Aborigines were 'hardly human'. But Pickering, whose host in New South Wales was Lachlan Macalister, reported that the blacks were highly regarded in the colony for their ready adaptability, their facility with language, and their amiability. Where Hale saw protruding abdomens, thick skulls and retracted jaws, the combination making for 'a distorted and hardly human appearance', Pickering's Aborigine was 'the finest model

7 In contrast to Sievewright's account, William Tennant Dawson was told by the Aborigines of Western Victoria that 'the body was eaten, with no desire to gratify or appease the appetite, but only as a symbol of respect and regret for the dead'.

of the human proportions I have ever met with; in muscular development combining perfect symmetry, activity and strength; while his head might be compared to the antique bust of a philosopher'. Hale clearly struggled with his preconceptions: on one page he described 'downright childishness and imbecility' among them, while on the next he wrote that they were 'extravagantly proud. The complete personal independence to which they are accustomed gives to their ordinary demeanour an air of haughtiness and even insolence. Nothing will induce them to acknowledge any human being (of their own age) their superior, or show any mark of deference.' John MacCulloch of course had noticed the same trait among Scottish Highlanders.

Pickering did not seem to have the same problems. He thought the notion that the Aborigines were low on the 'scale of civilisation' was nonsense. And he confronted another key assumption in the Europeans' pretence of superiority, *and* the consequent belief in a sovereign right to take the Aborigines' land. Pickering admired the use the Aborigines made of the land. 'I have sometimes doubted whether any different branch of the human family could have maintained its existence on the slender natural resources of interior Australia.' That was a profound observation. It was one thing to wax lyrical about the hunter in a natural world, or to lament his extinction by progress; it was something else altogether to recognise him as the manager of the estate.

Paul Strzelecki, the Polish explorer, wrote in a vein that was at once benign and clinical. Had his subjects been European the language he used would only have befitted a post mortem. The face had 'an angle of between 75° and 85°. It is marked by a low forehead, eyes large, far apart, and half covered by the upper lid, with a conjunctiva of the purest white, spotted with yellow . . . a nose broad and flat, the frontal sinuses being remarkably prominent . . . the lower jaw unusually short, and widely expanded anteriorly.' They must have all been cast from the same mould. The women were low in stature, 'the head short, and the features masculine: the mammae, instead of being hemispherical, are, in marriageable persons, pyriform, and soon after marriage become flaccid and elongated'. The 'foot [is] large, flat, and invariably turned inward', wrote Strzelecki. But he had more to say than this. He challenged the philistine view that the Aborigines were 'savage, debased, unfortunate, miserable'. The philistine travelled with his eyes closed, said Strzelecki: had he travelled with them open he would have seen, as Strzelecki had, that Providence offered as many roads to contentment as there were races of mankind. And when he beheld the Aborigines,

> the serene, calm, mild, yet lively countenances . . . their dance and song, those uncontrollable manifestations of attained felicity, he finds really in the scene a corroboration of what otherwise a mere inference, from the goodness and omniscience of the Creator might have taught him to believe.

The Scot, Sir Thomas Mitchell, perhaps the most meretricious man in the colony, had shot a few blacks in his day. But he had no time for the idea that they were in any way inferior. 'They have been described as the lowest in the scale of humanity,' he wrote, 'yet I found those who accompanied me superior in penetration and judgement to the white men composing my party.' There were a few Rousseauian flights in Mitchell's description, but it was not Rousseau which put him at odds with colonial opinion. It was observation of Aboriginal society. It seemed to him that they experienced 'a level of health and an intensity of existence . . . far beyond the enjoyments of civilized men'. And like Pickering, Mitchell would not accept the notion that the Aborigines' unwillingness to till the land had any consequences for their rights to it.

Mitchell was enlightened, even philanthropic, though he doubted 'our pretensions to improve and benefit the race'. He was intrigued by the technological ingenuity of the Aborigines. His patented screw propeller, the boomerang propeller, drew on the blacks' mastery of differential calculus, he said. In 1850 Mitchell read a paper to the Australian Society in which he suggested that there might be some knowledge of the occult or of freemasonry among Aboriginal 'priests'. He knew the blacks possessed secrets beyond the grasp of Europeans.

Had he spoken to Sir Thomas Mitchell, a newcomer to Sydney might have gained the impression that the Aborigines were a people to be admired. He might have seen beyond both the popular literature of the day and the derelict society before him. But even had he managed this, it was, as Mitchell's life itself had shown, no guarantee against murder. The most charitable of men in 1838 could still not rid themselves of morbidity when they thought about the Australian Aborigines for very long. It did not seem to matter whether they thought them the highest or the lowest on the scale of civilisation, or whether they felt compelled by Christianity to care for them or not; they still felt that an Aborigine's life was worth less than their own. They thought them as good as dead.

North of Sydney at Myall Creek, in the year of Angus McMillan's arrival in New South Wales, the settlers decided that to ensure the safety of their cattle they would 'exterminate the whole race of blacks in that quarter'. And they proceeded to do so. It was not long after the massacre at Myall Creek that Thomas Mitchell sent off a parcel to a scientific friend in London. It contained 'a memento—the sad emblem of mortality—a skull, being the head of a young Australian female—who was killed for some trifling offence by her brutal husband, or rather master. It is interesting for the uncannily fine set of teeth.'

EXPLORING

It is well known that when a settler or squatter in Australia discovers an eligible tract of country, he is generally in no hurry to let the world know of it, but rather endeavours to keep it concealed, that his own flocks and herds may luxuriate on the rich grass it produces as long and as quietly as possible without interruption.

J. D. LANG, *PHILLIPSLAND*, 1847

I was suddenly confronted by numerous blacks, who stared at me with astonishment, but when I dismounted and moved my hands in friendly salutation they fled in all directions.

ANGUS McMILLAN, 'JOURNAL OF AN EXPEDITION IN GIPPSLAND', 1839–41

The Portuguese probably saw Gippsland first, but if they ever bothered to set foot on it they left no trace. Cook saw it from the deck of his ship on 19 April 1770, but he pushed on up the east coast without landing. In 1797 George Bass charted its coast in his whaleboat, and is said to have left convict castaways on the shore. If he did, they were never heard of again. There is another tale (it may be a version of the same one) that four survivors of a wreck in February 1797 walked from a point west of Cape Howe to Port Hacking where they were rescued. Whalers and sealers operating in Bass Strait used Gippsland's coves and inlets where they found both seals and shelter. Wilson's Promontory provides superb shelter. Deposits of whale bones can still be found in its havens. It is believed that a Captain Stevenson settled east of the Promontory sometime before the Hentys settled at Portland in the Western District of Victoria. He left no trace. By the 1830s the scene had been thoroughly gazed upon from a distance, but there had been few intruders and all traces of them had vanished.

The mountains they saw from the coast are modest in altitude but marvellous in design. From a distance they are blue: even in the midst of the bush blue sometimes seems to dominate. If squatters and explorers ever noticed that blue prevails in the Australian landscape they rarely mentioned it. In Gippsland the Scots among them saw similarities with their homeland in the juxtaposition of mountains, rivers, lakes and sea. But in the bush it was very different. They were used to a green and tawny treeless landscape. In the Hebrides the view was horizontal. In the Gippsland bush it was all vertical. In some places they could barely see the sky.

A man of any era standing on a mountain top in these ancient ranges was likely to reflect on the Creator. In the bush on a black night or a moonlit one he was bound to feel with some intensity that he was in the hands of his Maker. To emerge from such a place into open hills and plains running down to the sea was doubtless a blessing with profoundly religious dimensions.

In the Gippsland ranges stands of box suddenly give way to iron-bark and stringybark, or expanses of messmate and shining gum. The gullies are often thick with acacia, sassafras, lianas, mistletoe, and tree ferns as high as 15 metres, all living in a slowly rotting world of fallen timber overgrown with moss. Elegant, brilliantly white gums rise out of the lower orders, seeming brittle against the impervious hulks of grey and yellow-box. It was very easy to get lost. An Englishman, John Pettit, arrived in Gippsland in 1854 and in his first years there spent much of his time trying to find his way out of the bush or from one point to another within it. He was sure many people must have perished in the attempt:

> 'A "new chum",' he said, 'cannot help being struck with the great sameness and painful stillness of the Australian bush generally. No birds warbling or other cheering sound. In some of the huge, deep and comparatively narrow gullies it is fearfully still and solemn and sombre yourself apparently the only living creature.'

The dingoes did not go into the gullies it seems. Elsewhere they followed nervous 'new chums' like Pettit as they rode through the bush at night, and set themselves up around the camps howling 'hideously and discordantly'. Higher up in the hills the undergrowth is missing. The light of late evening or early morning reveals rock beneath the trees. The hills turn grey-blue, and at some mysterious moment when the sun is neither up nor down the ridges light up for a moment, magically pink.

Lachlan Macalister's friend and neighbour, James Macarthur, first saw Gippsland from the sea in 1839. He was lying off the coast west of Cape Howe in HMS *Pelorus* which could make no progress against an easterly gale. It is said that through the mist he noted that the ranges 'receded considerably' towards Wilson's Promontory and he wondered if there might not be ample room for sheep. As the ship beat its way to Sydney he planned an expedition.

In 1841 an 'annihilator of space', 'a condenser of time', the new steamer, *Clonmel*, washed up on Gippsland's shores. This 'Argo which would have brought many a Jason to our modern Culchis ...' did the run from Sydney to Port Phillip in three days. The people of Port Phillip mourned the loss of the ship, but the passengers and their rescuers returned with stories about a likely looking port. The Kurnai were just becoming aware that they faced an invasion.

High up on the northerly side of the ranges, on the Omeo Plains, James and Malcolm MacFarlane, natives of Glenfalloch, had established a cattle run among the Yaitmathang in 1837. They had pushed down from the Monaro. George McKillop, late of Calcutta and later of Edinburgh, a man with interests in Port Phillip, Hobart and the Monaro, had travelled to Omeo as early as 1835. He left his name on the map in the magnificent gorge of the Snowy River where, lined with blue pine, it meets the Deddick. Also by 1837 there were men in the vicinity named Pendergast and Livingstone; and further to the west at the foot of the ranges which form the headwaters of the Tambo, an Irishman, Edmund Buckley, was grazing cattle. In 1838, James MacFarlane's nephew, Walter Mitchell—who had travelled with McMillan on the *Minerva*—found a route through to the Tambo and travelled as far as Buchan, possibly even as far as the Gippsland lakes.

On the eastern flank, a Scot named Peter Imlay was expanding his already large holdings at Twofold Bay. And Andrew Hutton, known as 'The Hie'landman', drove 500 cattle along the coast as far as the lakes before the Kurnai drove him off and plundered his stock. Perhaps he only got as far as the lower Snowy which would have been a formidable barrier to his herd, but Hutton always maintained that he reached the lakes.

Captain Lachlan Macalister was trying to escape the drought in New South Wales. He had already pushed into the Monaro. The recent arrivals from the Highlands were invaluable to him as God-fearing labour: a family of Mackenzies from Skye were at Goulburn, and Lachlan Morrison and his family were minding his sheep and cattle south of the Molonglo.[1] Dr Alexander Arbuckle, the son of a North Uist minister and a medical practitioner for four years at Portree, was at this time enjoying Macalister's hospitality and advice prior to embarking on a new career in medicine and cattle. Arbuckle had his two-year-old daughter, Flora, with him. He was a widower and a very resourceful will o' the wisp. But there was none so resourceful among Macalister's recruits from Skye as Angus McMillan.

'While you are on the voyage you cannot realize the distance; it is only when you set foot on shore that you can comprehend and feel it,' a Highland emigrant wrote home in 1850. When Angus McMillan arrived in Sydney on 23 January 1838 he had surely comprehended the distance. Fourteen passengers had died of the fever, and to aggravate the agony the *Minerva* was put in quarantine, where more passengers fell ill and died. The *Colonist* thought it was madness to put ships in quarantine: this 'gaol or typhus fever' only increased in virulence until passengers were allowed ventilation and exercise. When he finally set foot in Sydney, McMillan can have been in no mood to forgive any signs of a moral dunghill. Emigrants were advised by both the pious and the pragmatists not to linger in the town where ne'er do wells and reprobates would enfeeble their fibre. Head straight for the country, they said. The country held out hope if not redemption.

Yet the Sydney press did not carry much suggestion

1 Morrison feared God a little too much for Macalister's taste. It is said that when Macalister instructed him to work on Sundays on the grounds that there was no Sabbath south of the Molonglo, Morrison replied that he had taken it with him when he crossed it. Morrison died in 1840, just three years after his arrival from Skye.

of a cesspool and more than one Scottish emigrant noted a higher moral tone than that of Glasgow. Perhaps everyone was too busy making money. D. M. Sinclair, who arrived in May 1839, wrote to a Glasgow minister that the place had the virtue of sobriety and the vice of mindlessness. 'As to literature, nothing is ever heard of it here. Money is everything with the mass of the people . . .' One J. Fowles, who arrived a year earlier, was surprised to see the cove 'alive with boats plying to and fro', the wharves swarming with merchants, and the shores of the harbour dotted with their mansions. In the midst of this bustle Sinclair felt an 'oppression' at the thought of making his way in the world.

On shore the *Colonist* was telling its opponents what Lang had told the Molesworth Committee on transportation—that the convict system was a moral plague to be extirpated only by the mass migration of Highlanders. It was also warning that it had been recently shown that excessive laughter could cause death. It was writing of the 'beautiful delineation' of women's role in Protestantism, which placed more emphasis on the intellect than the heart, and more on practical accomplishments than adorning ones. And the *Colonist* had just received word of the discovery of the horrible practices of the Meetawallers of Patua and Sarun.

Angus McMillan had survived the gaol fever but he was going to run no further risk of contamination. He passed quickly through the streets of Sydney and made for the bush. The whipper-in for the Sydney hunt was also leaving town, hobbled in an iron gang. The Sydney bench said it was the only practicable punishment for a man who had stolen 36 pounds of meat and was too much accustomed to the whip.

With him McMillan carried a letter of introduction to Lachlan Macalister whose family seat in Skye was a day's walk through the Cuillins from McMillan's birthplace at

Glenbrittle. Macalister took him on as overseer of his home-station, Clifton, near Picton. It was a relationship not unlike that which the McMillan family had been used to in the Hebrides: McMillan played tacksman to Macalister's laird, though of course by traditional standards both were pretenders. But Lachlan Macalister was one of those Highlanders who imagined rebuilding the clan's fortunes in Australia and the reproduction of clan relationships must have suited his ambition. The bonds between him and the new immigrants were built on loyalty as well as money. The poorer Highlanders, Presbyterian but not much improved, continued in their roles as proud but faithful workers.

McMillan left no trace of the first twelve months of his life in Australia. He was soon out on the Monaro with Macalister's stock and searching for pastures unaffected by the drought. Had he thrived on civilised company he might have suffered the same mental agonies as Farquhar MacKenzie endured: but McMillan was hardened to loneliness before he arrived, and did not much care for civilisation.

In February 1839 he reached Carrawong, the most northerly of MacFarlane's stations. We do not know who else was there, but many years later McMillan said it was from discussion with the Monaro blacks that he learnt about the good land in the south they called *Cabone Benel* and the barbarous tribe which inhabited it. That makes for a good saga of exploration but it is more likely that he heard about it from white settlers there, and that it was with them he discussed a foray. However, he chose a Monaro Aborigine, one of the very few survivors of the tribe, to accompany him. His name was Jemmy Gibber (the Scots had obviously named him) and McMillan later said it had not been easy to persuade him to go. Jemmy was said to have an ancient fear of the Kurnai. He had been employed by a squatter on the Monaro named Edward Bayliss. He has often been referred to as 'Chief of the Monaro tribe', but Aboriginal tribes did not have chiefs. Whites created them from among those who survived their conquest of the land. They granted them special favours and responsibilities, gave them brass plates which were worn around their necks and *said* they were chiefs.

Carrawong station lies in a frosty valley on the Carrawong Creek a few kilometres east of the Delegate River. It is a silent place, except for the screech of cockatoos which gather and sit perpendicular in the trees at dusk to catch the last rays of the sun. Grey-backed magpies still make their way across the valley in silent spurts, like airborne squid. The low hills to the south do not look impregnable.

McMillan rode back to his master at Clifton to seek approval for an expedition and funds to supply it with provisions. Lachlan Macalister was enthusiastic. So in June McMillan was ready in the Carrawong Valley. He had arms and provisions and Jemmy Gibber to help him find his way through the hills.

After four days' travelling Angus and Jemmy reached a hill near the Snowy River about 10 kilometres from Buchan. McMillan named it Mount MacLeod. From the top he said he could see as far as Corner Inlet. After four days in the bush he could now see a man's domain; he could have his own little dream of empire. He should also have seen John Wilkinson, who had been at Buchan at least a month with his stock.

Wilkinson had arrived there a day ahead of Edward Bayliss. Bayliss had actually been there first, but he had gone down to the Ninety Mile Beach and the lakes to look for something better. Finding Wilkinson had moved his cattle into Buchan, Bayliss went further north to Gelantipy and in the same year he formed a station there with eight men and 715 cattle.

Apparently oblivious to the congestion, McMillan pushed on with his explorations. But Jemmy Gibber, it seems, had different ideas. Many years later McMillan described the incident:

> My friend was beginning to get alarmed, and wished to return, but seeing me determined to proceed he threatened to leave me. On this night I was nearly paying dearly for placing so much confidence in my companion. Whilst lying at the campfire I was aroused by the circumstance of his raising his club to strike me. I had just time to present my pistol to his breast: he begged for his life, saying he dreamt a blackfellow was taking away his 'gin', and he wanted to kill him. I was satisfied that he intended to kill me, and report that I had been killed by the blacks of the district.

The peculiar side to this story is that Jemmy had been through this country before with Bayliss and there is nothing to suggest that he took fright then. Perhaps McMillan inspired less confidence. We can't be sure that the Aborigine's pleadings were successful. McMillan said later that Jemmy had deserted him shortly afterwards and he 'never heard of him again'. As there were few Monaro blacks left by 1840 it is difficult to imagine where Jemmy might have taken himself without being noticed. If he lived to tell his side of the story it was, of course, never recorded. Instead we have the explorer's tale of why he turned back so soon.

McMillan set off the next day for Omeo and reached it in six days. Here he heard about Walter Mitchell's journey, and left immediately for Clifton where he received 'every encouragement to explore the country'.

McMillan now recruited another of Bayliss's men, Edward Bath. 'Old Bath' was a stockman of vast experience on the Monaro. McMillan enticed him with an offer of higher wages, Bayliss said. They set out from MacFarlane's on 16 September. After three days they were forced to return when one of the horses was staked. They made their way up the Tambo Valley, finding a suitable place for a station at Numbla Munjee (later named Ensay). At this stage of his life, at least, McMillan was dogged rather than skilful. Although he had been told the route through the Tongio Gap he lost the way and found himself obliged to pass through the much rougher country at Bindi.

Macalister's cattle were duly driven to Numbla Munjee, and the station became a base for further exploration. However, there was no future for Gippsland until a port was found. In January a party was formed consisting of McMillan, Bath, John Cameron (a stockman), two Omeo Aborigines named Cobbon Johnny and Boy Friday, and Lachlan Macalister's nephew Matthew. Was Macalister getting impatient with McMillan? There is some reason to believe that Matthew Macalister was the senior partner in this undertaking.

Descending the Tambo Valley 'over some of the worst description of country McMillan ever saw', the party reached the lakes on 16 January 1840. On the day before they arrived they made their first contact with the Kurnai. McMillan described it years later:

> This day we were met by a tribe of the wild blacks who came up quite close to us, and stared at us while we were on horseback, but the moment I dismounted they commenced yelling and took to their heels, running away as fast as possible; and from the astonishment displayed at the circumstance of my dismounting from the horse, I fancied they took both man and horse to be one animal.

In another account he said it was not until later that he 'learnt' the reason for their behaviour.

To reach the lakes they passed through country which McMillan described as 'open forest, well grassed, the timber consisting chiefly of red and white gum, box, he- and she-oak, and occasionally wattle'. In the evening they reached a 'beautiful sheet of water' and called it Lake Victoria. It was not the source of the Nile but it was a splendid sight to graziers' eyes, and 'covered with wild ducks, swans and pelicans'. And on the north side lay 'beautiful open forest, and the grass was up to our stirrup irons as we rode along, and was absolutely swarming with kangaroos and emus'.

Travelling east, the next day they came to a river as large as the Tambo, and were forced to track upstream to find a crossing. All day they heard at a great distance the blacks 'coo-eeing, and the cries and wailing of women and children'. It was hot and the meat went off: 'We were, however, fortunate enough to find some wild ducks, upon which we made an excellent supper.' The explorers named the river after a friend of Lachlan Macalister, Dr Nicholson of Sydney. They rode on. After 11 kilometres they came to another large river; they named it after the father of Macalister's brother-in-law, Sir Thomas Mitchell. If these names exclusively reflected the circle of acquaintance of the Macalisters, McMillan might have had his way at a morass a little further on: his horse, 'Clifton', was nearly lost in it. They gave the name 'Clifton' to the bog. And the next day also belonged to McMillan. On the other side of the Mitchell they pitched camp:

> In the evening I ascended a hill near the camp, from the top of which I obtained a good view of the low country still before us, of the high mountains to the north-west, and the lakes stretching towards the sea-coast in a south and south-easterly

> direction; and from the general view of the country as I then stood, it put me more in mind of the scenery of Scotland than any other country I had hitherto seen, and therefore I named it at that moment, 'Caledonia Australis'.

It is the habit of explorers to compose their finest thoughts on hill tops, or at least to locate them there in their memoirs. Gullies do not encourage the sense of man's domain or favour a friendly communion with God. This was land, said McMillan, 'sufficient to feed all my starving countrymen'. He determined to take up a sizeable portion for himself as well as Macalister. He now had an ennobled sense of his mission. 'It was then I keenly felt that I had a noble and glorious task to perform, and that I was only an instrument in the hands of the Almighty to accomplish it.' It was in this spirit, presumably, that the next creek they came to was named Providence Ponds. They must have been doing something right.

Now with a name for the land they traversed, they rode through open forest to a lake they took to be a continuation of Lake Victoria. In fact it was Lake Wellington. They followed another river towards the mountains. 'The country around and beyond the place where we crossed . . . consists of beautiful, rich, open plains, and appeared, as far as I could judge at the time, to extend as far as the mountains.' The stream was called the Avon, probably not after the Scottish river, but the English one which runs through not only Stratford, but Clifton, near Bristol, where Macalister's regiment had been based. McMillan would make his mark, however—these plains would become his home. In the meantime they named the highest peak Wellington and another Ben Cruachan, which could offend no-one. Further west they struck yet another river and called it the Macalister.

Now they turned south and met a stream which they called the Thomson after the Colonial Secretary; they followed this to its junction with another of at least equal volume which was named Glengarry after a true Highlander who was soon to be in their midst. Where the rivers met they came upon another group of Aborigines, about 100 McMillan said. As the whites approached, the natives 'burnt their camps and took to the scrub'. The whites pursued them, as McMillan described it:

> We managed to overtake one old man that could not walk, to whom I gave a knife and a pair of trousers, and endeavoured by every means in our power to open a communication with the other blacks, but without success. It was amusing to see the old man. After having shaken hands with us all, he thought it necessary to go through the same form with the horses, and shook the bridles very heartily. The only ornaments he wore were three hands of men and women, beautifully dried and preserved.

At all times on this journey the blacks apparently ran away. They would never make friends, McMillan said. In retrospect at least he gave the impression that this was a cause for regret among the party. It may well have been.

Beside the Glengarry that night they tried unsuccessfully to make a bark canoe. It was probably as well that they failed. McMillan thought that Corner Inlet was only a short distance away. In fact it was nearly 100 kilometres through dense scrub which would later defy their axes. They had only five days' supplies left. At least this was the reason given for hurriedly returning to Numbla Munjee where a message was sent immediately to Lachlan Macalister. No-one uttered a word about their discoveries. Within six weeks McMillan had a track cut through the mountains to the 'park-like land' on the Avon. In October he drove

500 cattle down to establish a station for Macalister.

Macalister now sent a friend, a Lieutenant Ross, to assist in finding a route through to Corner Inlet. The next expedition consisted of Ross, McMillan, Matthew Macalister, Bath, and another Highland stockman, Colin MacLaren. To McMillan's chagrin, Ross was in command of this mission. It was a failure; they turned back about 32 kilometres from the inlet.

There was a growing sense of urgency in all their activity. McMillan returned to Monaro, it is said to legally secure some of the land around the Avon. He was told that he was beyond the law and must make his own arrangements. Returning to the Avon he found the new station deserted. Matthew Macalister and his men had been driven off in an Aboriginal attack of 'unexampled ferocity'. McMillan gathered his men together and re-possessed the land in what was variously described as a 'desperate skirmish' and a successful defence against a 'second attack' by the blacks. But there can be no doubt that the blacks were pursued and that when they were caught there was no mercy. The Briakalung tribe were never a problem again.

It took just five days to reach Corner Inlet. McMillan's crew beat their way down the valley of the Albert River and arrived in the mangroves of Port Albert on 14 February 1841. The port had been given a name eight days earlier by a party of squatters who had formed the Gippsland Company and arrived on a chartered boat.

It was not El Dorado. McMillan later said the immediate hinterland of the port was fine country, but others said it was a 'useless barren tract'. In fact the soil varied from rich to poor, from sand to swamp; and the vegetation was tall and impressive in some areas, while elsewhere low gums, she-oaks, honeysuckles and grass trees predominated.

Had McMillan had a tall tree to climb, he might have been able to see far enough south beyond the mudbanks and mangrove islands which stud the inlet to the narrow entrance from Bass Strait; and west over Sunday Island to the southernmost point of the mainland, Wilson's Promontory, where whalers still gathered. Looking about him he might have noticed the riches of bird life and fish. But he had meat on his mind, not fish. This was to be a port for the export of cattle.

For sixteen months McMillan had not slept on a bed, or even in the comfort of a tent, he said. He had erected gunyahs like the Aborigines. The desperate slog was over. He bathed his 'worn and weary feet in the sea'. 'This was a happy day,' he wrote, 'having accomplished my object, I had great cause to be thankful to Him who guarded me and shielded me from many a danger.'

Just how great those dangers were is uncertain. In a diary McMillan showed another Scot, Richard MacKay, 20 years later, he referred to an attack on his party by about 60 blacks at Clifton Morass in October 1840. Only he and Arbuckle were armed. They fired but did not kill any of them, McMillan said. A little later they were confronted by them in 'hundreds'. It was a classic confrontation if we are to believe McMillan's account. McMillan sought to make peace. He dropped his gun and walking towards them motioned to the blacks' 'leader' to drop his spear. The Aborigine appeared to do so, but when McMillan was within about 20 metres of him, his men realised that the black man was dragging his spear through the grass with his toes. The white men fired. All the Aborigines fell on their faces, McMillan said, then 'seeing their leader killed, they bolted in confusion'. Nothing more was said. No-one offered a reflection on the incident.

They were simply too busy to reflect for long. It

remained to cut a track. By now McMillan's team of Highlanders and convicts must have been ferociously efficient at chewing their way through bush, and the track was cleared in three weeks. James ('Mark My Word') Lawrence, a convict of Macalister's, drove a bullock dray through to complete an extraordinary journey from the station at Clifton.

Lachlan Macalister had not told his friend James Macarthur about the exploits of his brother and his overseer, or about the team of free Scots and assigned servants working for him in Caledonia Australis. Macarthur reached Sydney on the *Pelorus* determined to mount an expedition. With a young Englishman, James Riley, two Aborigines from his Goulburn Plains station named Charley Tarra and Jacky, and three servants (one of them 'an Affrican', James Riley said) Macarthur set off for Yass.

Here, on 5 February 1840, he added to the party a new and charming oddity in New South Wales society; a man with whom he had been much impressed when he met him in Sydney. He was an explorer, indeed a 'scientific explorer of considerable experience in other parts of the world', and he had most of the social graces. He travelled under the name of Count Paul Edmund de Strzelecki but he was not really a count. His father, of Galician descent, was Francis de Strzelecki, and his mother was Anna Raczynski. They were genteel but no more than cottagers. The family lived in the town of Gluzyma near Poznan in Prussian Poland. Paul was born in 1797. At fourteen he was sent to school in Warsaw, but soon after he had to be rescued from an affair with a married woman. Four years later he began courting the 15-year-old heiress to a large estate near his parents' home. She was Aleksandryna Katarzyna Turno—Adyna. Her parents warned off the penniless Paul, but he would not be deterred. The couple eloped but were overtaken before they had gone more than a few kilometres. At the age of 22 Paul left Gluzyma wounded and disgraced.

Strzelecki found potentially lucrative employment managing the vast but decrepit estates of a Prince Francis Sapieha. It was a major task but, Strzelecki claimed later, he stood to earn 180,000 florins for doing it well. Perhaps he did it a little too well, for the Prince's son began a campaign to have him removed. It was claimed that he was transferring considerable portions of the estate to himself and two friends, and it was also alleged that he was the bastard son of the prince, or the product of a union between his mother and her godfather, an archbishop. Strzelecki said this was all because his improvements had upset some families. Years later he described the affair in detail to Adyna:

> Francis Sapieha, owner of immense estates, loses his credit, his fortune is tottering, he is surrounded by thieves, there is systematic pillage; he sees the whole country in a plot to ruin him. He trusts himself to me, an obscure individual, without recommendations or connections; gives me full power to act, *carte blanche* for the sale of 12,000 peasants and the administration of all his affairs. I drove away the rabble, baulked the creditors' conspiracy, sold 10,000 peasants, paid the debts, established his credit and triumphed just where humiliation was to have been expected. Many families, feeling wronged in their interests, were roused by this, and drew Eustache Sapieha the son into their group. The struggle breaks out; Francis Sapieha leads, and I tumble down with all possible hubbub, all the chicanery of lawyers and lawsuits; the remuneration of 180,000 florins which the father promised me was cancelled by what the son took upon himself to have against me. In a country where venality constitutes the administration of justice, he being rich, won. Being without means, I lost. Peace was made on the judicial front. I renounced my real claims, he, his pretended ones, and I left the Sapiehas after four years

> tribulation, like that Jack who went away in the same state as he came.[2]

So Strzelecki left Poland with neither Adyna nor the 180,000 florins. He had managed to save enough to assure himself of a private income of £300 a year which enabled him to travel and to be a gentleman among gentlemen. He mastered geology, mineralogy and a number of other disciplines, in addition to several languages. Adyna was a memory to whom, for more than 30 years, he sent his love in letters addressed M-selle Virginie d'Aimée. His own title became Monsieur le Comte. As a compatriot noted in the Alfred Club in London in 1833, it was not uncommon: 'The harder up they are, the more they puff themselves up with titles,' he said. Strzelecki at other times was happy to be known as a political exile from poor Poland.

In 1830 Strzelecki was in Scotland making notes on the correct management of sheep, pasture and shepherds; comparing innovations in the Highlands with the improved pastoral economies of Silesia and Poznan. His model was that of the man who had almost doubled the size of the cheviot fleece and halved the number of shepherds, Mr Patrick Sellar of the Sutherland estate.

It had been 15 years since Sellar had carried out his factorial duties when Strzelecki came to see him. The sheep

2 The original letters, in French, are in Poland: the typescript copies in the Mitchell Library were lent by Mr Geoffrey Rawson whose 1953 biography of Strzelecki contains an extraordinary discrepancy. The copies read '. . . je chasse la canalle, reorganise l'adminstration, dejoue le complet de crediteurs—vends 10,000 paysans, payant les dettes etablia le credit et triomphe la ou il n'y avait que humiliation a attendre.' Mr Rawson translates this as '. . . I remove the scum, re-organise the administration of the estates, thwart the plot of his creditors, restore 10,000 peasants, pay their debts, re-establish their credit, and triumph where only humiliation awaited them'. It seems impossible to deduce such philanthropy from the words Strzelecki used, irrespective of one's attitude to the ethics of improvements such as those Strzelecki undertook.

were doing well; careful application of scientific breeding techniques was 'ennobling' their blood and the management of their pasture was unparalleled. Another 15 years on and Strzelecki was to write that Mr Sellar's system was 'likely to answer best for all the exigencies of an Australian grazier'.

On 8 June 1834 Strzelecki left from Liverpool for the United States. He trooped all over the North American continent, and then 'explored' the south. He interested himself in things both social and geophysical. He wrote to Adyna of a visit to a captured slaver in Rio de Janeiro, writing in detail of the slaves' sufferings and of 'the avarice and barbarity of Europeans, greater cannibals than those who bear the name'. And in Buenos Aires he witnessed the public execution of 110 Indians. He imagined an Indian uttering 'an invocation of the vengeance of his race upon the white man. Perhaps in the rage of despair he rejected the God of the Christians from ever being his God.' Strzelecki's lifetime experiences conspired over the years to destroy his faith in God; he put it instead in science and social reform.

In Mexico he found an example of an improving landlord who might have been a model for Europe. Without the mechanical innovations developed in Europe this man had nevertheless quintupled the value of his farm and spread the benefits evenly among his labourers.

> Don Joaquim de Astiazaran is, in his physiognomy and manners, his thoughts and actions, a true picture of a kind-hearted country gentleman, in harmony with himself and with all about him. Far from the tumult of active life, undisturbed by the thirst of fame or power, he tranquilly spins the thread of his days in the happy uniformity of pleasures which the cultivation of the soil affords and the domestic comforts which his fortune procures him.

Strzelecki believed that life's fundamental relationship was between man and nature. If nature could be understood it could be managed, and if it could be managed material abundance and human happiness would flow. No political re-ordering would do. For Strzelecki, one suspects, there was a natural order to be discovered and allowed to flourish. Only tyrants and villains opposed him on this.

He left America and sailed through the Pacific Islands to New Zealand, gathering specimens of rocks and ores, analysing soils, assessing winds and waves, peering into the craters of volcanoes. He even analysed the dust on the sails of his ship for its proportions of aluminous and siliceous matter. By his expertise in mineralogy and geology he earnt, as he put it, 'a certain rank', which his relatively meagre finances would never have allowed. And the sale of his specimens paid for his explorations. On 25 April 1839, about nine years after he left Poland, it was announced in the *Sydney Gazette* that 'Monsieur le Comte Tralski (late of the Polish Army)' was a passenger on the *Justine* recently docked in Port Jackson. Strzelecki wrote to Adyna: 'I've been everywhere cherie':

> I've crossed the equator six times. Seen much, felt more, never losing one grain of the love I bear for you . . . which is more extraordinary than everything else I've done. Putting aside the seductiveness of Europe and America and that of the perfect nakedness displayed by the women of the Pacific Islands powerful enough to bowl over all but the least sensitive and most constant of loves. I prefer you before all women and believe that you are above them all. That is my belief and as it is said that belief is salvation I do not despair of mine.

He swore that neither in the Duchy of Gosen nor in the Sandwich Islands had he had an 'intimate or confidential relationship with anyone'. She must not believe the words of his detractors.

He arrived in New South Wales with a letter of introduction from George Pritchard, missionary and British Consul in Tahiti, who described him as a 'Polish nobleman and scientific traveller'. In New South Wales Strzelecki soon became friendly with 'Pure Merinos' and the Governor's circle. He was much impressed by the Macarthurs. At the Vineyard, the German families whom Macarthur had brought out reminded him of his own roots and also, perhaps, of the farm of Don Joaquim de Astiazaran. Soon he took to the Blue Mountains, exploring and fossicking and measuring. He was afflicted by the same hot wind which Barron Field said made parrots drop from trees, and which had kept Strzelecki's ship out of Port Jackson for two days. It blew at sea and at 1,500 metres: it blew sometimes by a 'ricochet movement' and sometimes 'by puffs': it withered grapevines and laid waste to potatoes and wheat alike: like the sirocco it produced in men 'a feverish heat, and determination of blood to the head': it blew as if fired by 'a huge electric apparatus, highly charged'.

He was not always hot, however. He descended into 'stupendous rents in the bosom of the earth' where his clothes froze and rattled on him 'like the scales of a rattlesnake'. The great gorges of the Blue Mountains were proof of the fantastic antiquity of the earth. They also convinced John Dunmore Lang that the word 'day' in the Mosaic account of creation was not to be taken literally. Lang had no fear of the geologists.

At more comfortable times he wrote down his thoughts on civil society. It was all very well for the genteel women of the colony to devote themselves to 'biblious contemplations, retrospectious and prospectious . . .', but what about poor Strzelecki who could not kindle his 'amorous disposition or propensities at the torch of such devotion'. He found the women of New South Wales, in both Sydney and the bush, 'shut up hermetically within a dry circle of utility and most infernally innoculated with the disease of domestic felicity'. This was all 'perfectly correct', but for a 'poor perigrinating solitary dog' like Strzelecki such 'a system of life [did] not leave even a bone of all that happiness they enjoy'.

No-one could have set Angus McMillan's Scots Calvinist qualities in such sharp relief as Paul Strzelecki. They had nothing in common at all. When Strzelecki dreamt of doing great works he saw admiring faces and his ears rang with the sound of applause: at similar moments McMillan's ears rang with the bleating of his flocks and he saw himself among Highlanders in Heaven. The difference showed in the ways they explored. Travel for McMillan was a nightmare which only God could see him through. He closed himself off and did God's will. Having less fear of God, Strzelecki did not fear the world as much. He explored with wonder, and took notes, whether he was peering at a volcano, a merino, or a woman. Strzelecki's explorations were always partly explorations of himself: McMillan saw himself as a threat to the accomplishment of the task. In the end only Strzelecki was an explorer. True to type he was also part fraud. McMillan was an incomparable bush basher, but he only became an explorer when the mission was complete and the community decided that he had been. And at that moment, of course, he too became a fraud.

So while the perils of the bush, the power of nature and the terrible loneliness drove the Scots to wonder how they might best assure themselves of a place in the next world—how to appease God; Strzelecki wondered how he could come to some arrangement with genteel society—

how to satisfy his desire. He wished he could be like the celebrated ornithologist, Mr Gould, whose wife remained at the campfire each day stuffing parrots, while her husband went out to kill them. But he maintained that it was not thoughts of other men's wives which animated him. It was Adyna. 'What would I be without you, without this idea of possessing you, of ending my days with you?' he wrote to her. Despite what she may have heard he possessed no desire for glory. His work was for her, and their future together. He was nothing if not cosmopolitan. He thought they might settle in France: France was cheaper and the 'centre of European civilization'. These thoughts enlivened him. He was 'far from dried out—well muscled, broad shouldered, powerful chest, full of fire and strength'. And, he promised her, 'saving for the future'.

Grandson of Alexander Macarthur of Argyllshire and son of John Macarthur of New South Wales, James Macarthur was just a year younger than Strzelecki. Macarthur was an 'exclusive', a man of great standing in New South Wales, but on the expedition to the Australian Alps he conceded leadership to Strzelecki. In later years he maintained his loyalty to him at times when it might have been tested. He was an unhurried man who gave the appearance of preferring to avoid confrontation wherever possible and was unwilling to think ill of a friend unless it was impossible to think well. When his 'old friend' Macalister told him nothing of the early ventures into Gippsland before he left with Strzelecki, Macarthur said he 'assumed that at that time he was really ignorant of the fine grazing country that his friend Mr McMillan subsequently occupied with his [Macalister's] stock . . .'

The party left Hannibal Macarthur's Ellerslie station in a 'gay mood'. Macarthur said it was 2 March 1840.

Strzelecki said it was 15 February. Macarthur was right, it seems.

They followed the valley of the Murray and, on 10 March Strzelecki and Macarthur left young James Riley in charge of the convict servants and started off with the two black guides for the highest range in the Australian Alps. The weather was hot and they travelled a good deal in the cool of the night. On the twelfth they camped at a spot where the Aborigines of the high country were reputed to hold their seasonal feasts on the Bogong moths. The next day they ascended the Munyang Range through thick 'gigantic' grass and 'flying mist, occasionally accompanied by keen, freezing air'. The two blacks, Charley Tarra and Jacky, were left to form a camp while the two white gentlemen climbed the summit. But it was not the summit: they found six points, and the one they stood on was not the right one. Strzelecki was determined to reach the point he calculated to be the highest. Macarthur decided to find the camp before nightfall and before he left, Strzelecki told him the name he intended to give the peak. 'I could not but respect and feel deep sympathy for my friend,' Macarthur said, 'when with his hat off, he named the patriot of his country.'

Macarthur, an almost insouciant explorer, descended to the camp 'leisurely enjoying the ample supply of fine water-cress that abounded in every crevice', and enjoying the flowers in full bloom. It was dark before he found the natives' fire. Some time later Strzelecki scrambled into the camp bearing a rock, the very highest rock on the continent, he said. The snow was perpetual he assured them: the regular hissing they heard was the sound of gas escaping from the rocks. As they sat by the fire the 'air was alive with the Bogong moths causing a deep-sounding humming noise like that of a gigantic beehive'.

Having left Macarthur when the day was 'far advanced', it had probably been well into the afternoon when Strzelecki reached the summit, but in his report he thought it more appropriate to put the time as 'about noon'. 'I found myself on an elevation of 6,510 feet above the level of the sea, seated in perpetual snow, a lucid sky above me, and below an uninterrupted view over more than 7,000 square miles.' He saw the 'windings of the Murray', and allowed his eye to be 'seduced even beyond the required limits of survey'. He was reminded of Poland, he said:

> The particular configuration of this eminence struck me so forcibly, by the similarity it bears to a tumulus in Krakow over the tomb of the patriot Kosciuszko, that, although in a foreign country, on foreign ground, but amongst a free people who appreciate freedom and its votaries, I could not refrain from giving it the name of Mount Kosciuszko.

Later he sent a flower from the summit to Adyna, and hoped that it would remind her of 'liberty, Patriotism and Love'.[3]

---

3 Adyna may have been the first Polish woman to receive such a gift, but Strzelecki was not the first Pole in the Australian Alps. In 1834 John Lhotsky stood on what seemed to him the highest point that any European had ever reached in Australia. In 1969 two writers argued that Lhotsky had in fact reached Kosciuszko. That now seems very doubtful, while it seems certain that Strzelecki and Macarthur were the first Europeans to go beyond the tree line. Lhotsky's long forgotten journeys are another example of Australia's perambulatory mode of discovery, and a small chapter in the long chronicle of private fantasies and public brawls in the history of exploration. Lhotsky, a rude iconoclastic Pole who offended the settlers as he went, probably was the first to reach the point on the Snowy River which now bears the name of George McKillop. And it was possibly the valley of the Deddick River near there that he imagined to be a pass which might one day link the Murrumbidgee with the coast. He did not name it after a Polish freedom fighter, but called it Pass Britannia; and he called his peak Mount King William IV. If the pass was in the Deddick Valley it now bears only a cairn commemorating the passage of Angus McMillan.

The day after the ascent Strzelecki completed his computations. As we have seen he estimated that Kosciuszko was 6,510 feet (about 1,980 metres) above sea level. Macarthur, however, gave the altitude as 7,800 feet (about 2,380 metres). Strzelecki's 'official' estimate was given later than Macarthur's, which was recorded on the spot in his day book; just as Macarthur also recorded the date they began their journey as 2 March while Strzelecki seemed to be convinced that it was 15 February. The heightened sense of the dramatic with which Strzelecki invested his account of naming the mount and so many more of his descriptions—he told Adyna that the mountain 'towers over the whole continent'—does not explain these discrepancies. Nothing seems to. The conflicting figures have sometimes been used as evidence to suggest that Strzelecki had not picked Adyna's flower from the tallest peak at all; that he had climbed Mount Townsend instead, and that Townsend, a government surveyor who followed Strzelecki, was in fact the first to stand on Kosciuszko.

After a day's rest the party set out on the second object of their mission: in Macarthur's words, 'to explore the country between Omeo and Port Phillip', in Strzelecki's, to explore *'terra incognita'*. On 27 March they were at the station McMillan had established for Macalister at Numbla Munjee on the Tambo. McMillan was on the Monaro, and Matthew Macalister was in charge. He gave the Strzelecki party provisions and a camp kettle. The amount of information he gave them is harder to gauge.

McMillan and Matthew Macalister later said that they told Macarthur about the nature of the country they had recently traversed, the route they had taken, and the names they had given to the rivers and the lake. McMillan added that Macalister had informed Macarthur of the name he had given the entire district, 'Caledonia Australis'. Macalister said that Macarthur had noted this in his memorandum book.

Macalister went a day's journey with them along McMillan's route, and described where they might cross the rivers. 'So soon as I had discovered the country I gave information of it shewing thereby that I did not wish to conceal it to the world,' McMillan said in 1856. He gave the date of Strzelecki's arrival as 7 March: Macalister recorded it as 27 March.

Macarthur's recollection of the meeting was quite different. He acknowledged, charmingly as always, 'the kind attention and aid from young Mr M'Allister', but he claimed that where Lachlan Macalister had told him nothing of the land McMillan had explored, Matthew Macalister had told him a good deal less than he later assured the world was the case. From Matthew Macalister they had learned that 'Mr McMillan had penetrated to fine grazing country about a week previously (in the direction we intended travelling), but the party had been obliged to return for want of provisions.' But the trip to 'Caledonia Australis' had been made in January. Someone's memory had failed them.

In 1856 Matthew Macalister insisted that Macarthur came with 'foreknowledge of the discovery of Gippsland by Mr McMillan'. According to Macalister, Macarthur stated that he 'understood that our party had discovered a fine country, and that he was on his way thither in quest of runs, and wished to know the position of the part of the country that Mr McMillan had fixed upon for occupation, so that he in taking up his position, might give them a wide berth'. Macalister said he supplied Macarthur with this information. Before leaving, Macarthur 'advised the most profound secrecy to be observed, and that no marks should be made by which our route could be traced until we were in full occupation of the newly discovered land: but this advice . . . was treated with the contempt it merited by the discoverer'.

Thus, by 1856, McMillan had been cast by his supporters as the magnanimous explorer and settler; Macarthur as the meretricious and mendacious ingrate; and the Pole was almost beneath contempt. That at least was the view from Gippsland.

Macarthur and Strzelecki very nearly did not live to tell the tale which made them so unpopular. The party followed the tracks which Matthew Macalister had told Charley Tarra about, until they reached the Nicholson River: from here on, Macarthur said later, they saw no trace of McMillan's tracks. It was the same sort of country they advanced across, however; 'beautiful country', Macarthur said. Macarthur and Riley presumably noted the density of the kangaroo grass under their horses' feet and wondered how many bullocks could pass between the trees, while Strzelecki insisted that 'all possible means were put in requisition to get an insight into the physical structure of the country'.

However, between the Thomson and the Glengarry rivers they ran into dense scrub, and by the time they crossed the Glengarry, 48 kilometres upstream from where McMillan had forded a few months before, the Strzelecki expedition was in considerable trouble. Strzelecki decided not to proceed to Corner Inlet, there was no food awaiting them there, but to make straight for Westernport where they knew there were settlements. Strzelecki described their dilemma later:

> The utter exhaustion . . . of the horses began to impede our progress; in a few days, after crossing the river it was necessary to abandon them. The men, too, who for five weeks had

> already been on half allowance (one biscuit and one slice of bacon per day) manifested symptoms of wear and tear, which, coupled with the loss of the six horses and packs, and the remainder of our provisions being only sufficient for four days, forced me with regret to relinquish our intended course, and to take the nearest one to Western Port, where new supplies might have enabled me to prosecute my researches into the geognostic nature of the coast range . . .

Strzelecki's account here maintains the classical form it assumed after he reached the top of Kosciuszko. This was the crisis point in the expedition; it called on the leader's decisiveness and derring-do.

But why had they been on one biscuit and one slice of bacon for five weeks when just four weeks ago they had been given provisions by Macalister at Numbla Munjee? James Riley told his mother that the daily half rations consisted of two pounds of bread for three people (Charley Tarra and the convicts presumably made their own arrangements), and 'three thin slices of bacon'; and he remembered an assessment of the rations as being enough for eight days, not four. In either case the expedition was extraordinarily under-provisioned, for even had they not run into difficulties after crossing the Thomson, and arrived safely at Corner Inlet, they had no reason to believe that they would find food there. They did have food: sliced into strips and dried or smoked, horses were almost a staple of Australian explorers, yet they had left them behind on a grassy patch in the scrub. It may be that Strzelecki's instruments—those he had not left with the horses—were wrong, or more probably, Major Mitchell's maps. He thought they were only a week's march from Westernport. In fact it took them three weeks to walk the 96 kilometres, and at the end of it the Pole was in no condition for further geognostic surveys.

The bush in the hills they entered is indescribably

dense. Settlers did not enter them until the 1870s and very soon it drove many of them out. J. J. O'Conner arrived at Narracan, a spot close to Strzelecki's route, and found that in 'no place could you see more than 50 yards ahead of you, and in many places you could not see the sky'. There was nowhere a horse could make its way. Blackbutt (mountain ash) grew to over 90 metres in this forest: their girths measured up to 18 metres. When hollowed out, the settlers found them sufficient to accommodate a store or religious congregation. Strzelecki spoke of 'gigantic trees, fallen and scattered in confusion'. It was the vegetation below the blackbutts and blue gums which gave the most pain—or pleasure. Lucy Bell remembered

> ... the mountain ash, draped with lace curtains of 'supple-jack' (clematis), hazel scrub musk with its strong sweet scented woolly backed leaves, blanket wool, cotton bush, Christmas bush with masses of white flowers in the hot weather, and sassafras, another scented leaf, many kinds of wattle ... 'prickly Moses' ... Purple sarsaparilla, decorated some of the trees, small wildflowers grew around, maidenhair fern and little flat rockferns, grew along the creeks, and tree ferns by the thousands ...

George MacDonald, a surveyor, found scenes 'of the most enchanting beauty'. Women and surveyors might admire it: J. J. O'Conner thought it was 'appalling'.

It was through country such as this that Strzelecki led his party at a rate of no more than two or three kilometres a day: 'scrub, wet, hunger, destitution, exhaustion, sight of Port Western and the periwinkles, and the tail of a kangaroo wrested from a native dog', he reminded Macarthur years later. Charley Tarra saved them. He caught koalas when they had nothing else to eat. In England, Mrs Riley read that her son had been eating an animal 'the size of a small dog which lives in trees—a monkey or native bear'—and eating it *raw*. The undergrowth was generally too wet to light a fire.

When they reached the hut of three runaway convicts at Corinella on Westernport, they were starving. They made their way to the station of a respectable settler at Tooradin and recuperated over several days. Melbourne greeted them on 19 May as heroes—Strzelecki in particular. 'We have sincere gratification in announcing the arrival of Count Strzelecki the enterprising pedestrian naturalist,' the *Port Phillip Herald* said, 'and his friends and compagnons de Voyage, Messrs Macarthur and Riley, from an exploratory trip through the terra incognita of the south east coast of New South Wales.'

Melbourne was civilisation to Strzelecki's party, but in 1840 it was still a scruffy gimcrack town. There were five to six thousand people—most of them young, male and free—living there amid what the educated liked to call 'the grandeur of nature'. Just five years before on the Yarra River nature had been undisturbed except by the Aborigines of the Wurundjeri tribe who had been living there for 20,000 years or so. Now English, Scots and Irish were taking tea and port in the bush and the Aborigines fighting among themselves had become a British spectator sport. Summer turned the town into a dust bowl, winter turned it into a bog. But civilised intercourse flourished through it all: gentlemen's clubs were formed, duels were fought, and in three newspapers, the *Port Phillip Gazette*, the *Port Phillip Patriot* and the *Port Phillip Herald*, English Tories fought with Scottish radicals and the Irish fought with both. Being so isolated, and surrounded by nature so pristine, drove some of the inhabitants to rapture, some to mayhem and a few to insanity. It drove others to establish order, rationality and respectability. 'Melbourne was like an unreformed public school before the tone had been elevated by a middle class Arnold,' Paul de Serville has said. Strzelecki was not Arnold but for the moment he served as civilisation's triumph over nature. Just when standing on Flagstaff Hill and looking south to Port Phillip Bay for ships from the Old Country had become a Melbourne custom, three gentlemen wandered in from the wild country in the east.

Strzelecki was not averse to lionisation. The bush had not been so tough, at least for him it had not been: '. . . the ridges through which I wound my course, requires only the occasional clearing of the bogs, and in some parts of the brush, which last, though exhausted during four weeks of starvation, I was, however, able to break, bend or open to those more exhausted who followed me in the exploration'. A few years later one of the settlers they met at Westernport recalled: 'Mr Macarthur and Mr Riley reached a station occupied by myself about 12th or 14th May, 1840. Count Strzelecki being too ill, from want of the common necessities of life, and fatigue, to accompany them.' Strzelecki took full responsibility for the success of his expedition and, the party having survived, did not need to accept any blame for the near disaster. Not all explorers were so fortunate.

While Strzelecki wrote his report of the journey and enjoyed the attention of Port Phillip's gentlemen, Riley returned to the place where they had left the horses and brought them back, with Strzelecki's instruments and specimens, to Melbourne. He was accompanied by one white bushman, Charley Tarra and another Aborigine. It was a strikingly efficient operation, but if it called into question the leadership of the earlier trek, this went unrecorded—at least until Strzelecki's reports reached the ears and eyes of the Scots in Gippsland.

If Matthew Macalister had told him of the names McMillan's party had given the rivers of Gippsland, Strzelecki took no notice of them. The Tambo he named after Deas Thomson; the Nicholson after Riley; the Mitchell after Macarthur; the Avon after Mr Dunlop of the Parramatta Observatory; the Macalister after Major Barney of the Royal Engineers; the Thomson after Alexander MacConochie: and the Glengarry after the Superintendent at Port Phillip, Charles Joseph La Trobe. The naming of natural features in Australia was even more arbitrary and arrogant than the explorations themselves: rivers and lakes and mountains which had borne names of profound meaning to the Aborigines who had lived near them for thousands of years were in an instant renamed to honour some hubristic bureaucrat or benefactor of the expedition, or a niece or nephew of the explorer, none of whom meant much to the new inhabitants of the district and nothing to the old.

Strzelecki described the country glowingly. Even the terrible forest they had staggered through, '. . . for its valuable timber of blue gum and black butt [had] no parallel in the colony'. The 'valleys large and deep' held out 'high expectations for the cattle breeder'. He knew of no place in New South Wales on any scale which could 'boast more advantages'. He added a summary of the results of his geognosy.

It was in his report to the Governor, however, that he committed his greatest offence to the Scots. 'On account of the cheering prospects which this country holds out to future settlers, and which it was my lot to discover, I took the liberty of naming it in honour of his Excellency the Governor, Gipps Land.' This shrewd but prosaic title stuck and McMillan's 'Caledonia Australis', an El Dorado for hungry Calvinists, slipped away from all but a few minds.

Both in this report and in his statements to the Melbourne press Strzelecki claimed discovery for all of Gippsland. He freely acknowledged that Matthew Macalister had assisted him on the first day, but thereafter he believed all was new discovery. He never answered his critics. He hardly needed to. His supporters included Macarthur, H. F. Gisborne who was Crown Lands Commissioner, and the Governor Sir George Gipps. McMillan had a little support from Lachlan Macalister, and a good deal more from the Reverend John Dunmore Lang. Macalister objected to Strzelecki's claims first, but Gisborne quickly wrote to the *Australian* in defence of his Polish friend:

> It is not my intention to . . . enquire who has the best claim in the gratitude of the public—he who 'naturally' wishes to be the first to benefit by the discovery HIMSELF, and, of course, feels it in his interest to keep his information to himself, or he who having discovered and surveyed in a thoroughly scientific manner, a fine country naturally wishes it to be made useful to his fellow creatures, and accordingly takes the only steps within his power for the accomplishment of that object—viz—the publication of his travels.

In proclaiming the purity of Strzelecki's aims, Gisborne did not mention the motives of the Count's companions: Riley had freely acknowledged them, to his mother at least: 'We then follow the snowey mountains down on the Eastern side to Wilson's Promontory or Corner Inlet, where we intend to form our stations. We send a dray by the road to Melbourne there was no road and then take our Men to Make Huts, yards, &c, and also prove psesion till such time as we come down with the stock [*sic*].'

But Gisborne's point did not concern Strzelecki's companions. Strzelecki was the benefactor of society; McMillan was a self-seeker. Gipps gave his official seal of approval.

In his despatch of 28 September 1840 he wrote: 'Although a cattle station has been pushed beyond these mountains by a gentleman by the name of Macalister, the country between them and the sea, was altogether unknown until the month of March last, when the Count Strzelecki, a Political Exile, who since the latter misfortunes of Poland, has devoted himself to the pursuit of science, attempted and achieved the exploration of it.' For the supporters of Strzelecki the argument rested not only on who was first into the country but who was first to talk about it. As Sydney's *Colonial Observer* put it, McMillan was disputing Strzelecki's claims 'on the fact of his having formed a cattle station there! In so far as the rest of mankind are concerned it might as well have been undiscovered still.' Who was serving mankind and who was serving Mammon?

The *Colonist* entered the fray peacefully enough. It published an account of McMillan's exploits and hoped that Strzelecki would promptly acknowledge 'the mistake he made in confounding himself with the real discoverer'. When Gisborne replied in another newspaper and from a salubrious address, the Australian Club, the *Colonist* pulled out some hoary old antagonisms. 'It may correspond with Strzelecki's notions of honour to usurp or pirate another man's discovery, but it is anything but handsome in the estimation of genuine Englishmen.' So the Scots were genuine Englishmen but Strzelecki was a Pole. McMillan was a struggling Highlander, a simple man of God; Strzelecki was an eloquent darling of the Establishment. Strzelecki's friends wanted to continue the infamous system of transportation because it suited their venal interests; McMillan was an embodiment of Lang's alternative to that abomination, he was a sturdy and moral Highlander.

In the end neither man had much cause for distress. Strzelecki went to Van Diemen's Land and received renewed patronage for his researches from Lord and Lady Franklin. His reputation went with him and never failed to win him the favours he needed. By 1844, at least, McMillan was acknowledged as Gippsland's discoverer by those who mattered to him. That year he asked a visiting minister to proffer his thanks to Dr Lang, '. . . for advocating for him the honour, which he is due, as being the discoverer of Gippsland in opposition to the arrogant assumption of Count Stralesky'. The deeds had already swelled in McMillan's mind, just as they did in Strzelecki's every time he wrote to Adyna. Now McMillan was telling people that '. . . years before the Count set foot upon this district [he] by night and by day, accompanied sometimes only by a solitary black, surveyed and explored its scrubby ranges and beautiful plains; and that at a time when even Mr Macalister, who was at that time his employer was as ignorant of it as a child who has never been beyond the circumscribed precincts of its limited domain in sea-girt Iceland'. And, the Reverend Walter Robb told the Reverend Dr Lang, all who knew the truth or wished to know it were aware of this.

The Gippsland pioneer, E. W. Bayliss, did not know it. Many years later when an old friend of McMillan was putting his case in the press, Bayliss wrote to say that neither McMillan nor Strzelecki 'had anything whatever to do with the discovery of Gippsland'. He was not claiming to have performed any 'wondrous deed' but he had been there well before either of them, and so had Andrew Hutton and John Wilkinson. Both claims, he said, were preposterous, though Strzelecki's was the more so and he had been ungenerous and a bad bushman to boot.

In fact there is little doubt that Strzelecki's party traversed entirely new land from the Macalister on; from the La Trobe River to Westernport it is certain that they did.

And McMillan's explorations—those which were not led by Matthew Macalister or Lieutenant Ross—comprise no more than the easy country between the Tambo and the La Trobe. Perhaps the two camps quarrelled because each knew the other's motives through recognition of their own. The object of both enterprises was to secure profitable land, although Macarthur and Riley never took up land in Gippsland. There was only one genuine explorer among them (even Charley Tarra pioneered at Port Albert), Strzelecki: and, like a genuine explorer he was genuinely vainglorious.

Perhaps Charley Tarra, the silent indefatigable Aborigine from Goulburn—'clever and good fellow', Strzelecki said—deserves the most credit. Perhaps he never sat on a log beside James Macarthur in the hour of trial and said 'Me nebber leave you, massa,' as the *Port Phillip Herald* reported on 10 July 1840, but skilled and faithful servant he had been.[4] Having travelled through territory as unfamiliar to him as it was to his European companions, he set off on 6 February 1841 on board the ship *Singapore* with another group of Europeans, the Gippsland Company. On the day that McMillan reached the coast the *Singapore* was in the port itself. The Gippsland Company men named it Port Albert and also gave Albert's name to one of the streams that flowed into it. And, in a rare acknowledgement of Aboriginal services to Australian pastoralism, they named the river to the east the Tarra.

4 The *Herald* continued: 'The fervour with which the unsophisticated son of nature expressed his determination to share the fate of his young master touched the hearts of his companions in distress, and encouraged them to persevere in their efforts to overcome the obstacles which lay between them and safety. We love to record such deeds as these when performed by our sable brethren. Who can say after perusing this interesting anecdote that gratitude dwells not in the heart of the savage?' The *Port Phillip Herald* was the paper of the Melbourne Club and, oddly, the Catholic Irish: presumably it was Melbourne's Protestant middle then which held that savages were genetically ungrateful.

Guided by Charley Tarra, the men of the *Singapore* explored not just the port but the land around it as far north as the La Trobe River and the lake it flowed into, which they named Wellington. Three members of the party returned to Melbourne in the *Singapore* after forming a depot at Port Albert. The remainder, led by William Brodribb, followed a more southerly route than Strzelecki's through the hills to Westernport. Strzelecki's account combined with the sinking of the *Clonmel* to excite interest in the new province in Melbourne. If Melbourne pastoral interests did not act smartly, the *Port Phillip Herald* said in August 1841, the land would be taken up by the Monaro settlers who had by now also seen Strzelecki's report.

Port Albert was satisfactory but not as good as those who explored it from the sea suggested. The man who led the expedition to rescue the *Clonmel* passengers, a Captain Lewis, described it as a 'noble, inland lake, capacious enough to ride a fleet of shipping secure from any storm'. In 1843 a visiting journalist said it was a better harbour than Liverpool. If these were errors of perception, Lachlan Macalister's remark to an Immigration Committee in 1846 that it was a better harbour than Port Phillip was probably more calculated: Port Albert simply was not a port to be compared with Liverpool or Port Phillip. But Gippsland was a frontier community now, and myths were inevitable and possibly essential to comfort people confronting a grim reality, or to confuse governments in whose hands lay the interests of frontier proprietors.

McMillan and Strzelecki had served their purpose. It was not just that they had opened up the land for settlement. That was bound to happen, in fact, was happening before they made their journeys. They had created a wonderful climate for legendeering. The stereotypes were there: man of science versus man of action, the ethereal versus the material; or alternatively, dour impoverished crofter against flamboyant Polish aristocrat, the downtrodden and the upstart, the cattle yard and the salon, the man of women and the man without them, the man of God and the man without Him. Although he has always had his detractors McMillan was bound to win the contest. Scottishness was in his favour, and his mythical poverty. Being Polish told against Strzelecki and so did the fact that he was an intellectual—if he was an intellectual he could not be a bushman. Ludwig Leichhardt's reputation suffered for similar reasons. It did not matter that both were proven bushmen, just as it did not matter that Strzelecki was no more a man of means than McMillan—or that they were fundamentally improvers, with different styles.

Perhaps it seemed to colonial Australians that there could be nothing genuinely Australian about men like Leichhardt and Strzelecki. By nationality they were outsiders in a British enclave, and also by habit; for like the Aborigines, they did not farm the land or conquer it, they just passed through it. Perhaps such people could not be trusted, being without God or commercial interests. A legend grew in Gippsland, a simplification of the argument in the city newspapers. McMillan had reached Port Albert and cut into a tree the words 'Caledonia Australis': the Polish impostor came down later and, on seeing McMillan's tree, cut it down and rolled it into the sea. Into another tree he cut the words 'Gipps Land'.

PIONEERS

They are almost all Highlanders here, and one hears lots of Gaelic. People are very anxious that we should get a station here (we are such pleasant fellows!) but there is nothing to suit.

ALICK HUNTER, SCOTTISH COLONIST, IN GIPPSLAND, 1844

Met Mr Tyers looking very miserable. He and his people have had nothing to eat for four days except one scone each. Two of their horses died, one was lost and all the rest were knocked up and left in the ranges on the bank of a creek so steep that the horses could not lie down. Some of the men were so knocked up that they wanted to be left to die where they were. They were all obliged to lie down and rest every ten minutes, and their boots were all cut to pieces by the sharp stones and rocks. They made Jordan's last night: a dead heat between the Commissioner, Marley and a Scotch policeman. The rest came in by ones and twos for the next two hours, and a corporal was distanced. He is going to be turned out of the police force for wishing to die without leave.

JAMES HUNTER, SCOTTISH COLONIST, ON THE FAILURE OF THE CROWN LANDS COMMISSIONER TO FIND GIPPSLAND AT HIS FIRST ATTEMPT, 1843

I now availed myself with the little eloquence it has pleased God to bestow upon me, to read those portions of the gospels relating to our Lord's calming the tempests, and remarked on our utter dependence on the Almighty now and ever, and our utter inability to help ourselves.

THE REVEREND WILLOUGHBY BEAN, ATTEMPTING TO ENTER PORT ALBERT IN A SQUALL, 1848

As they rode around their lush new domain the first white men in Gippsland sometimes forgot their own financial interests and had the same visions of Arcadian industry as those which transfixed the improvers in the Scottish Highlands. Angus McMillan and Lachlan Macalister saw it feeding all their starving countrymen. Paul Strzelecki and the first Crown Lands Commissioner, C. J. Tyers, agreed that the district's future lay in agriculture: 'the salubrity of the climate, the absence of hot winds and . . . frosts, the copious supply of summer rains, the fertility of the soil . . .' would make it 'the granary of Australia', Tyers said. The Anglican minister, Willoughby Bean, imagined a railway from the port to the lakes, and there a town, and steamers plying up and down the rivers.

The men of Gippsland had no doubts. They remembered the injunction: 'Be fruitful and multiply, and replenish the earth, and subdue it.' Informed by the likes of McMillan and Archibald MacLeod who had come down from Lake George, John Dunmore Lang thought Gippsland had been created by the Almighty expressly for the white man's plough 'and all the kindred arts of his wonderful and complicated civilization'. The vision grew in Lang's mind: 'Each of these solitary valleys would ere long have its village, and each village its school house and church, while the Sabbath bell would be heard in its most secluded wilds, and that "multitude be seen going up from its hamlets", to the house of God . . .'

It was with an idea rather like this in mind, and in the hope that his clan might be re-established in Australia, that Aeneas Ranaldson MacDonnell, 16th of Glengarry, arrived in Gippsland early in 1841. In the familiar pattern, his father had left him the ancestral estate so encumbered by debt that the young Glengarry was obliged to sell in 1840. As Glengarry sailed to Australia Lord Cockburn passed by the lost lands in Scotland and beside the 'great man's gate' saw 'mud hovels . . . and beings with the outward forms of humanity within them, which . . . the Esquimaux would shudder at'. He had heard that the young Glengarry was a vast improvement on his father and hoped that he would be successful in his Australian venture.[1]

With about 30 men and women, mainly Highlanders, Glengarry arrived at Port Albert early in 1841. He selected a run on the Tarra River, later known as Greenmount. He built a house, huts and a stockyard and awaited the arrival from the mountains of 500 dairy cows for which he had paid £10 each. It is likely that most of them were bought from MacFarlane of Omeo. In 1842 the establishment bore certain outward similarities to the surroundings of his ancestral seat. 'Glengarry's establishment consists of five or six miserable Esquimaux-looking huts, covered with bark,' a reporter from the *Hobart Town Courier* wrote. There was also 'a dairy, a stockyard and an uncomfortable English house painted white. A pond of water lies in front and a

1 The fifteenth Glengarry had surrounded himself with every affectation of Highland authenticity he could muster; from the sentinels he kept at his door to the military language he used. In 1815 he formed the Society of True Highlanders. Membership was open only to those who had 'proved' their breeding. Walter Scott used him as a Highland specimen in *Waverley*, but Lord Cockburn thought him 'a paltry and odious fellow'.

small attempt at a garden, a few cabbages, has been made in the clayey mire.' For about a year the men bailed up the cows and the milk maids milked them, and everyone ate the butter and cheese. Glengarry's father would have been aghast. This was a profession worse than one might have expected of the 'unnobilitated squires of the south'. The old Glengarry thought a true Highlander could live only in a mountain glen. A true Highlander, he told MacLeod of Dunvegan, was 'as untenable in the resorts of population and the subjugated Fields of the South, as would be the saucy pride of our Native Eagles, or of our Mountain Stags ...' But even if he had tried to recoup the clan's fortune in something so ignoble as milking cows, the young laird was still cutting an imposing figure in the colony. It was reported in the *Inverness Courier* that a Highlander had met the chief in a colonial inn; 'The chief was fully armed and his countryman took him for a bushranger.'

The venture at Greenmount was a failure. Perhaps Samuel Johnson was right when he said the pastoral way of life in the Highlands did not favour dexterity. Glengarry and his clansmen failed to transplant. He sold his cows to an Englishman named Long Mason, a friend of P.C. Buckley and a brother of Leonard Mason who was to end up in gaol for killing a Scottish overseer in a boundary dispute. Glengarry sold his cows for £2 7s 6d a head. At his farewell at Port Albert, the Highlanders became drunk and tried to drown Long Mason and his friends in Corner Inlet, but at this they also failed. Glengarry went home to Scotland in 1842. As members of the acclimatisation societies which burgeoned in the mid-nineteenth century discovered, it was often difficult to induce exotic species to take root in Australia: the same people also discovered that once acclimatised their habits were altogether different.

For all their talk about a Protestant yeomanry and

their visions of rural industry the Gippsland squatters never found the prospect of agriculture attractive. But pastoralism was second nature to a Highlander and commonsense to a capitalist. The squatters craved land to run cattle and sheep, and tilled the land only to provide for their own needs or the requirements of their stock.

The settlement of Gippsland was a rapid yet casual affair. By 1842 the heart of the province had been taken up by a handful of men, the majority of them Scots. Soon they walked domains, not cattle runs. In 1844 just 40 stations were supporting a population of 327 people, 20,000 cattle and 62,000 sheep. A year later the Crown Lands Commissioner had to report that Gippsland was a 'full house'. By the Order in Council of 1847 the squatters on those runs were effectively granted security of tenure. They now built great houses and brought in wives and servants. Small farmers would have to wait almost two decades for the *Selection Acts* to grant them access to the land; and few of them ever saw a return on the great labour they put into clearing marginal hill country. Nor, for the most part, did the succeeding generation.

By the time the *Port Phillip Herald* had advised Melbourne pastoral interests to hurry into Gippsland or the Scots on the Monaro would, McMillan had already taken up much of the land along the Avon for Lachlan Macalister. This was Boisdale (named after the tiny port on South Uist a few kilometres across the sea from Barra), 23,000 hectares of rolling park-like pasture. The official description suggested the ancestral seat of a clan, as no doubt Macalister fancied it. It was bounded by natural features of great dimensions: 'on the N. by a river called the Avon and ranges; S. by the Macalister river; E. by a plough furrow across the "big plain" from the Macalister river and a continuation of the same line nearly E. and W. to Lake Wellington; W. by ranges'.

Lachlan's brothers and nephews went down to Gippsland, but the great man himself preferred to maintain his seat at Clifton, and visited Boisdale only for the shearing.

The Scots took up the high country. The MacFarlanes ran cattle about the headwaters of the Thomson and Macalister rivers. They named two of their runs after their ancestral home, Glenfalloch, and for some reason called another Glenmaggie. These 'dry, matter of fact Scots gentlemen' prospered in the hills for years. Long after he had thwarted the provisions of the *Selection Acts* James MacFarlane was droving his Herefords about the mountains in a gig tied up with greenhide.

'Came on down to Heyfield, which MacFarlane made up his mind to occupy,' wrote William Pearson. 'Came on to Kilmany Park which I made up my mind to occupy. Returned to Lindenow and brought our stock down.' Pearson made a fortune out of Gippsland. Not that the journey in 1841 had been easy. Without McMillan's help Pearson thought they might have perished from want of food or at the hands of the blacks.

Clannishness was invaluable. Alexander Arbuckle first threw in his lot with Macalister, then took a share in a run with John Campbell, a shipmate of his on the voyage from Tobermory. Campbell was the son of a Highland gentleman from Tiree, but the family had come from Glencoe originally so he named his run on the banks of the La Trobe river Glencoe. Adjoining that run another passenger on the *British King* from Tobermory, Alexander MacDonald of Skye, and his brother John, ran cattle on land they called Armadale. Alexander MacDonald married Arbuckle's daughter, Flora, and the Skye connection was made complete.

Archibald MacLeod also came from Skye and the Skyemen went out of their way to help him when the drought drove him in from the Monaro. It had been an epic trip with his stock, three bullock teams, 36 men, four women and six children. Progress was slow in the mountains and MacLeod must have sensed that time was running out. He left his party and with two men went on ahead. Robert Thomson told him that most of the good land had been taken up. But Angus McMillan and his friend Arbuckle spared no effort to help him. Arbuckle took him to the Mitchell a few kilometres from its mouth. Charles Lucas had settled here, or at least he thought he had. He was away when MacLeod arrived: when he returned he found the MacLeod family in legal possession of his run. The family had come on down, leaving 1,000 lambing ewes at the now abandoned Numbla Munjee station, which MacLeod took up and renamed Ensay after the birthplace of his sister-in-law. No-one left more traces of Skye on Gippsland than the MacLeods.

Archibald was lean and pious and hungry. He was the fifth son of Captain Norman MacLeod of Bernisdale on Loch Snizort. Like MacLeod of MacLeod a few kilometres away, his interests had long been pastoral and military: Archibald had chosen the former. In 1822 he emigrated to Van Diemen's Land on the *Lusitania.* His wife, Colina Campbell, bore him 15 children of whom 11 were still alive when she died, aged 40, in 1839. She was buried at Parramatta. Archibald named his boat after her. His son extended the family's holdings in Gippsland. John took up a station on the Snowy River plains and named it after William MacLeod of Orbost, his uncle who had married the young woman from Ensay.

Robert Thomson was another Highlander to make his way from Monaro. Thomson was the son of 'one of the most popular and striking preachers in the west of Scotland'. '. . . a man of great information and full of unction'. On the

Monaro Robert Thomson had been in partnership with Robert Cunninghame who came from a substantial Ayrshire family connected to Thomson on his mother's side. The two of them came to Gippsland in 1843 and acquired excellent land from Macalister on the banks of the Lower Avon. It was called Clydebank. Thomson and Cunninghame prospered. In 1848 Thomson returned to Scotland to collect an inheritance and a wife. She was Margaret Louisa Campbell whose mother was a MacNeill and whose father was 'a splendid specimen of a Highland gentleman'. The family came from Islay where the best whisky is made. Robert Thomson had a great liking for whisky and brought it into Clydebank by the drayload. Later he was joined by a nephew from Canada, and Cunninghame's brother Boyd arrived as well.

They were not all Highlanders of course. William O'Dell Raymond, a Protestant Irishman of superior education, read Strzelecki's report on Gippsland while his stock languished in the drought-stricken Wellington Valley in New South Wales. Within three weeks he had 8,000 sheep on the road and they travelled the 1,130 kilometres in four months. Raymond put his flocks on the land between Macalister's and Thomson's, a place which eventually became the site of Stratford. Later he built a magnificent home from the local red gum lower down the river and called it Strathfieldsaye. Another member of the Irish ascendancy, William Montgomery from Strabane, settled on land adjoining Thomson's Clydebank and stretching to Lake Wellington—a lush primeval setting. The station he managed was called The Heart, perhaps because it was the heart of Gippsland, perhaps because it was there that a band of squatters believed they found a heart drawn upon the ground just after they scattered a group of Aborigines. William Montgomery became a stalwart of the Presbyterian

Church in Gippsland. If they weren't all Scotsmen along the Avon, they were all Presbyterians.

On the banks of the Mitchell 50 kilometres away there settled Irishmen of a different stamp. John Michael Loughnan, born of a well-connected London family and formerly a captain in the 10th Bengal Cavalry, bred Arab horses at Lindenow for the British Army in India. Men like Loughnan rarely put their swords away, especially in a district of Protestants. He had a protracted dispute with an Englishman over the ownership of his land which only ended when a Scot, John Campbell, took the Englishman's side and broke Loughnan's sword with a hurdle. He offended Lachlan Macalister in 1847 and Macalister challenged him to a duel, but it came to nothing.

Edmund Buckley and his stepson, Patrick Coady Buckley, were Catholics at the nether end of the social scale. Patrick was born on St Patrick's Day in Newgate Prison and it took him a long while to escape the stigma. The Buckleys had stations at Tongio Munjee and Benambra in the mountains when McMillan passed through, and by 1844 had taken a substantial part of the windswept strip of scrub and grazing land along the Ninety Mile Beach. When Glengarry left, and Loughnan and James Davis moved in, and all kept Irish overseers and workers, the strip became a Catholic enclave. On the land where Glengarry had hoped to rebuild the fortunes of his clan, a Catholic cemetery appeared.

Thus when the adventurous Hunter brothers came down from Devils River in the Victorian Alps to Gippsland in 1844 they could not, despite the efforts of their countrymen, find a suitable run. After 1844 only those who were quick with large amounts of capital made headway in Gippsland. New squatters with limited resources of capital and stock suffered severely on the fringes. The process of occupation had been exceedingly fast because the stakes were exceedingly high. First drought had driven them, and then the Depression. When he had visited Melbourne in 1843, the gentleman civil servant Robert Russell was staggered by what the Depression had done: 'Melbourne is no longer Melbourne,' he said. 'No money, no credit, no trade, nothing but failures, the sheriff's officers the only active men in the community.' Russell decided to move to Gippsland.

The Depression created opportunities for men with an eye for the main chance. Several properties in Gippsland changed hands as squatters who had over-extended their holdings were forced to retreat, and men with capital advanced. Peter Imlay departed from his station, Fulham: John King, grandson of a governor of New South Wales, entered. Gippsland had a number of advantages—albeit some, like its agricultural prospects, were illusory. Port Albert was three days' sailing from Hobart, and in Hobart there was a demand for meat. Keen-eyed capitalists in the Gippsland Company, led by the irrepressible family of squatters, the Brodribbs, had moved into Port Albert and now sought land on which to graze their surplus stock. James MacFarlane advertised in the Melbourne Press that he was 'ready to treat with parties desirous of purchasing cattle from his herds at Omeio or Maneroo [*sic*] deliverable to Gippsland'. At the other end of the process John Orr, a merchant from Edinburgh, selected on behalf of the Company more than 2,000 hectares between the Albert and Tarra rivers. The Company said it hoped to be granted a special survey and thence to establish a town, and sell the land in small allotments to recoup some return on their outlay. The Company's critics said it planned to tear 'the very vitals' out of Gippsland.

The cattle came in from the north and went out

through the port. Gippsland was fed by a road between Port Albert and the junction of the Thomson and La Trobe rivers, near which arose the town of Sale. With their Gaelic, Aboriginal and ticket-of-leave stockmen the settlers now drove their beasts to the port and hoisted them aboard boats bound for Hobart. Gippsland was fed by that road in more than one sense. To provide lodgings, food and drink for the stockmen, inns were established along the way. They were cultural waterholes too: it was in them that experience was related, facts and ideas exchanged, floated and invented. It was in them that Gippsland's frontier history was written.

Hobart's beef market was one answer to the Depression. Tallow was another. Almost as soon as the first settlers arrived in Gippsland boiling-down works were established, first at Port Albert and a little later near the site of Sale. Soon after the squatters themselves installed the yards and vats necessary for this simple operation which was insurance against low prices for meat and wool, and, later, a means of recouping something on flocks stricken with catarrh and influenza. The Gippsland Aborigines must have marvelled at people who would commit murder to avenge a sheep or steer speared for food, yet who would take their precious beasts and boil them down into drayloads of fat.

They were indeed hard and hungry men. The time when gentility could be affected was a little way off. And no-one was looking in any case, so there was no need to draw the curtains. Patrick Coady Buckley had a boiling-down works on a site called Poison Hill, so named, it is said, because he fed poisoned meat to the Aborigines who gathered there. A pastoral culture ascribes its ultimate values to animals and the weather. Buckley kept a journal in which he spoke more about heifers and steers and dingoes and bulls than he did about the people he visited almost daily. There was no mention of a man's character, or the nature of Miss Ricketts with whom for two decades he regularly rode on the Ninety Mile Beach. When he found Long Jack dead under the wheel of a dray, killed a horse which had bolted on him, or shot 'a very fine fat native dog amongst Loughnan's cattle', it was simply recorded along with the weather—'d.fine, d.cool, d.wet', etc. On the day after his stepmother died he wrote: 'Mrs E. Buckley died. Started down to Green Mount to attend Mrs E. B. funeral sold 200 bushels of wheat to Montgomery at 9/6 per bushel.'[2]

In the years before they gained a secure title to the land, the squatters lived rough. Some stayed under no more than canvas for years. Huts were built from local materials—stringybark, paperbark and wattle mixed with mud ('wattle and daub'), or from slabs of eucalypt with roofs of thatch or shingle. Single men tended to build less substantially than those, like Archibald MacLeod, who had brought their families with them, but each run needed accommodation for several stockmen and shepherds and housing generally took a similar shape. When he visited MacLeod at Bairnsdale in 1844 the Crown Lands Commissioner found 36 people, including a number of children, living in 13 huts and a head station: 'No land in cultivation—no pigs—20 sq. miles—Blacks about—do no harm,' he added. The pattern was the same at McMillan's Bushy Park and Macalister's Boisdale on opposite sides of the Avon. The stations seem to have evolved along semi-feudal lines. Macalister had 150 milking cows at Boisdale in the 1840s. They were milked, George Dunderdale said, by 11 men

2 Late in his life Buckley rewrote his diary. It is not then the most reliable of sources and we are left to wonder whether he embellished the tale or trimmed it. Whatever changes he made, he did not hide his brutal estimate of life on Gippsland's frontier.

and women 'superintended by nine Highlanders', who sat on the toprails 'discoursing in Gaelic'. There was one MacDonald and the rest were Macalisters, Gillies and Thomsons. Dunderdale found the mode of operation as quaint and curious as Tyers had found MacLeod's:

> The stockmen were convicts, and they lived with the Highlanders in a big building like the barracks for soldiers. Every man seemed to do just what he liked, to kill what he liked, and to eat what he liked, and it was astonishing to see so little discipline on a station owned by a gentleman who had seen service both in the army and in the border police.

It was somewhere between pastoral democracy and pastoral despotism. While status and power inevitably derived from land ownership on the frontier, the Highland landlords at least seem to have reproduced something of that social bonding which derived from a sense of land held in common in clan society. Labourers on the frontier were often referred to by given names alone, as the property of their employer (Smith's Jack) or by their trade or some peculiarity (Jack the Stripper, Long Jack), but the Highlanders generally kept their full names regardless of their rank.

McMillan took on Highlanders almost exclusively at Bushy Park. (Some said later that he cared for them at the expense of his own financial interests.) At Loy Yang in the west of the district John Turnbull, though a Lowlander, ran an establishment that earnt him the name 'The Laird of Loy Yang'. An old settler recalled that there had been 'barracks for overseers, Colonial youths and other yokels who drifted out from good homes in the old countries . . . and there was a colossal size men's hut for the "olla padrida" who roamed about in those days'. On the big man's frontier it served a small man well to be a Scot.

For a stockman or a squatter it was not such a terrible life in the bush, chasing cattle and sheep. The horse gave a man a status in the frontier community which the shepherd or labourer did not enjoy. The stockmen were a wonder to the English 'new chum', John Pettit: 'In riding in horses and cattle they go full gallop thro' the Bush no matter how thick the trees turning sharp around them almost touching, jumping all fallen logs in the most astonishing manner going over such ground as would capsize any horse not up to it,' he wrote to his father in England. The exhilaration of the chase, and the pride in possessing a unique skill no doubt compensated for the dangers. For the Australian bushman did fall off his horse occasionally. In fact the three doctors at Sale treated more shoulder injuries than any other.[3]

There were worse hazards on the runs. Twice within six weeks in 1849 Dr Robert Ewing went to McMillan's station; the first time to treat a man dying from burns, the second to attend to Fry the blacksmith who had shot himself through the mouth. A month later he found a child dying from burns at Raymond's station.

Ewing's clinical descriptions did not disguise the tragedy any more than the witness to Henry Meyrick's tragedy did. Meyrick had made a terrible journey overland from Melbourne and set up in North Gippsland at Glenmaggie. Lewis Desailly came by in May 1846 and asked Meyrick to go to Alberton to fetch help for his wife whom

3 Between March 1849 and November 1852 Dr Robert Ewing kept a record of his practice at Flooding Creek, Sale, Victoria. Extracts from the journal are held in the Port Albert Museum. The other doctors in the district were Dr Alexander Arbuckle (when he was not attending to his cattle), and a man named Lightfoot, who was said to bear a striking resemblance to George III and was believed to be his son.

he feared would die in childbirth. Meyrick agreed unhesitatingly. At the age of 29, Meyrick was already crippled with perhaps the most common disease among bushmen, rheumatism. Ignoring Desailly's advice to cross at a more distant but safer place, Meyrick rode his horse into the flooded Thomson River. He was pushed downstream but seemed certain to make the other shore when he suddenly threw himself from the horse and started to swim. Then 'an astonishing and inexplicable' thing happened as Desailly watched:

> When he was within a few feet of the bank, to my great astonishment he turned right round and swam out into the middle of the river, where to my horror he sank. There was nothing I could do. He never rose to the surface. The last I saw of him was his hat floating about in the spot where he had sunk.

In the previous eighteen months or so, Henry Meyrick had seen three men die suddenly. There had been George Bolton Eagle, his close companion; a man who was thrown from his horse 'and went tipsy into the presence of his God'; and a man by the name of Stewart who, as Meyrick wrote, 'was about to cross a swollen river, and to those who tried to dissuade him answered, "I will cross tho' I should go to hell on the road". He pushed his horse in and was drowned.'

The rivers of Gippsland brought many to sudden ends, as did the Depression and the fatal impulses which seem to have overtaken Stewart and Meyrick. Women faced the same dangers, and one other. A few days after Meyrick drowned, Mrs Desailly died in childbirth.

In Gippsland's history Mrs Desailly's death is a footnote to the tragedy of Henry Meyrick. The death of a woman in childbirth was never so melancholy an affair as the accidental death of a young gentleman. That was partly because there were more deaths in childbirth than there were drownings of gentlemen, and partly because a man's labour on the frontier was valued more highly.

Agnes Buntine was an exception. As Agnes Davidson she had married an Ayrshire tilemaker named Hugh shortly after his arrival in Melbourne in 1840. Hugh's first wife had died and left him with five children. They arrived in Port Albert in 1841 and started an inn—the Bush Inn—which Tyers said was filthy. Tyers thought Hugh was a man of doubtful character (despite the fact that he was connected by marriage to J. D. Lang), and suspected him of selling sly grog. But Hugh was not well. Agnes raised his five children and five more they had together. And she ran a bullock team. She wore both leggings and a dress, and when she went to the gold fields in 1851 she carried two pistols in her belt. 'Nothing could exceed her dignity and bulk,' said William Howitt, 'except it were a Turkish dome or a steam boiler on horseback.' When Hugh Buntine died in 1867 Agnes married a 29-year-old man. She did not die until 1896.

For every Agnes Buntine there were hundreds of women who went unnoticed. The values of 'manliness' were paramount on a frontier which prized physical achievement above all else. The physical achievements of women were therefore cast as manly or not recognised at all. Notions of 'womanliness' were also held dear of course, at least by the genteel and those who aspired to gentility. It was a fact, after all, that the decorous treatment of women was a significant measure of the level of civilisation. Archibald MacLeod was too much a Presbyterian and too little a Victorian to put his women on a pedestal. They were his women nonetheless and they were required to suffer his patriarchy. The Anglican minister, Parson Bean, was impressed; he found Miss MacLeod an 'excellent, religious, charitable lady, attentive to her domestic duties, whilst Miss Williamina appears equally so in her department, that of instructing the younger members of her family'. By the time Bean observed the MacLeods at home, Archibald's wife was long dead, having borne him 15 children. The cemeteries of Gippsland contain the graves of numerous women who died in childbirth; beside them their husbands lie, and not infrequently just beyond them their second wives who had borne them yet more children.

To have women with him made Archibald MacLeod an unusual figure in the first few years of settlement. The squatters tended to wait until their land was secured before they searched for wives. The landless also preferred to be set up. So long as the sexual imbalance remained, an even greater burden of work, child rearing, sexual abuse and loneliness fell on the women who had come into the district early. The high-minded men who said the frontier was no place for a lady did not see even half the problem.

The weight fell heavily on Aboriginal women too. They were used by white men until such time as civilisation was sufficiently advanced in the province to permit the entry of civilised white women. The Aboriginal women were murdered by white men, raped by them and poxed by them. Dr Robert Ewing treated more cases of venereal disease than any other ailment in his three years at Sale, 1849–52. The most respectable citizens of the district were among them—indeed at £10 a cure one wonders if any but the respectable attended for treatment. The doctor seemed to know where they were getting it from: when a man presented himself with two-thirds of his penis sloughed off Ewing assumed that he had had intercourse with a black woman. No-one asked where the black women contracted it.

As they used the women so they used the land. Nothing emerges so strongly from the thin records of settlement in Gippsland than that, judged by their own standards, the Europeans did not belong there. Nothing they did proclaimed a 'natural' right, nor any claim by the fashionable criterion of improvement. They did not understand the land and that sometimes cost them their lives. But there was not much need to understand the land in a pastoral economy. They simply ran their cattle on it, let them breed and sold them or boiled them down. They lived off the land as long as the land could stand them. Patrick Coady Buckley lived in a fantastic natural world but in more than 20 years he scarcely offered a thought on it, except when the fires of Black Thursday in 1851 terrified him.[4] Within a decade of the Europeans' arrival the land was riddled with thistles, and within two decades with rabbits. The watercourses eroded to several times their original size: rivers like the Avon which had been navigable for 16 kilometres from the mouth became too shallow for any craft. The wildlife rapidly disappeared.

But even in 1862 the *Edinburgh Review* was still prepared to believe that settlement had not spoiled the 'Arcadian beauty' of Gippsland.

By comparison with the succeeding generation the pioneers of Gippsland were in some ways people of leisure. Buckley could write happily of visiting Hobart, visiting Melbourne, visiting neighbours: riding with Miss Ricketts on the beach, bathing with her on the beach, boating with her on the creek: he enjoyed 'pleasure parties' with his neighbours during Christmas holidays, took part in the

4 Buckley's diary for 2 February 1851 read: '. . . about 2.o.c.PM the day took a most frightful appearance the air full of smoke fires breaking out in all directions the wind scorching hot the air thick with smoke and ashes. About 3.o.c.PM the Sun disappeared and the evining became as dark as night.'

occasional kangaroo 'battue'. It was the next generation who had to cope with weeds, pests and erosion, extend the fences, and improve the quality of the stock. The first settlers could afford to be generous to travellers and neighbours, not least because loneliness was as great an enemy as nature in those days.

When Robert Russell came to Port Albert in 1843 he waxed lyrical about the pristine beauty of the surroundings. He described the scene on the Tarra River.

> Here the fern tree and creepers of the Illawarra district wave and twine, and the quick descent, free from rock, and available to the margin of the cool stream, overlooks the rich variety of foliage on the opposite bank, where flowering shrubs backed by the deep green of the tea-tree, and still higher by box and stately gum, render the solitude pleasing; high fern and the indigo plant here luxuriate in profusion, and on the river's bank the lightwood tree lifts its flowering head.

Russell had no doubt that South Gippsland was 'likely to be about the best agricultural district in the colony', and he was at first elated to think himself a part of its progress—a subduer and a replenisher. He wrote to a friend about the blessings of agricultural life: 'With our cows, pigs poultry, garden and an occasional kangaroo, ducks, quail, with wood and water *ad libitum* how little is left for money to purchase.' Gippsland even inspired in him a certain optimism about the Depression: the importation of some 'respectable capitalists' and an adequate supply of labour would soon have the colony on its feet again, he thought.

The Port Albert district had indeed been founded by respectable capitalists with the improving concept of agriculture ostensibly in mind. While the people without capital or anywhere else to go lived on roast flathead, birds' eggs and large amounts of fat, John Reeve, who had already taken up a run on the La Trobe River, was working out a way to make the best use of the land. Reeve took up a special survey to the east of the Tarra River and advertised the lease of 50-acre (20 hectare) farms at the annual rent of a bushel (60 pounds) of wheat. He wanted to establish a respectable tenantry, he said. A township, Tarraville, grew up among the tree ferns and creepers at the crossing on the river and became the gateway to the hinterland.

Five kilometres up the Albert River the government township of Alberton was laid out on splendid lines among the gum trees. Alberton was gazetted in September 1843. Plans for an adjoining township called Victoria were also drawn up and 23 half-acre (2,030 square metre) lots were sold. Governor Gipps envisaged a town on the lines of Melbourne. Thomas Mitchell thought that if it grew to such dimensions it might be called 'Gippolis'.

But Alberton and Victoria were beyond the point where ships of any size could go, and they were on the wrong line for commerce with the inland. Their future was limited, and so was that of the old port, close to the mouth of the Albert River. In 1841 a channel deeper than that at the old port was found a couple of kilometres to the south. Even allowing for the absence of fresh water there it was the obvious place for a government township. In 1843 Major Alexander Davidson, who had arrived in Melbourne with Indian servants, coolies, deer, cows and Arab horses, bought the 180 acres (73 hectares) of Orr's Special Survey at auction for £1 an acre. Davidson was a 'dummy' for Turnbull, Orr and Co. who 'bought' it from him soon after. Even before then they had begun to erect a store on the land. Thus began Turnbull's monopoly of commerce in Gippsland. It was not until 1857 that any of the land was sold again and long before then, it was said, there was not a man in Gippsland who was not on the company's books.

Nothing could have been more appropriate than the name the port went under for the first few years—New Leith.

Some of the respectable capitalists flourished at Port Albert. John Gellion, late of Inverness and the West Indies, made his way overland from Westernport with a friend. It was a terrible journey.[5] Gellion and his friend dragged themselves into Port Albert in the winter of 1844 and pronounced it 'the most miserable place ever man set foot in'—that remark was probably made somewhere every day in the empire. Gellion stayed, however, successfully grazing his cattle on the lowlands and maintaining a hotel at the port.

But for years the disreputable remained as Raymond had found them in 1842. The dregs of Van Diemen's Land came in with the Hobart commerce. There were 30-odd convicts among the 206 Raymond counted, and 26 women. Some had come expecting to buy land and found none. Some were in service, others were living on the beach, 'God knows how,' Raymond said. He thought the place needed a magistrates' bench and suggested to the Superintendent of Port Phillip that he and two other squatters, John Reeve and Walter Curlewis, should fill it.

Port Albert became the most disreputable town in the colony. Robert Russell found that the state of morality there was 'pitiable in the extreme'. Summing up a trial for a murder in the little settlement of St Giles near Tarraville a judge said the place was 'pandemonium on earth'. It was a great source of notoriety for the Melbourne press. Dr Fishender treated the poorest—or wickedest—of the

5 Raymond, Pearson, Brodribb and Raymond's Aboriginal had made the trip in 1842 and like the Strzelecki party were reduced to eating parrots and koalas. Squatters William Scott, Montgomery and Robert MacLure had an even worse time in the scrub and water and were obliged to eat their dogs before they scrambled into the port. The trip killed MacLure. He died soon after of consumption. They rowed his body up the Albert River and buried him on the banks.

citizens until 1847 when he fell from his horse and broke his neck. He was on his way to treat a man who had suffered a similar injury at the 'jollifications' after a wedding.

Jollifications were common. Mother Murden threw the first ball in the district. It was a great success, although everyone had to step over Neddy who was prostrate in the doorway. Neddy, on a conditional pardon, was an amiable accomplice of Joshua Dayton who was then stealing cattle and boiling them down at a hideaway in the tea-tree. When morning broke at the ball, 'Mother Murden came to the door with a tumbler in her hand, containing a morning nip for Neddy, "to kill the worm", as the Latins say: but the worm was dead already. The merry makers stood around; the men looked serious and the ladies shivered. They said the air felt chilly, so they bade one another good morning and hurried home.' For George Dunderdale the town was more tragic and funny than it was wicked: 'It is hard to say why one sinner is taken and the other left,' he said.

There were plenty of sinners left and they were not all living in St Giles. In 1851 a letter appeared in the *Melbourne Morning Herald* which charged that some of Gippsland's most respectable citizens—among them magistrates—were living 'in a state of fornication and adultery'. Tyers forwarded a confidential letter to the Colonial Secretary assuring him that all the gentlemen in question had declared that the charges were 'without foundation'.

When Gippsland was proclaimed a district on 13 September 1843, Charles James Tyers was appointed Crown Lands Commissioner.[6] He was 37 when he set off to find a way in across the swamps from Dandenong, but the water

6 Tyers had been an officer in the Royal Navy, serving on HMS *Alligator* off the north coast of Australia between 1837 and 1839. He had been a surveyor in the Portland area for three years after that. Tyers loved astronomy, geography and measuring things.

drove him further and further north and he was forced to retreat. The party staggered into an Irish settler's garden and were mistaken for bushrangers stealing peas. When Tyers got back to Port Phillip people were asking if the place existed that he was supposed to police. But he took a ship to Port Albert, and on his arrival on 13 January 1844 a flag was raised and the cannon fired. The harbour pilot, who was soon being asked to pay £20 for the hut he had built three years ago, said the shot signified the death of liberty at the port.

The government granted Tyers two horses and a cart, and in this he toured the district, extracting the government's due from the squatters, and telling each settler what his rightful boundaries were. As he went he noted, as a surveyor would, the character of the settlers, the manner in which they kept their homes, the number and type of their livestock and so on.

It was Tyers's duty to regulate affairs between gentlemen as much as between ordinary men. He settled quarrels over boundaries and stock, and when, at a race meeting, Mr Pearson horsewhipped and otherwise assaulted Mr Desailly, and insulted an Irish magistrate and other gentlemen, Tyers bound him over to keep the peace, remarking that magistrates would not attend the races if they were going to be treated like this. Robert Turnbull and Angus McMillan paid Pearson's sureties.

To aid Tyers in his duties a Court of Petty Sessions was established at Alberton in May 1844. The prominent gentlemen of the district (the likes of Edwin Hobson, John King, Robert Thomson, John Reeve and James MacFarlane) were appointed magistrates. Tyers was given a native police force which was based at Stratford. Police stations were set up at Sale and at Eagle Point, a place with a fine view at the mouth of the Mitchell River. It was at Eagle Point

Tyers settled, after marrying a squatter's daughter, Georgina Scott. Tyers was a lover of the good things in life, as the dashing Alick Hunter observed after drinking a lot of his claret in 1844. But he was always circumspect and no reputable man had much to fear from the Crown Lands Commissioner in those first few years.

They might have had more to fear from a Presbyterian minister. The Reverend James Forbes brought the new district to the notice of the Kirk in 1841, but the Disruption was occupying the minds of Presbyterians then, and Gippsland was left to find its own way in the world. The Gippslanders did, and when the Reverend Walter Robb travelled there at J. D. Lang's behest in 1851 he found 'open profanity and great immorality'. Still, he vowed to Lang that it was worth his life to eradicate it, even though he would be 'sadly stricken with penury' and 'drag out an existence unaffected by the dainties of the rich'. In fact Robb did not stay long at all, despite the kindness and the absence of profanity he encountered at Angus McMillan's.

In the ten years between the notification of the Kirk and Walter Robb's visit, the Presbyterians of Gippsland had to be content with instruction from Anglicans. Edward Gifford Price arrived from the Monaro with an Aboriginal boy in 1846. He baptised as many white children and dispensed as much legitimacy and respectability in the woolsheds as he could, but he seems to have found the task as thankless and unnerving as Reverend Francis Hales did after him. Hales was deeply distressed by his inability to induce the settlers to observe the Sabbath, or even to get their families together for prayer. Mr Bayliss spoke of showing him the door. Hales was no missionary: 'I feel that I am sadly deficient and often blame myself for undertaking an office for which I feel myself so inefficient,' he wrote. Even Angus McMillan, whom he preferred to any other settler in the district, and who paid at least some respect to the way of God, was of limited comfort to the minister. For all his virtue, McMillan was 'a man who has not thought much about the deeper things of life', Hales said.

The most popular and imposing clerical figure in Gippsland was the Anglican, Reverend Willoughby Bean. He was posted there in 1848 after the Bishop of Melbourne had decided that Hales had suffered too much: 'The state of the people was such as to render the country an unfit residence for a young married clergyman.' In November Bean hurtled through the entrance of the port aboard Archibald MacLeod's *Colina* and spent his first night in Gippsland aground on the mudflats.[7] MacLeod was also on board.

At first Bean was distressed by the immorality, and almost as much by the demeanour of the pious:

> I was much struck, and painfully so, with the air of apathy and indifference with which the service was gone through . . . I appeared to be the only person present engaged in prayer. All the rest sat with their eyes fixed on me, as though astonished at so strange a display or occupation . . . it was perhaps not surprising, when one considers that most were Presbyterians who use no forms and stand in prayer, and the rest Episcopalians who had forgotten the routine of the service.

---

7 The voyage, which usually took two days, took 13. A howling westerly gale almost blew them on to the rocks off Wilson's Promontory: they lost their anchors trying to shelter near Rabbit Island, and they were blown past Port Albert, though close enough to the bar to see clearly the wreck of the *Clonmel.* They were blown more than 320 kilometres, almost to Twofold Bay, and it was now thought prudent to make for Sydney for a new anchor; but an easterly blew them back towards Port Albert, MacLeod pointing out his runs to the minister as they sailed past. This time it was calm as they approached the port entrance, but a sudden squall came up and nearly wrecked them on the bar, before blowing them out to sea again. Bean prayed for the ship's company. The wind changed and they entered the port, only to run aground.

> My heart yearned to be back to my little flock at Williamstown; and yet I was determined to teach these how to pray in that posture most natural and fitting for a true penitent and supplicant at the throne of mercy and grace.

It was a determination that he should have known would soon fade; the Presbyterians of Gippsland were hardly going to become more suppliant while mercy and grace were manifestly bestowed on them. Yet, while Bean was 'astonished' by their unbent knees, he found among the Presbyterians 'more devotional feeling' than among those of his own church. He became known as 'Parson' Bean and in time he was hardly less popular with the Presbyterians than he was with the respectable Anglicans of the district. He liked brandy and porter and curries. Long after the oyster beds had gone from the port, it was said that Parson Bean knew where to get himself a bagful.

The real founder of the Presbyterian church in Gippsland was Reverend William Spence Login. Login had been born in the Orkney Islands and educated at Edinburgh. He was the minister at Papa Westray in the Orkneys before emigrating to Port Phillip with his wife and four children in 1853. He was Free Church. His first service in Gippsland was held in the Royal Hotel, Tarraville, in January 1854. The gentry of the lower district and even some from The Heart were there, and their names were recorded as they were now accustomed to hear them: Thomson of Clydebank, Montgomery of The Heart, Pearson of Kilmany, Campbell of Glencoe, MacDonald of Armadale. Login was soon on his way into the interior. He stopped at Flooding Creek where he gave a service and was filled 'with wonder' by the superior dairy cows of the town's founder, a blacksmith from Skye named Archibald MacIntosh. The next day Login lost himself in the bush on the way to Bushy Park.

A shepherd, a crippled veteran of Copenhagen, gave him the directions and after more than 30 hours' wandering he arrived in time to give a short service at McMillan's.

Login rode all over Gippsland performing services and telling settlers the future of the Church depended on their support. The Presbyterian station lords built a bark church on a block of Robert Thomson's land, and there the families of Gippsland's heart worshipped for four years until a new church was built in Sale. But the station homestead or woolshed was used for services in outlying areas, and settlers like the MacDougalls on the Tambo and Isaac Buchanan at Roseneath made their buildings available to Login.

The settlers also co-operated in other ways. Several of them married the women with whom they had been living 'in sin'. Others, after a reminder from Login, put an end to their illicit connections by sending the women away. The choice rested at least partly on questions of breeding. One man even gave up the booze for Login. Quite soon it seemed to the minister that things were changing for the better. His work, as he said later, had been more missionary than pastoral.

Fifty years after his arrival in Australia, the Reverend W. S. Login was convinced that Presbyterians should reunite. 'The desire for it is of the Lord and he will fulfil it,' he said. There was no longer any need for the 'Contendings' of the previous 50 years: 'Like storms in the economy of nature', they had cleared the air. The Presbyterians were breathing freely. There seemed to be very little evil in Australia, as far as Login could see, and what there was could readily be eradicated by educating working men to shun alcohol and light reading, both of which drove the fear of God from their minds, and by instructing them to save their wives from any toil beyond the raising of families. The Lord had smiled on the Australian working man by placing a high value on his labour. Capital and labour seemed reconciled in mutual interest. Soon all should be living in a state of grace. So a descendant of 'the men' had become a spokesman for middle-class egalitarianism and a friend of the lairds of Gippsland. It was the way of the Lord in Australia.

Providence smiled on the respectable capitalists of Gippsland, though it cast only a passing glance at the agriculturalists, the oyster farmers, the bark strippers and all the other 'kindred arts' of the white man's civilisation. By the 1850s Robert Thomson had a coat of arms which read 'Robt. Thomson of Glasgow and Gippsland Victoria Australia'. At his back door the Avon was deep enough for a boat: supplies could be brought in across Lake Wellington, and the gentlemen of the river could take their families for holidays across the lake. Robert Thomson virtually defined the high spots of social life in Gippsland in those days. A 171-kilogram pillar of Presbyterianism, his house on the Avon was the centre of Highland gentility and boozing. When Robert Thomson entered the Victorian Legislative Council in 1856 the celebrations at Clydebank went on for days. The balls there were large and frequent. A. W. Howitt attended one and then found himself stranded by the weather. He described the pleasures of it in a letter to his wife:

> My friends are devoted to 'horses' and are great racing people, very kind, nice people and very rich so that it is a pleasant idle house where people come and go as they like and the gentlemen congregate in a house called the 'barracks', and talk of such subjects as interest us here—the American war—the weather—the floods—pleuro pneumonia—fat cattle—sheep—horses—and I am sorry to say, very rarely of books. It may not be a very intellectual life but it is without trouble or care. It is a fearful place for 'nobblerizing'—it goes on morning, noon and night . . . they dance to a harp, a melaphone and an accordion every night.

The Thomsons were as flamboyantly Scottish as their affluence allowed. Perhaps they were ostentatiously so. It was common in the colonies for Scots to seem larger than life, as it was in Edinburgh and London. The Caledonian societies of which many of the Gippsland settlers (including McMillan) were members were ideal vehicles for parading a brand of Scottishness which owed more to homesickness and Walter Scott than the realities of life in Scotland. But the culture was fed by contact with home, and in Thomson's case it was by no means all affectation. Indeed, back in Argyllshire the *Oban Times* seems to have admiringly monitored their lives in Australia.

Gold had disturbed the pastoral industry but the impact was not fatal. Those without property went off to western and central Victoria, or sought new fields in the Gippsland hills. The pastoralists of Gippsland replaced their labour with Aborigines, until such time as more Highlanders arrived on the famine ships. They also imported Chinese to solve the 'domestic problem' and to work as shepherds. A typical shipping manifesto at Port Albert thus read: 'Mr King and 1 Chinaman. Mr Disher and 1 Chinaman. Mr Nielsen and 1 Chinaman'. Angus McMillan put his Coto to work at Bushy Park: he was a remarkable man, the Reverend Login said, a man of 'indomitable perseverance'.

In 1855 the *Gippsland Guardian* emerged in Port Albert to announce that the 'night of ignorance and barbarism' had been chased from Gippsland 'by the cheering influences of civilization'. The *Guardian* promised its readers much the same diet as the *Inverness Courier* had promised Highlanders 50 years before. There would be foreign and domestic intelligence. Shipping Intelligence and Prices Current would appear regularly. There was Longfellow's *Hiawatha* and Prince Albert's *The Toy of the*

Giant's Child. The *Guardian* promised that it would not hesitate to 'raise its voice against every species of oppression and injustice'. The year 1855 was also splendid because the goldfield markets had almost doubled the price of beef.

In August of the following year the newspaper reported that a party had been held at Thomson's on the eve of his election to the Legislative Council. Such a 'galaxy of beauty and refinement assembled would have graced a similar gathering in any part of Her Majesty's dominions', the reporter from Sale wrote. The 60 guests had danced till almost dawn. They had danced most impressively, particularly when doing the Scottish Reel—a 'justly celebrated dance' the reporter said, and one for which the guests at Clydebank had a 'propensity . . . natural to the sons and daughters of old Scotia'.

Up at Bushy Park Angus McMillan was being smiled upon. In 1856 he was one of the district's most propertied citizens. The man who had come from a society in which half a dozen cows constituted a herd now had 2,400 head of cattle. Where a flock might have meant 50 sheep to him in his youth, he now owned 9,000. He had 50 horses as well, and five runs, the biggest and best of them, Bushy Park, nearly 6,500 hectares.

On the banks of the Avon, Angus McMillan had built himself a large house—not of stone like Thomson's downstream, but of wood, and he had surrounded himself with Highlanders. The Macalisters had left Boisdale at the end of the 1840s, Lachlan having decided to cash in on his investments in Gippsland.[8] It was a splendid setting for a Highlander—a stream, 'like a Scotch burn', at the doorstep;

8 John Foster took up Boisdale from Macalister. He had begun buying into Gippsland in the mid-1840s and he added more stations after Macalister's. In the next decade Foster became the truly big man of Gippsland, and built a large house on an imposing site overlooking the Avon River flats.

in the near distance blue mountains, one of them bearing the name Ben Cruachan; and a company of loyal Highlanders with the Gaelic. His brother Donald had joined him sometime in the 1840s. He also employed MacKays, MacLeans, MacDonalds, MacIntyres, MacLarens and Morrisons. Some of them had almost certainly arrived on the ships of the Highland Emigration Society.

McMillan had a universal reputation for generosity to his countrymen. 'If hospitality be a virtue his was unbounded, and he exercised it continuously,' Richard MacKay wrote in his *Recollections of Early Gippsland Goldfields.* McMillan had an arrangement with the Port Phillip Club Hotel in Melbourne to see that newly arrived Highlanders were cared for until they found employment in the country, 'and at his own home . . . he was never without visitors—shame to many of them his too liberal generosity was too frequently abused', MacKay said. Among those Highlanders only Colin MacLaren left a testimony to McMillan's virtue. MacLaren had been with McMillan on some of his early explorations, and in Gippsland he remained a stockman of renown. In his old age, living on an island in the lakes with an Aboriginal skeleton wedged in a tree trunk as his only regular company, he remembered McMillan with 'boundless respect'.

Not all McMillan's workers felt the same way. Two cases suggest that he did not always extend his generosity beyond his countrymen. One, Charles Lamb, remembered a strike at Bushy Park during a harvest when McMillan reneged on his promise of two whiskies a day. James Kelly, shepherd, took McMillan to the Alberton Magistrates' Court in 1847, alleging that he had been underpaid. The Justices of the Peace, Raymond and King, found that the pastoralist was justified in requiring the shepherd to 'work off' the price of the 47 sheep he had allowed to stray. McMillan was not a JP, and not quite of the society which comprised men like Raymond and King, but he was a man of means.

John Morrison was one of those Skyemen who had come to New South Wales to work for Lachlan Macalister on the Monaro. He had brought the first sheep into Gippsland with McMillan and remained with him at Bushy Park as a stockman for some years. Highland stockmen earnt a degree of recognition that evaded the general labourers. The colonial-bred bushmen were not honoured in any sense. The men with names like Robinson the Splitter, Jack the Devil and Dick Drive Hard provided the indispensable labour on every station but they faded rapidly from memory and the public record.

It was the same with the women. John Morrison married a Presbyterian Englishwoman named Betsy Latham who had come to Gippsland with her first husband in 1849. Her husband took an immediate dislike to the district, returned to Melbourne and died. Betsy Latham raised eight children in the scrub of Sandy Creek, McMillan's run adjoining Bushy Park. She had an accommodation house there, and her girls worked as shepherdesses. McMillan's kindness to her was famous, as were her own exertions. It is said that one Christmas McMillan gave her a turkey, a live one, and she carried it 25 kilometres home to Sandy Creek.

The men of Gippsland did not send for women to civilise the community. They thought that they had completed the task. They sent for women to service them and provide *proof* of civilisation. In the 1850s the women came through the port in hundreds, nameless like the Chinese. In 1858, for example, more than 200 arrived, and 'they have all gone like smoke', John Pettit said a year later:

> They engage as servants and get spliced very soon afterwards. I know some few instances, where men have lagged out in

> their best, walked into the Depot and after looking around upon the fair damsels enquire if 'any of you young women [who] want a husband will take me'—sometimes the labourer deputes his employer to choose one. As soon as the ceremony is over everyone gets *mortal,* or in other words *groggy,* often there is no accounting for what may take place.

John Pettit, however, was not going to get spliced until he was well set up. Not that he didn't like 'young ladies', he assured his father: 'Bless their dear little hearts, no!' But in Gippsland it would be folly to bring out a wife who was 'well bro' up'.

Many of the women were Highlanders who had arrived in the colonies on Highland Emigration Society ships and followed their kinfolk to Gippsland, or had gone there under contract as domestic servants to Highland settlers. We know next to nothing about those famine victims, men or women, who came to Gippsland, but the experience of Highlanders and Islanders in South Australia, where some research has been done, might offer an insight.

To begin with, it is clear that the belief that Highlanders would settle rapidly into Australian colonial life and fill a vital gap in the labour market was either too sanguine or disingenuous. It was one thing to encourage whole families to emigrate, it was another to keep them together. The Highlanders were prone to typhoid fever and 'pulmonary' diseases. Frequently one or both parents died on the voyage or soon after arrival. Young children often found themselves in the Destitute Asylum a few weeks after they disembarked.

By the mid-fifties the squatters' demand for labour had diminished and it proved impossible to keep the families usefully employed as groups. The families found themselves required to labour in fields which were foreign and quite unlike anything they had been promised. The Highlanders did not take kindly to it. Their supervisors soon attributed their diseases to 'the uncleanly habits of these Gaelic people'; and their inability to adapt to work and separation from their families to the 'incomprehensible and intractable' characteristics of the race. They were 'as near an approach to barbarism as any I have ever met with coming from Great Britain', the South Australian Comptroller said.

So people like John MacLeod and his family came from destitution on a Hebridean croft to break stones at Dry Creek, South Australia. John MacLeod died after a few months in the colony. His wife continued to break stones until, after six months, her own health failed.

The Highland women who came to Gippsland cannot have suffered such afflictions. The concentration of Highland old hands must have made life easier. But it is still reasonable to ask how much better off than John MacLeod's widow in South Australia was the widow of Angus McMillan. Christina MacNaughton, a native of Argyllshire, arrived in Australia in 1849. There is no record of her landing in Port Albert. She went 'like smoke' it seems. It might have been in 1852; the year when Angus McMillan bought for the first time from the store at Port Albert large quantities of gingham, calico and thread. Christina MacNaughton became Angus McMillan's housekeeper. With Coto the Chinese as well, life at Bushy Park must have been very comfortable for the squatter.

In 1858 Christina bore Angus a son which they named Ewen. She bore him another, named Angus, in 1861. The precise dates of the births are not known—there are no birth certificates. Angus and Christina were married by Reverend Login at Bushy Park on 30 March 1861.

No-one knows why it had taken Login so long to convince one so God fearing as McMillan that, if he was not to burn in hell, he should marry Christina or send her away. It may have been that she was beneath McMillan's rank—in Scotland and Australia. On their marriage certificate her father, Angus, of Kilmorie, is termed 'Farmer': alongside Ewen McMillan's name is written 'Sheep farmer'. Christina was probably illiterate. Her witness, Catherine Cameron, was, and Christina's name is written, in a laborious hand, 'Christion'.

In the records of Gippsland, Christina McMillan does not utter a word until the day of her death. She outlived her husband by 19 years, raising her sons in poverty and living for the most part it seems off the charity of friends and what wages she could earn from domestic duties. Early in January 1884 she left her own home in Sale for the house nearby of Scottish friends. She stayed for only a few weeks before taking a room in the Victoria Hotel on the banks of the La Trobe River. She fell into 'acute melancholy', the proprietress said later. Christina told her one day that she was too much of a problem for anyone to care for. She had become 'unhinged', her friends said. For several days she sat on the veranda. Then, on 29 January, she drowned herself in the river.

The Coroner at Sale, A. W. Howitt, declared that Christina had been of 'unsound mind' when she killed herself. He found that her heart was enlarged, her brain softened, and her womb chronically displaced—'of years standing', the examining doctor said. The Gippsland papers said that her depression might have been brought about by the fact that £2,000 granted to Christina and her sons by the government after her husband's death in 1865, and held in trust by Login and Isaac Buchanan, had not been paid—six years after the eldest son had reached maturity. The newspapers also mentioned, without explanation, that Christina had once had a daughter who had died in Melbourne at about the age of twelve. They did not say who the father was but it cannot have been McMillan, and it just might have been the presence of this child which so long delayed his decision to marry her. Christina was 60 years old when she died. There must have been times in the last half of her life when she wondered if things could have been worse on an Argyllshire croft.

Yet, in the 1850s, it was on women like Christina MacNaughton that the reputation of the white community of Gippsland was substantially dependent. Women were a measure of civilisation. Gippsland was now a place for a lady.

White society was flourishing; Aboriginal society was dying away. The pox and 'pulmonary diseases' raged through the black community. The blacks seemed so ineffectual to newcomers. As she accompanied her husband around the district the wife of Reverend Login wondered why they were so feckless. It was too late for women like her, arriving a decade after settlement, to know the reasons, and the men were unlikely to tell them.

But it is possible that the women sometimes gleaned what the surviving Aborigines knew—that their husbands and masters had once all been much the same. The dashing Hunter brothers, the brutish P. C. Buckley, and the kindly Angus McMillan, had all shared a common characteristic on the all-male frontier—they had all been prepared ro destroy without mercy.

Towards the end of the second decade of settlement the gentlemen of Gippsland grew very pleased with the progress of civilisation. A mood of self-congratulation grew. They might have looked to the men and women whose labour was an indispensable commodity in their society, but they could not honour a labourer. It was much the same with capital, the other indispensable commodity. They could hardly honour a capitalist. How else to honour themselves, then, except as the benchmarks of civilisation—and they threw in a toast to the ladies to prove it.

In 1856 William O'Dell Raymond was leaving the district. A dinner was held in his honour at the Royal Hotel, Alberton. The wines were excellent and Mr Thomson of Clydebank was in the chair. The diners toasted the Queen, Prince Albert and the Royal Family, his Excellency the Acting Governor, the Army and Navy, and so on, and all these toasts were met with 'that loyal enthusiasm which has ever characterized the true Briton'. They also toasted Mr King MLC, Mr Tyers, the press, the Ladies and the Chairman—and 'Mr McMillan, as the discoverer of Gippsland'. McMillan now wore much the same title to such dinners as he was invited to at Clydebank.

Angus McMillan's work could be honoured because he was also a gentleman—and one who had served both labour and capital. If he had been a father to his poor countrymen in Gippsland, Angus McMillan had been something of a factotum to these men. He had shown some of them where the land was. He had beaten trails. He had remained in Gippsland and given loyal and dedicated service to the district: he was a member of the Church, the Caledonian Society, the Acclimatization Society; he supported schools in the area; he was an Honorary Protector of Aborigines. His work lifted burdens from others. The gentlemen of Gippsland recognised a loyal tacksman when they saw one.

They held a dinner for McMillan at John Gellion's Hotel at Port Albert on 3 March 1856. There were, no doubt, the same toasts as Raymond had endured. The Chairman, Dr G. D. Hedley, a distinguished citizen of Port Albert, proposed the toast to the guest of honour.

We have gathered here, to do honour to a great man, one to whom each of us owes more than we can ever acknowledge. In the eighteen years since he came to New South Wales Angus McMillan has won a reputation as an intrepid explorer, a successful squatter and a citizen of whom the colony may well feel proud.

In all that he has accomplished he has not sought personal aggrandisement. Indeed, we know him to be the most modest of men. In an age when so many have spent their lives in accumulating possessions he has spent his years in service.

To each of us, gentlemen, Angus McMillan is a true friend and companion in whose presence we inevitably feel inspired to higher things. In the manner in which he has overcome difficulties and setbacks which would have crushed a lesser man, in the manner in which he has stamped on this province the indelible mark of a fine Scottish gentleman, honour him today, confident that history will accord to him his rightful place as the discoverer of Gippsland. It is my fond wish—and in this I am sure I voice the sentiments of many—that Angus McMillan will one day represent Gippsland in the Parliament of this State.

From behind the British flag a portrait in oils was revealed. McMillan responded with the story of his exploration. There was talk of erecting a monument—a stone pillar—to the explorer. The respectable folk of Gippsland were about to enshrine McMillan, their history and, as the natural heirs of both, their own virtue.

CHAPTER EIGHT

REMOVING ANOTHER RACE

The manifold calamities, but more particularly the decrease and final annihilation of the great majority of indigenous races which has followed, and always does follow, the approach of the whites—is a fact of such historical notoriety that the melancholy instance of the Australian natives affords but a further corroboration of the fearfully destructive influence which the one race exercises upon the other. Those in whose eyes the question of decrease and extinction has assumed all the mournful interest and solemnity which it merits, have inquired into the nature of that invisible but desolating influence which, like a malignant ally of the white man, carries destruction wherever he advances; and the inquiry, like an inquest of the one race upon the corpse of the other, has ended for most part with the verdict of 'Died by the visitation of God'.

P. E. STRZELECKI, *PHYSICAL DESCRIPTION OF NEW SOUTH WALES AND VAN DIEMEN'S LAND*, 1845

There are minds which may be still more affected by gazing on beauty in sorrow, and feeling that pity, that desire of comforting the lovely mourner, which the poet has described as so nearly akin to love.

WALTER SCOTT, *ANNE OF GEIERSTEIN*, 1829

There might have been a second, unspoken, debt acknowledged when the gentlemen of Gippsland toasted the hero of their little nook of empire in Port Albert in 1856. They all knew that Angus McMillan had been a lion in more fields than discovery and track cutting. They all must have been aware that as much as anything else they were celebrating the passing of the bad old days of settlement, the days when they all carried a brace of pistols in their belts. The dinner was a collective sigh of relief. It was a wake. They had buried their memories—and the fact that only 100 Aborigines in all of Gippsland had survived their invasion.

On 28 December 1840 a letter had appeared in the *Sydney Herald* from 'Augustus McMillan of Gippsland or South Caledonia'.

> Started from our station, to discover a road to the coast with the view of running along the Long Beach to Shoal inlets, then to Corner Inlet,—same evening came upon a camp of twenty-five black natives, chiefly women, who all ran away on our near approach, leaving everything they had behind them except some of their spears. We then searched their camp, where we found European articles as underneath described, viz: several check-shirts, cord and moleskin trousers, all besmeared with human blood; one German frock; two pea-jackets, new brown Macintosh cloak also stained with blood, several pieces of women's wearing apparel, namely, prints and merinos; a large lock of brown hair, evidently that of a European woman; one child's white frock with brown velvet band, five hand towels, one of which was marked R. Jamieson No.12, one blue silk purse, silver tassels and slides, containing seven shillings and sixpence British money, one woman's thimble, two large parcels of silk sewing thread, various colours, 10 new English blankets perfectly clean, shoe-makers awls, bees'wax, blacksmith's pinchers and cold chisel, one

bridle bit, which had been recently used, as the grass was quite fresh on it, the tube of a thermometer, broken looking glass, bottles of all descriptions, two of which had castor oil in them, one sealskin cap, one musket and some shot, one broad tomahawk, some London, Glasgow and Aberdeen newspapers, printed in 1837 and 1838. One pewter two gallon measure, one ditto handbasin, one large tin camp kettle, two children's copy books, one bible printed in Edinburgh, June 1838, one set of the National Loan Fund regulations, respecting policies of life insurance, and blank forms of medical man's certificate for effecting the same. Enclosed in three kangaroo skin bags we found the dead body of a male child about two years old, which Dr Arbuckle carefully examined professionally, and discovered beyond doubt its being of European parents; parts of the skin were perfectly white, not being in the least discoloured. We observed the men with shipped spears driving before them the women, one of whom we noticed constantly looking behind her, at us, a circumstance which did not strike us much at the time, but on examining the marks and figures about the largest of the native huts we were immediately impressed with the belief that the unfortunate female is a European—a captive of these ruthless savages. The blacks having come across us the next day in numbers, and our party being composed of four only, we most reluctantly deemed it necessary to return to the station without being enabled to accomplish our object. This was the more painful to our feelings, as we have no doubt whatever but a dreadful massacre of Europeans, men, women and children, has been perpetrated by the aborigines in the immediate vicinity of the spot, whence we were forced to return without being enabled to throw more light on this melancholy catastrophe, than what I have detailed above.

It was the juxtaposition of savagery with the personal inventory of a civilised family—a Scottish family by implication—which was so shocking. There was no 'evidence' of a massacre at all. But massacres of Europeans were to be expected of savages, and it would have been more surprising if McMillan and Arbuckle had *not* deduced from the scene they described that a great bloodletting had taken place. It was not the massacre which lingered in the public mind, it was the thought of the white woman—the 'idea that a female of European birth is detained in durance vile by these ruthless savages', as the *Port Phillip Herald* put it in February 1841—that was so horrifying.

Robert Russell repeated the story in the Melbourne press in 1843, but little more was heard of it until late in 1845. Then the likes of 'Homo' asked in the Melbourne *Argus*, 'Unhappiest of the fairer kind; who knows the misery of thy mind':

Exposed to insults worse than death
Compell'd to breathe the pois'nous breath
Of a rank scented black;
To yield to his abhorr'd embrace,
To kiss his staring, ugly face,
And listen to his clack.

A white woman enshrined the highest virtues of civilisation, the Aborigines of Gippsland the deepest vices of humanity. No doubt she occupied the minds of the lonely men of Gippsland in a variety of roles. The blacks had stolen one of their women. Nothing could have been so well calculated to bring out the warrior in a man. Civilised squatters became crusaders, and unoffending Aborigines their heathen prey.

But for the time being it was enough that the blacks were stealing and spearing stock. That had always been enough for a Highlander.

The Kurnai had merely observed when the Europeans arrived. They attacked when the whites made it plain that they intended to stay. Hutton and his cattle were driven out. McMillan was threatened when he built a hut and brought in stock. Within six months most settlers in Gippsland would have contested Paul Strzelecki's claim that the blacks were 'peaceable' and 'inoffensive'; that they could be 'easily tamed and secured by trifling articles'.

The Aborigines attacked stock and drove them off. They murdered shepherds—they killed four at least in 1843 and they were still killing them on the Snowy River runs in 1851. They directed their resistance at the squatters' weakest points. When he arrived in 1843, C. J. Tyers found himself in the middle of a war, albeit a very one-sided one.

There is no doubt that internecine war, largely precipitated by the breaking down of traditional barriers to communication, was a major factor in the destruction of Kurnai and neighbouring tribes. The process was accelerated by the custom of payback killing. As disease spread through the tribes, we can presume that the process quickened; each inexplicable death being blamed on a member of a hostile tribe and avenged. The white invasion triggered a self-destructive mechanism inherent in Aboriginal culture. There was a terrible battle between the Omeo and Bruthen blacks sometime in the 1840s. In 1844 George Robinson reported that the Westernport tribes had been all but wiped out by the Brataualung of the Port Albert area. And Tyers reported that the 'Melbourne blacks' led by Lal Lal and Billy Lonsdale had killed at least 30 Brataualung in about 1847. He knew of a similar massacre of upper La Trobe people by, he thought, Westernport or Melbourne blacks, when the upper Gippsland road was opened. Tyers, who thought the Gippsland blacks were irredeemably low on civilisation's scale, always maintained that it was internecine war, disease, and the indiscriminate brutality of the native police which accounted for the drastic decline in the Kurnai population.

But Tyers was disingenuous. His reports to La Trobe concealed more than they revealed. There can be no doubt that to some extent the Kurnai tribes did tear themselves apart, and were consumed by diseases to which they had little resistance. But it is equally certain that a substantial proportion of the original population was slaughtered by whites. There were at least two massacres in 1840–41. The 'defence' of Bushy Park was a massacre and everyone in Gippsland must have known it when the Crown Lands Commissioner arrived. The Briakalung were driven down the Avon to a point near the mouth at Lake Wellington. In 1844 George Augustus Robinson saw 'many Human Bones and Skulls' there. Twenty years later the missionary, John Bulmer, had gathered that a 'great many Aboriginals' had been killed on the spot. It was known as Boney Point. The 'defence' extended beyond Lake King. Colin MacLaren, McMillan's stockman, recalled that a party from Bushy Park had pursued the blacks to a place which was known for a while as Butcher's Creek, near present day Metung. As they apparently had been at Boney Point, the Aborigines were trapped by the water's edge and shot down. There was only a handful of men at Bushy Park then, Colin MacLaren among them. Angus McMillan was their leader.

Tyers must have known. Yet at no point in his accounts of contact with the Gippsland Aborigines, over more than a decade, did he name a single white in specific connection with the death of a black. In 1849 he wrote in his journal that it had been reported to him that Lal Lal (or Yal Yal), a Port Phillip black, had led a party of 13 or 14 whites in a massacre of eight blacks near McMillan's Straits. The bodies had been hung from nooses attached to a hide rope stretched between two trees. He had heard of skeletons and bodies being found. But he wrote with great care.

In 1844 he had been told of a punitive raid on the blacks after some of MacIntosh's cattle had been speared: 'Mr McMillan and others pursued them and came up with them on the Ranges—Blacks poised their spears—party fired—not known if any blacks were killed. Number of blacks said to be 200.'

On another occasion in 1844 Tyers accompanied McMillan and some other settlers, including Hobson, Brodribb and King, in pursuit of blacks after they had speared cattle belonging to King and Macalister. The Commissioner's account is worth quoting:

> After tracking through the scrub, crossing and re-crossing the river several times came upon them at 10 o'clock in thick scrub, where they had evidently recently arrived and were setting to cook their midday meal. It was my wish to endeavour to take some of these prisoners to be dealt with, and in accordance thereto I issued orders to both the Border Police and the Blacks not to fire except in self-defence, but to rush upon them and take them by surprise. When approaching the scrub however . . . one of the party fired and was followed by the whole. Not seeing the Blacks myself in consequence of the thickness of the scrub between us, I was for a moment at a loss to know whether my orders had been disobeyed or if spears had been thrown. From inquiries I subsequently made I could only learn that a native had been seen brandishing a spear, but whether with the intention of throwing it was uncertain.
>
> The natives being taken by surprise fled through the scrub, leaving everything behind them.

Tyers made a detailed inventory of the goods left behind: 60 spears, 'clubs of various kinds', '6 English tomahawks . . . 24 stone do . . . some old knives and a fork, pieces of iron' and 12 cwt of smoked beef. He concluded his report: 'As a punishment and to show them these depredations will not be allowed in future to be committed with impunity, I caused their spears and the beef they had taken to be burned on the spot.' There were at least nine men in the hunting party. It may be that when 'the whole' of them fired they all missed their targets, but it is unlikely. Tyers was meticulous in discovering and recording the number of cattle speared, the quantity of meat in the Aboriginal camps, the number of weapons. But when there were respectable settlers involved, he was never able to ascertain the number of blacks killed, or say what was done with the bodies, even in the parties he personally supervised. He did not say there were no deaths. He simply did not mention the subject. It might be reasonable to assume that the bodies were burnt with the beef.

In Gippsland, as in other parts of Australia, it seems that the Aborigines thought the white invaders were 'jumped up white fellers'; in other words, the ghosts of their own people. This was not an unreasonable interpretation. There were plenty of people in Britain to say that emigrants were gripped by 'a fatal spirit'; that they had committed an act tantamount to suicide by severing the cords with their native land. There were those who said they had done something analogous to bleeding. It was not so unreasonable then for the blacks to think of them as 'grinkai'—peeled corpses. It may even have been perspicacious. The whites thought they had left their past well behind, but they had brought with them some of their ancestors' habits of mind. It was perhaps because they sensed their past that the Scottish settlers of Gippsland took to the Kurnai like the Sassenach, 'Butcher' Cumberland, had taken to their ancestors. Like Cumberland they justified their destruction of an ancient way of life in the name of an advancing civilisation. Perhaps it was patricide. Or Cobbett may have been right the first time, and the first generation of settlers had severed the cords which bound them to humanity, including the cords of memory.

Early in 1843, shortly before Tyers arrived in Gippsland, the Port Albert blacks had made the tragic error of killing not just a sheep or a shepherd, but the nephew of the great man, Lachlan Macalister. There are numerous explanations for the death of Ronald Macalister. It has been said that some stockmen had thrown hot coals at a group of Aborigines; that Macalister had made a target of an Aboriginal boy and eventually killed him; that Macalister had fired casually at a group of blacks 'without any provocation'; that it had in fact been the stockman, John Morrison, who had caused the trouble. Whatever the offence the blacks decided to take their revenge. In or near the paddock where Lachlan Macalister kept his cattle before shipping them out of the port, Ronald Macalister was speared to death as he rode home one night. Most accounts say his body was mutilated—'in their usual fashion', Dunderdale said. There are as many variations of this story as there are reasons for the murder: they range from the tidy removal of his kidney fat to one which has Angus McMillan, or his Aboriginal 'boy', Friday, finding nothing more than Ronald Macalister's two legs—and those consisting only of the portions below the knee, the blacks being unable to remove the leggings. The *Port Phillip Patriot* let its imagination go:

> Mr Macalister was dragged off his horse and cruelly murdered in the township of Alberton, his head being so totally disfigured that his countenance could not be recognized amongst his most intimate friends this outrage being committed by those harmless innocent citizens of the wilds of Gippsland bearing the anomalous cognomen of Her Majesty's most liege subjects (we give it as our gratuitous opinion, most bitter enemies).

For the Brataualung the result of this action was catastrophic. It was said that 'every Scotchman who had a horse and gun gathered'. The company they formed was known as the Highland Brigade. The blacks were cornered at Warrigal Creek to the north of Port Albert and close to the Ninety Mile Beach. Dunderdale said the number of men, women and children killed was probably less than 60. 'Gippslander', who wrote many years later, said the figure was somewhere between 100 and 150. He described it this way: 'The brigade coming up on the blacks camped around the waterhole at Warrigal Creek surrounded them and fired into them, killing a great number, some escaped into the scrub, others jumped into the waterhole, and, as fast as they put their heads up for breath, they were shot until the water was red with blood.' His informants were two survivors of the massacre who had been boys at the time. One of them, with a slug in his eye, was captured 'and made to lead the brigade from one camp to another'. His name was 'One Eye' or 'Bing Eye'.

It was impossible to establish the number killed. Dunderdale's estimate, as the Gippsland historian Peter Gardner has pointed out, would approximate a family group; that of 'Gippslander' would be typical of a division, that is, three or four family groups gathered together as they often did for warfare or defence. It may have been the biggest single massacre on the Australian frontier, but because the men who had roped together, murdered and burnt 28 Aborigines at Myall Creek in 1838 had been hanged, no-one was going to talk about the Warrigal Creek affair. It was one of the great ironies of Australian history that Governor Gipps's determination to see justice was administered equally between blacks and whites, did nothing to halt the flow of blood on the Australian frontier, and may even have encouraged settlers to be more thorough as well as more secretive. Edward Deas Thomson, the Colonial Secretary, tried valiantly to prevent a bloodbath after the attack on George Faithfull's party on the Ovens River, but in the end Faithfull could say that he had given them 'a notion of what sort of stuff the white man was made of, and my name was a terror to them ever after'.[1]

We know few of the details of the Warrigal Creek massacre, but it was certainly a very Scottish affair. McMillan probably organised the 'Highland Brigade'. (It has often been called McMillan's Highland Brigade.) He had demonstrated both an unswerving loyalty to Macalister and a ready will to destroy any resistance to settlement at Bushy Park. No doubt he was joined in the Highland Brigade by other loyal servants of Macalister: men who felt they owed him their livelihood since they had arrived from Scotland, men for whom 'fidelity to superiors and their trusts' was still a fundamental principle, men who had developed something resembling an 'habitual attachment' to a prosperous 'laird' who had yet not forgotten his duties to his kin. Macalister himself seems to have taken part at Warrigal Creek. George Dunderdale left a blunt hint from stories he had heard about the port: 'The gun used by old Macalister was a double barrelled Purdy, a beautiful and reliable weapon, which in its time had done great execution.'

1 On 13 April 1838, 300 blacks attacked Faithfull's party on the main stock route from Sydney to Port Phillip. Eight whites were killed. Thomson gave strict instructions to the police magistrate aimed at containing the inevitable punitive action. The magistrate was to discover the causes of the attack—had Faithfull's or a previous party been harassing the Aborigines or interfering with their women? Prisoners were to be taken but no more than the number of whites shot. There was to be no indiscriminate shooting. The hunting party was to keep within set bounds. The blacks were 'in every respect to be considered subjects of the Queen and not as aliens against whom the Queen's troops may exercise belligerent rights'.

Everyone in Gippsland knew of the massacre, and it remained a part of folk memory. 'As far back as I can remember,' one old resident wrote, 'there were all sorts of tales in connection with this killing business, and it seemed to me that everyone was more or less ashamed of the affair.' Sometimes the bones emerging from the sandhills jogged the memory. 'They drove the abos in to a bend beside Warragal [*sic*] Creek homestead and killed all that were there. Then they loaded the bodies into bullock drays and took them up into the sandhills about half a mile away and buried them,' another man said.

The folk history of Gippsland, for all its variations on detail of the massacre, is consistent on two issues. First, that the Ronald Macalister murder was a reprisal either for the actions of other Europeans in the area, or for his own actions. Second, that the slaughter did not stop at Warrigal Creek. George Augustus Robinson, the Protector of Aborigines, who passed through Gippsland shortly after the massacre, illustrated the suppression of this information from the very beginning. While in the vicinity of the port he wrote that there had recently been an 'unprovoked murder' of a white man, and the blacks 'as might have been expected were completely dispersed'. In colonial argot 'disperse' always meant to shoot; to 'thoroughly disperse' meant to shoot on a considerable scale. By the time he reached the ranges Robinson had changed his story. Now he had learnt that 'some depraved white men had in a fit of drunkenness, shot at and killed some friendly natives'. So Robinson conceded that the murder was a reprisal; but it was not for actions of a nephew of Lachlan Macalister, rather for those of the nameless and depraved. Similarly, the massacre, like the other 'mischief' being done to the blacks in the district, was inflicted by the 'lawless and depraved who had infested the Port from Van Diemen's Land'.[2] The irony, not to say the injustice of this account is heightened by the fact that until the Macalister incident the blacks at the port had lived amicably with the whites—the 'depraved' whites included. It seems that at the very beginning of settlement the squatters of the Gippsland Company had established their authority in the area without resort to violence. 'We occasionally fired off our rifles at marks on the trees,' W. A. Brodribb said, 'or empty bottles suspended in the air, to show that we had arms to defend ourselves. We brought with us a small cannon, which we loaded and fired off towards the bay, and they saw the double shot strike the water.' There is no suggestion of bloody conflict.

The Warrigal Creek massacre and subsequent black hunts were not isolated acts in the seizure of the land by force. They were acts of genocide, and like other acts of genocide they were occasioned not by reason but by unreason. They were gratuitous acts triggered by impulses which possibly even the participants did not understand, but which could be justified by any amount of spurious racial and religious thought. Nobody really had to justify it. No-one could afford to. Tyers sent an obtuse report to La Trobe in February 1845. 'In the early part of 1843,' he said, 'as far as I have been informed, some of the Corner Inlet tribe were occasionally employed by the few settlers at Port Albert in carrying firewood and in other light works, for which they generally received payment in flour etc., but since the unprovoked murder of Mr Ronald

2 Robinson's ambitions in Gippsland are not entirely clear. He collected 8,000 words of Aboriginal language and complained that 'depraved stockmen' had added blasphemies to it. G. H. Haydon, who travelled to Gippsland at about the same time, said Robinson's efforts 'like everything else undertaken by the protectors amounted to little or nothing'.

Macalister by them at Port Albert about that time they have not been seen in the neighbourhood.'

There were three types of squatters on the Australian frontier: those who thought that their right to the land was qualified by an obligation to treat the Aboriginal inhabitants with kindness; those who believed that their right was conditional only on extermination; and those who combined murder with kindness. Those differences had parallels in the three broad ideologies of the age. Christianity could instruct settlers in the language of the Song of Solomon or the Book of Job. It could inform Europeans that the Aborigines were 'black but comely' (a fact which many squatters had discovered for themselves), 'our sable brethren', 'our dusky neighbours'; or it could underpin the idea that the blacks were born to suffer as an accursed race, the sons of Ham. Social Darwinism legitimated extermination policies in some men's minds, but not all; it was also the basis of the uniquely nineteenth-century idea of making life comfortable for a dying race, 'smoothing the dying pillow' it was called. Similarly, imperial ideology expressed itself in philanthropic terms, often even while pursuing its most venal ends. When the natives resisted, the balance of all three views swung heavily towards murder. Whether it was at 'Cawnpore' or Port Albert, an act of rebellion was an act of suicide.

So long as they had not mastered the environment or the interest on their loans, the squatters of Gippsland were fickle and dangerous. Henry Meyrick makes a good example. He was a devout and gentle man, on the surface at least one of the most appealing figures in the district's early history. In 1846, after a few months in Gippsland, he wrote that he had 'heard tales told and [seen] some things that . . . would form as dark a page as ever you read in the book of history'. He was convinced that not less than 450

Aborigines had been murdered. 'The blacks are very quiet here now, poor wretches,' he wrote, and continued:

> No wild beast of the forest was ever hunted down with such unsparing perseverence as they are. Men, women, and children are shot whenever they can be met with. Some excuse might be found for shooting the men by those who are daily getting their cattle speared, but what they can urge in their excuse who shoot the women and children I cannot conceive. I have protested against it at every station I have been in Gippsland, but these things are kept very secret as the penalty would certainly be hanging.

But Meyrick was as committed to his sheep as he was to Christianity. He could not shoot them in groups, but, he said, 'if I caught a black actually killing my sheep, I would shoot him with as little remorse as I would a wild dog'.

If it worried Meyrick to think of murder, and the members of the Highland Brigade were inclined to see it as their regimental duty, John Campbell MacLeod seems to have had a casual approach to the problem. When the Aborigines speared one of his cattle on the Snowy he went after them with a gun and found them on the other side of the river. He beckoned them to cross but they gestured that it was too high. They told him that they did not spear his bullock, and danced about 'slapping their legs in a token of defiance'. They thought they were out of range, he said. So MacLeod gave them a shot which sent mud all over them and frightened them 'out of their lives'. When they re-emerged from the reeds, they again swore they had not taken his beast and begged him not to shoot. 'So we fired three more rounds over their heads,' said MacLeod. It was not the most effective policy. 'From this time on,' as he said himself, 'they set to work—in one week of rainy weather, they killed twenty or thirty.' They killed even his quietest cattle, taking only the tongue, the tail and the kidneys. His black boy would not leave the hut. When MacLeod hunted them he found they 'could get over the river and through the high ferns like wallabies'. One day he was told that more cattle had been killed at the bottom of the run:

> I rode down unarmed as I had a young horse; about two miles or more from the hut I saw a native dog, and having no gun took out my stirrup leather intending to kill him with the iron, my horse took fright and pitched me and the saddle on the ground. Instantly the scrub between me and the river seemed alive with blacks, I am sure the whole tribe was there, the yells made my flesh creep, I was in a deuce of a fright but I always had a brace of pistols in my belt and this was known to the blacks. So I took out a round brass tinder box and holding it like a pistol, made the best of my way home, and although they followed me up in the scrub, I never saw one. I think the fright was mutual . . . When I got home we went out armed but could not fall in with any of them.

Tyers had to send the native police into this farthest frontier of Gippsland to deal with the situation.

Patrick Coady Buckley first mentioned the Aborigines down on the Ninety Mile Beach on 27 March 1844.

> Young Mason (Leonard) and myself to scrub below House where blacks had taken some sheep evening before went out scrub and on our way saw five Blackfellows about one hundred and fifty yards ahead, Mason and I fired at them and chased them but they got into the scrub. A good job we found the remains of two sheep they had taken the night before Mason and I had double barrelled guns. d.cool.

Three days later the Border Police[3] arrived and they all went off on a hunt, but they had no luck. 'We must have struck terror into them,' wrote Buckley, 'day showery.'

Buckley and his men went hunting again on 8 April. In the middle of the night Buckley mistook Mason moving about the camp for an Aborigine and nearly shot him. They were all very jumpy, Buckley wrote. The next day Mason nearly passed out from thirst in a morass. They went home after two days.

Buckley kept up his war for three years or more. Sometimes he was frustrated by his own incompetence. Too often the blacks saw him coming and got away before he could shoot them. One infuriating day he fell down and broke the stock of his gun while chasing them. The only compensation was to burn their spears—that and the sport. 'Took Betty the mare and went down to the beach . . .' he wrote on 18 January 1845, and went on:

> Just as I got on the sand hammock I saw two Blacks coming along the Beach from near the Creek. I waited behind the sand hammock until they came opposite me. I then rode towards them and they took to the sea. I had pistols with me and fired Blank Shots to keep them in the sea which I did for almost four hours and drove them along in the water to near the mouth of Merrimans Creek which is about a mile.

Perhaps the two were eloping. The man grew weak and Buckley motioned the woman to leave him. She would not until 'at last she thought there was no chance for him consequently she left him at this time he seemed nearly drowned in the breakers'.

---

3 This was a force organised to keep order in pastoral districts under the direction of the Commissioners of Crown Lands.

> I rode into the surf after him got a rein round his neck and pulled him out and nearly hanged him whilst doing so when I got him out on the land he pretended to be dead but when I pulled out his hands to look at them he jerked them in again I planted back of the Hammock for sometime but he would not move so I came away and left him. Only my mare was so frightened I would have brought him home to the hut.

For what purpose he would have brought the man home Buckley did not say. Three days later he rode back to the beach to see if the man was dead. He had gone.

With Marshall, William Scott, Henry Bayliss and Black George, Buckley was hunting blacks again in October 1845. On the first day they went 25 kilometres without seeing any. On the second day '. . . went about a mile along the Beach left our horses with Black George went in the scrub saw several places where they had camped about turning back when we saw two black Women walking towards us we waited until they came close up . . . then started back.'

The night afterwards they camped by the 'margins of the lake lined with dead fish Tons of them. Night very wet.'

If in life Buckley was a vicious man, in death he was a humbug. He was not the 'superbushman' the obituary writer said he was when Buckley died, rich, influential and almost respectable, in 1872. The writer referred to the man's 'prodigious strength and undaunted courage'. He said that Buckley prided himself on never using a gun against the blacks. (He did not mention poison.) Buckley, he wrote, used only a stockwhip to 'strike terror' into them. The estate realised £60,000. An old labourer fought a long battle for the money: he swore that Buckley had been terror stricken in 1844 and, fearing that the blacks would soon kill him, he made out a will in his favour.

Buckley never mentioned the captive white woman in his diary, but in 1846 the Scots in Gippsland started to see her again. She manifested herself to William Pearson, Hugh Reoch and John Turnbull: it was just like McMillan's sighting five years before—the blacks had 'driven her before them'. In August 1846 John MacDonald, proprietor of the Scottish Chiefs Hotel in Melbourne, wrote to the *Argus* to say that he had it on good authority from Gippsland that a woman named Anna MacPherson was a captive of the blacks there. She had been a passenger on the *Britannia* which went down off the Gippsland coast in 1839, he wrote. George Cavanagh, editor and proprietor of the *Port Phillip Herald*, said a friend of his had seen her name carved on trees in areas previously unseen by whites.

What *was* her name? For the Gaels she was Gaelic. For 'an Englishman' in the *Sydney Morning Herald* she was the Irish wife of a Sydney brewer who had survived the sinking of the *Sarah* in 1839—Mrs T. Capel. Others said her name was Lord, and that she was the wife of a Sydney merchant. Whoever she was, the white woman had been taken from a civilisation in which comfort and the respect of men were her birthrights, and forcibly held in one which, being primitive, abused her sex as a matter of course. The thought of her 'repulsive thralldom', her lost honour and her terrible melancholy was too much for any decent man to bear. 'The horrors of such captivity—an educated white female forcibly detained by a savage cannibal black—the helpless misery of her wretchedness—the bitter recollection of a former happy home . . .', excited the *Argus*; and the *Argus* hoped that the thought would excite 'the generous of all classes' as well. The gentlemen of Melbourne called a public meeting and began a subscription for an expedition to the 'fastnesses of Gippsland'. If it was too late to save her virtue there might still be time to save her life.

The private expedition was led by C. L. J. de Villiers, a former trooper and something of a bushman, and James Warman, a resolute humanitarian. The Melbourne commentator, 'Garryowen', thought Mr Warman was about the last man in Melbourne they should have appointed.

The party of five whites and nine blacks left Melbourne for Corner Inlet on 20 October 1846, nearly six years after McMillan and Arbuckle had first seen the white woman. In addition to fishhooks, lines, blankets and such other items as were 'esteemed by the blacks', they had with them a large number of handkerchiefs on which were printed, in English and Gaelic, directions for the white woman to look out for them.

> WHITE WOMAN!—There are fourteen armed men, partly White and partly Black, in search of you. Be cautious; and rush to them when you see them near you. Be particularly on the look out every dawn of morning, for it is then that the party are in hopes of rescuing you. The white settlement is towards the setting sun.

The Gaelic version of the handkerchief was addressed more specifically to 'Anna!'

From Corner Inlet the expedition hauled their whaleboats to the lakes, and in these for several months they made their way about the waterways of Gippsland. They soon found along the shores 'a great many skulls and human bones, which were remains of Warrigals who had been shot', Warman said. The Aborigines were now living in the most inaccessible parts of the ranges in winter and among the swamps in summer. They dared not show themselves in the open country. Warman believed, as did the blacks he spoke to, that the Kurnai tribes faced extermination. The blacks told him that the white woman did exist and that she was living with a man named Bunjeleene in the mountains. One of them hummed a tune which he said the white woman often sang. It was Psalm 100. He told them she 'plenty cry'.

It was extraordinary how the story reproduced itself in various places. In 1846 reports came into the Aboriginal Protectorate in Port Phillip that the Aborigines of the Wimmera had a white woman at their mercy. It was too much for the Assistant Protector, William Thomas, to believe. After interviewing several Gippsland blacks he wrote to George Augustus Robinson to say it was a myth.

Another expedition had been mounted by the combined exertions of McMillan, Tyers and the native police. This was the 'official expedition'. McMillan was the most active of the Gippsland squatters in the hunt. And even when he was not personally engaged in pursuit, that first sighting of his lived so keenly in his and other minds it was as good as a gun. He must have told the tale countless times. It was remarkable how the subsequent sightings bore such a resemblance to his.

The native police were an ancient invention and an ingenious one for turning the traditional animosities of tribes to the invaders' account. The English had employed the technique very effectively in the Scottish Highlands. The brutality of the native police compounded the European belief that all natives were barbarians by nature as well as habit, while indemnifying themselves against similar charges. In the Port Phillip district the native police were commanded by Captain Henry Edward Pulteney Dana, a member of the Melbourne Club,[4] and a squatter in his own right. His force had been used in support of the

4 Dana died in the Melbourne Club in 1852, as a result of exposure suffered in the field.

Orangeists against a Catholic mob in Elizabeth Street, Melbourne, in 1843, but such actions were not their speciality. They had recently distinguished themselves in the massacre of the Cape Otway tribe to the west of Melbourne. Gippsland was their next theatre: it was relatively convenient along the new road they had beaten from their base at Narre Warren about 40 kilometres east of Melbourne.

If they were not essential to European success on the frontier, the native police certainly made it very much easier to achieve. Tyers called for them immediately after his arrival in Gippsland, and soon after completing their first missions he called for them again, for the 'depredations' of the local blacks had increased to 'an alarming extent'. A Sergeant Walshe led them in Gippsland; he was a man feared by the Aborigines and favoured by the settlers. The settlers had little time for the humanitarian Warman and de Villiers.

Both the official and the private expeditions tracked their quarry to the Snowy River country. A member of the official party complained that they had been told a great many contradictory stories by the blacks. Some had said that the woman had not been seen because Bunjeleene never let her out of his camp; others said they had missed her at the camp because she had gone off digging roots with the women of the tribe. At the Snowy Dana and Walshe let loose on the Aborigines.

Taking some of the 'fine athletic race' with them Warman's party had explored Lake King and the Tambo and Nicholson rivers without success, but they were convinced by their conversations with the lake tribes that the woman did exist. They were much impressed by the blacks: 'Friendship and kindness for a year would make them demi-civilized,' Warman said. They were told that Bunjeleene was in the vicinity so five Aborigines were sent off to bring him in or to arrange a meeting. Pursuit of Bunjeleene led them, like the official expedition, to the Snowy. When they reached the mouth of the river in December they found what they took to be evidence of a massacre. Warman found one body with three gunshot wounds and a fractured skull on the banks of the river and eight more bodies in an Aboriginal camp nearby. He and de Villiers also freed two Aborigines who had been handcuffed together and left to stagger about the bush.

The leaders of the official expedition reported only that there had been some hand-to-hand combat on the Snowy and that some prisoners had been taken. Their explanation did not impress Tyers. Not that Tyers had much sympathy for Warman and de Villiers. He had been hospitable to them up to a point, but he had also refused them provisions and later accused them of 'rushing' a group of Aborigines near the lakes. Tyers must have known where the sentiments of the squatters lay and that he had to live with them. After hearing of the massacre from de Villiers and Warman, however, Tyers felt obliged to instruct the official expedition to withdraw. He estimated that fourteen Snowy River blacks had been killed by the native police.

Warman said the native police were 'harpies of hell, misnamed police and . . . one or two Europeans were not a whit behind these demi-civilized wretches'. Matthew Macalister and Octavius Sparks who had runs on the Snowy wanted Warman and de Villiers out of the district, and when the *Port Phillip Herald* published Warman's reports in January 1847 the squatters of Gippsland were furious. A public meeting was held in Port Albert and the chairman, W. O'Dell Raymond, wrote to the Melbourne press alleging slander.

The search for the white woman went on. The official expedition said they had seen someone carried off in a possum-skin cloak on which the native police later smelt a white woman. Walshe said he came within five metres of her. A black boy identified traces of her handiwork in the construction of a dwelling. One party saw her footprints, but thereafter, said the *Argus*, Bunjeleene put possum skins on her feet. The searchers were told that she had two children by Bunjeleene. Some said four. It was thought that he called her Toondegon.

There were some who said that she was no more than the figurehead from the *Britannia*. No, the figurehead was from the *Yarra Yarra*, and the woman was one of the Misses Sargentson, wrote a correspondent from the Duke of Kent Hotel in Melbourne. George Augustus Robinson said she was a fabrication. In March 1847 La Trobe told Tyers that her existence was 'strongly disputed by those whose opinions might be supposed to have weight'. She was the invention of 'a few waggish settlers' someone wrote in the *Port Phillip Patriot*. On the other hand, opponents of de Villiers and Warman accepted that she existed but called for stronger measures to secure her release: '. . . shall these babblers prate against *force* being used to release a British subject, and that subject a helpless woman, from a slavery worse than death', asked the Scots-run *Patriot*.

A more forceful expedition was sent out under the command of Sergeant Walshe,[5] and eventually contact was made with Bunjeleene. Trooper Cowan noted that he was 'a left handed man and rather old'. Bunjeleene offered the party a gin he had taken from the Port Phillip tribe. She had two children and her name was Loondegon. He said he had no other. Tyers was tired of being 'made sport of'.

5 Among their guides was the Aboriginal youth named 'One Eye' or 'Bing Eye' who had survived the Warrigal Creek massacre. In the course of the expedition he was attacked by two of the native police and died from the wounds they inflicted.

Bunjeleene was made to lead a party to the mountains where some believed his brother held the white woman. When the mountains refused to yield her, Bunjeleene, his two wives from his own tribe, Mumbalk and Parley, and Parley's two boys were taken to the native police headquarters at Narre Warren. Bunjeleene told his captors that if it was not Loondegon they wanted, he did have the figurehead of a ship, or so the *Argus* reported, and he added that it had become 'an idol' for his tribe, 'around which they danced the most solemn corroborees'.

Bunjeleene and his family were to be held hostage until the white woman was released. While the whites waited Mumbalk died, in August 1848, and Parley and the two boys were taken to Melbourne. On 21 November 1848 Bunjeleene also died, almost a year after Henry Dana had been authorised to return him to Gippsland.

The white woman had been put to death twelve months before, at least to the satisfaction of her original discoverers. Mr David Campbell had arrived overland from McMillan's station to tell the *Port Phillip Herald* that the 'remains of a white female and child' had been found at Jemmy's Point, about four miles from Tyers's place. McMillan and Arbuckle had been called to the inquest on the bodies at Eagle Point. After Arbuckle had examined the bodies he had declared that there 'could not be an atom of doubt of one of them being that of a white female, which was easily evident from her head'.

So it was not a 'joke of a few waggish settlers', the *Port Phillip Herald* declared triumphantly: 'She really did exist and lingered through a revolting bondage of several years, and has at length been *murdered* to satisfy the fiend jealousy of one of her black tyrants.' The *Herald* knew she had been murdered because a shepherd had told their informant.

When Bunjeleene had been arrested, their informant was told, the woman had been passed on to his brother. But the brother had a rival who defeated him in battle for the white prize and the poor woman became 'the lubra of the conquerer'. It was all 'according to barbarous custom'. It was hardly a surprise then that Bunjeleene's brother should decide that his rival 'should not long enjoy her. Accordingly, he lay in wait one night, he watched for a favourable opportunity and murdered the woman and her child.'

Tyers must have decided to let the Highlanders end to their own satisfaction the story they had started seven years before. It was the only hope of respite for the wild blacks. He estimated that no less than 50 of them had been killed in the hunts for the woman. If Arbuckle and McMillan were satisfied that the remains they saw at Tyers's house were those of the woman, the Commissioner himself was not. A decade later he wrote: 'My firm opinion is, and it was the opinion of Mr La Trobe, that there never was a white woman among the blacks.' Tyers believed it was the figurehead from a ship—it was no more than a representation of a woman.

Even in 1858 Tyers was anxious that the subject not be raised again. He knew by then how potent a myth could be. Two years after Tyers had killed the myth at Eagle Point, Robert Russell wrote a novel called *The Heart* which was based on McMillan's sighting. In 1866 Angus MacLean wrote a similar romance. For more than 100 years the tale was told periodically in the press. It was the *Oban Times* which had the happiest ending. In 1919 they reported that she had escaped, rejoined her husband in the Land of Lorn and lay buried, not at Eagle Point, but in the cemetery at Pennymuir.

John Campbell MacLeod was a direct descendant of the Campbells of Lorn. At the end of 1848 he was at

Buchan where he heard that one of the native police had found part of a bible at The Heart, and he went out looking for the white woman. In the course of his hunt he found some nice grazing country on the Snowy, and shortly after he 'went up with cattle and took possession'. The white woman served many purposes. MacLeod was always amused by the blacks. He 'used to laugh at them for hours'. But he found time to discover that the woman did exist, before she drowned with her two half-caste children in McLennan's Straits.[6]

It may have taken more to tame John Campbell MacLeod, but until real white women came to Gippsland the captive woman served as proof that the white settlers were civilised. So long as they pursued her they were worthy. So long as she sang Psalm 100 they were Christians. And so long as they thought of her they ceased to think of their own worst fears and their own desire. For the Highland men at least, 'Anna' was also a manifestation of their memories. She was proof of the power of nostalgia. She took them home.

George Dunderdale would not hear of the argument that because they were men of their time they could do no other. 'When a race of men is exterminated somebody ought to bear the blame,' he wrote; 'and the easiest way is to lay the fault at the door of the dead.'

The Gippsland Aborigines were asked to bear more blame than any race was logically capable of: they were charged with being both cunning and feckless, both savage and indolent. They had resisted the white invasion to the extent that they had put fear in the heart of P. C. Buckley,

6 When *Life* published an article on the white woman in 1916, MacLeod's daughter said it was all a 'fiction'. How could 'such a thing be hushed up or forgotten?' she asked.

but in the end white society judged them, as it did the rest of the Australian Aborigines, to have given in without a fight.

In fact the war in Gippsland went on for more than a decade. The blacks resisted with great ingenuity. John Campbell of Glencoe countered their mastery of the bush with a deerhound he trained especially for the task. Curlewis at Holey Plains was so impressed he asked Campbell to clear his run with it. While Campbell was away the blacks returned to Glencoe and bandicooted all his potatoes. For all John MacLeod's efforts to clear them off his Snowy River station they were still there in 1851: they burned his huts to the ground and killed one of his stockmen. In 1852 Tyers had to send police into the hills of Central Gippsland from whence he had received 'reports of murders committed, cattle and sheep stolen, and lives threatened by a tribe of Aborigines . . . many among them being armed with muskets and fowling pieces'.

White settlers used Aboriginal skills to explore the district and to tame it. Every settler had at least one 'boy' as a stockman, tracker and general labourer. McMillan, Raymond and several other squatters put Aborigines to work washing sheep. When shepherds left for the gold fields, Aborigines took on their jobs. They were excellent stockmen. Buckley used them for all sorts of tasks. Other settlers, Tyers among them, employed Aborigines 'even as house servants'. Frederick Jones told Tyers in 1853 that without them he could have neither washed his sheep nor shepherded them; he could not have harvested his wheat crop, 'nor carried on the ordinary work of the station'. Yet Tyers wrote to La Trobe in the old familiar language:

> Notwithstanding the opportunities they have had by their increased intercourse with the settlers, I cannot say they have

> made any progress in civilization. They still conform to their savage habits and mode of life. Too idle to cultivate the soil and to lay up provision for tomorrow they hold to their wandering propensities when employed by the White population, and are satisfied with the scanty food which their indolent life allows them to obtain from Gum Trees, or from the Rivers and Lakes.

It was a similar story in central Victoria where H. C. W. Smythe took them to task for not bothering to go to the gold fields: 'Even the allurement of Gold seeking cannot overcome the natural indolence of their disposition. The Chinaman, the Lascar, the New Zealander, Malay and African are seen to be working in parties, but in no case is the Aborigine to be met with.' Someone in Gippsland might have told him they were too busy on the stations to go to the gold fields. Or too busy maintaining a besieged culture. Or too busy getting drunk like so many others among the colony's dispossessed.

Drunkenness among the Aborigines appalled Tyers and La Trobe. The young 'do not live out half their days', La Trobe said. And now they did not even lament their dead but 'may be seen staggering around the scene in a state of intoxication vociferating most awful curses'. But the Governor thought he could see why alcohol was such a problem with them. This 'slavish vice binds many an intelligent European', he observed; it was little wonder to him that the effects were catastrophic on a people with 'unbridled sensual appetites'. There was little that could be done for them beyond setting aside places they could call their own and issuing provisions and a blanket each year. For the rest they were beyond the reach of civilisation. They would not even sleep indoors. They insisted on wandering about and sleeping under the stars in 'primitive wildness'.

Disease killed them too. To La Trobe it seemed the influenza which afflicted them was 'much resembling in appearance, and having the same effect as, the sheep catarrh prevalent in the Colony': another historic victory for sheep. And the 'loathsome disease' which afflicted Europeans was rife, as we have seen. Tyers believed it was inherent among the blacks, although he conceded that it had 'not been mitigated by their intercourse with the whites'. He was always careful not to offend.

Tyers counted the Gippsland Aborigines for La Trobe in 1853. There were 131, comprised as follows: Dargo; 18 men, 21 women, 13 children. Low country or Plain; 9 men, 4 women, 2 children. Tarra or Corner Inlet; 15 men, 9 women, 8 children. Mitchell; 6 men, 0 women, 0 children. Swan Reach; 11 men, 5 women, 4 children. Upper La Trobe; 3 men, 3 women, 0 children. When he counted again in 1857 there were only 96 left.

The Church did not express much interest in their souls until there were very few souls left. The diary of the Reverend Willoughby Bean was silent on their plight. The Reverend Login directed his missionary work to the station owners; although he arranged at least one marriage among the blacks—and his wife offered the useful observation that it was remarkable how 'slight and trivial' were the marks left upon the land by the Aborigines. It was more than 20 years before the Church began to minister to them. When it did, in the heads of Europeans and Aborigines alike the fantastic notion was cemented that the black men who had driven white men to a murderous frenzy at the thought of their violating a white woman, and the black women who had for a decade satisfied the white men's desire, were not men and women at all, but children.

When the mission, Ramahyuck, was established by the Presbyterian Church in 1862, the remnants of the

Kurnai, together with a handful of Aborigines from all over the continent, were dressed in the garb of Europeans so that they could labour in the fields for six days like Europeans, and on Sundays rest in the European clothing which pleased the Lord. They were given the names of European heroes and Old Testament prophets. And they were taught the same hymns and the same catechisms that had been employed on the Isle of Skye. 'Who made you?', they were asked. They answered, 'God'.

'What did Jesus Christ do for us?'

'He died for our sins.'

'Have you learnt any hymns?'

'Yes. "O'er the gloomy hills of darkness".'

The idea that Christ had died for their sins was perhaps no harder to accept than one put about at the time by the Home and Foreign Missionary Society of the Church of Scotland—that the people of any land who survived European conquest owed their lives to those whites who continued to assert the Christian belief that all humanity was descended from Adam and Eve and 'whatever appearances might say to the contrary, the conquerors and the conquered were originally of one race'.

Now when a Kurnai died the Reverend G. A. Hagenauer pronounced the New Testament blessing on the soul departed to the realms of bliss. To his great satisfaction at least one said before he died, 'I can see Jesus.' The 'grain of mustard seed began to grow', said the missionary, 'and the eye of faith saw, like the prophet of old, the little cloud arise, which should pour out the Lord's blessing over the poor Aborigines in God's time'. Perhaps the mission did little more than take the blacks out of the sight of ladies like the young squatter's wife, Mrs Campbell Coulson, who found them repulsive beyond words, and gentlemen like John Pettit who 'never saw such a stinking lot of wretches'.

But if Hagenauer's hopes were too sanguine, they were by 1862 the only states of grace on offer.

It was by then too late to act on the advice received by Gippsland's other missionary, John Bulmer: an Aborigine in New South Wales told him that the blacks were dying out because they had broken with the customs of their ancestors. A Calvinist might have translated that as punishment for their sins. It was too soon to see the irony in this; or in the fact that when an Aboriginal woman told Bulmer about the Aboriginal ghosts she heard, she described them as if they were akin to angels. She said she often heard 'a multitude' of *mraats* talking as they passed by in the sky, and a great noise as they alighted.

Far from being inevitable, the destruction of Kurnai society was gratuitous and grotesque. The Europeans made no attempt to come to terms with those they displaced. On spurious pretexts they even sought out and destroyed tribes whose land was useless for their sheep and cattle. It was too often murder for the whites to call it war, which is why they called it nothing at all and preferred to forget than to contemplate treaties. The Presbyterian missionaries thought it was a just redress to show the remnant blacks the path to heaven. George Dunderdale thought the whites might find justice in hell. It was 'the age of whitewash', he said in 1893. 'There is scarcely a villain of note on whose character a new coat has not been laboriously daubed by somebody, and then we are asked to take a new view of it. It does not matter very much now,' he said, 'but I should prefer to whitewash the Aboriginals.'

CHAPTER NINE

CIVILISATION AT LAST

It was only the other day that I saw the redoubtable explorer at Scott's Hotel; he was preparing to depart to the Crooked, and was full of high hope and confidence in the future of what might very appropriately be called 'McMillan's Land' instead of Gippsland.

A CORRESPONDENT IN *THE MOUNTAINEER*, WOOD'S POINT, 24 MAY 1865

It was a one roomed hut they were in, and during the evening his father's horse (the one he had ridden right through from Sydney) came up to the hut and his father then said he was sure there were blacks about. One of their number (Dr Arbuckle) who was unable to fight, was put in the fireplace, where he was to load the spare guns as they were discharged. The blacks attacked the hut in the morning and the order was given not to waste a bullet. The blacks fixed their spears to their woomeras and threw them, in reply to which a volley was discharged at them from the hut, and a second volley dispersed them. The men in the hut were a fine example of what the British Isles—especially Skye—could produce; and that little island of Skye had produced 50,000 soldiers for the British army, including several generals . . . These were the kind of men who had made this a great and good land to live in.

ANGUS McMILLAN'S SON RECOUNTING HIS FATHER'S PIONEERING EXPERIENCES. SALE, 1913

For years before the establishment of Ramahyuck in 1862, Bushy Park had been a gathering place for Gippsland Aborigines. Angus McMillan was the Honorary Protector there—the man who distributed supplies of food and blankets. Another party of blacks seems to have attached itself to Pearson's Kilmany Park. In May 1861 a group from McMillan's station attacked a group from Pearson's and killed two of the men, 'Toby' and 'King Charley'. Nothing much could be done. No whites had been injured, so they were not taken to court where they might be defended on the usual grounds for whites that the plaintiffs could not tell the difference between black men's faces.[1] Dr Arbuckle attended to the wounded and returned the bodies of the dead to the tribe. The *Gippsland Guardian* expressed admiration for their mourning; the 'wailing cry'—the 'similitude of prayer'—which they declared bore 'no small resemblance to the Keen', so frequently heard in the 'half civilizations of Ireland'.

When Billy Clark escaped from custody at Sale in 1861 it was at Bushy Park that the police found him. When two other blacks were imprisoned at Narre Warren, it was Angus McMillan who gained pardons for them. In a photograph taken after their release, McMillan, in his corduroy suit, sits between the two of them holding the hand of one firmly in his. He gazes at the camera in defiance of the irony that the man who had led the rout of their civilisation was posing as their benefactor. He was a man of influence then.

The Reverend Hagenauer thought that, as the blacks

1 A Dr Coombe defended Aborigines like this in the Alberton court in Victoria. The 'same difficulty existed with the Mongolian race', he said. It does not seem to have impressed magistrates, and men like Billy Clark were sentenced to three months' hard labour for stealing two pound notes and two sovereigns in the Club Hotel, Sale.

had long gathered there, Bushy Park would be the most suitable place to establish Ramahyuck. It also offered the potential for agriculture on the rich flats of the Avon River: and of course it was best that the Aborigines be engaged in agriculture. Not surprisingly McMillan opposed this idea at first, but in October four of his five runs passed into the hands of his Melbourne agents, Kaye and Butchart, and McMillan had a change of heart about the mission. Now he supported the proposal. Kaye and Butchart said he was acting out of malice but McMillan gave a different reason. He said he could not accept Hagenauer's alternative site, on the banks of Lake Wellington, because it was too close to a place called Boney Point, where 'a great many Aboriginals were killed and as the bones lay about it got its gruesome name'.

Boney Point was probably the site of the first massacre in Gippsland, the place where the Briakalung learnt what resistance to McMillan and his men would lead to; but just as the Briakalung had lost control of their destiny, so had McMillan. His influence had faded when he lost his land. For a Highlander the lesson had been well learnt. Hagenauer settled the Aborigines on a hill overlooking Lake Wellington close to Boney Point. The place was called Ramahyuck, the Aboriginal 'yuck' meaning 'the place of'. Hagenauer would have known from the *Book of Jeremiah* that Ramah had been the scene of a massacre of Jews.

If it was not the monument they proposed to build to him in 1858 which turned McMillan's fortunes to stone, it might have been his decision to enter parliament. He stood as the little man's friend. He would make it possible for the little man to buy small lots for agricultural purposes, and guarantee that each farmer was rewarded for improvements to the land. He had done this himself for his shepherds. McMillan stressed that he was not standing as the discoverer of Gippsland, but as its friend. He was not the dupe of Turnbull, Orr and Co., or the lackey of the big pastoral interests. He would not run away from his constituents. He was a Gippslander through and through. Like the best of lairds he said he would remain all his life with them.

But as his poor opponent noted, McMillan rode about with five hotelkeepers, seven storekeepers, the doctor, and most of South Gippsland's pastoral establishment. They presented him as a man of 'refined feelings, generous candour, scrupulous veracity, with a studious avoidance of giving offence to others'. A correspondent in the *Gippsland Guardian* stressed his generosity: 'His station at Bushy Park might well be called the Benevolent Asylum of Gippsland,' he wrote. McMillan's opponent was a lawyer, a 'Johnny-come-lately', a man from the town, and a stranger. McMillan's friends satirised Mr W. J. Walduck as a 'Novelty in Natural History', the 'Place Hunting Wilduck'.

When he began his campaign, however, McMillan had been poorly prepared and even his supporters had to concede that he had been obliged to alter his policies. The *Guardian* put it politely when it said he was a 'novice'. A correspondent wrote that he had been put up 'unfinished'. He had begun by attaching himself to the small farming vote by declaring that he was 'in favour of the agricultural land of the colony being at once sold'; but as one of his opponents said, no-one had the cash to buy—except of course the squatters. This correspondent to the *Guardian*, who signed himself, 'A Working Man', said McMillan was a rich man acting for the rich men of Upper Gippsland. He implied that McMillan was a stooge for the squatters' interests. His supporters had proposed him not on the grounds that he offered an opportunity for the struggling man, but on the basis of his past feats. McMillan's backers had told the electors that they were 'under great obligations to him for finding out the land, and . . . that if he was not returned they would be very ungrateful . . .' The land should be taken from the squatters, wrote the working man: 'Use it in the way providence intended it to be used, by cultivating it that it may produce food for the sustenance of man.'

McMillan had to change his tack and say the land would not be sold for cash, but on 'gentle' repayments as 'improvements' were made. He was offering the electors the 'key to the door' of Upper Gippsland. The problem remained, said the *Guardian* and one of its correspondents, that until there was cheap and reliable transport between north and south, and until the thistles were eradicated on the good agricultural land, there was no keyhole. But, 'unfinished' as McMillan was, this policy was enough to win him a seat.

That early strife was an indication of McMillan's ineptness in political life. At the end of 1860 he resigned from parliament without having made a speech. He went back to his people as he had promised, but ignominiously. Melbourne, it seems, had not agreed with him and his affairs in the country were in chaos.

The *Gippsland Guardian* had hoped that McMillan would take the acrimony out of politics. His supporters no doubt hoped that he would smooth over the differences in class which their ownership of the land created. In January 1860 a resident of Gippsland, signing himself 'A Scot', wrote to the newspaper complaining that the stone imported for the construction of roads from Port Albert to the hinterland was to be broken by 'fresh fools brought into the district to spend their money, hardly earned though it may be, in poisonous drink, and be left here a burthen on this already miserable district'. He was a Scot of a different class to the squatters and merchants; he spoke of his fellow workers in Tarraville seeing their families clothed in rags while newcomers were employed. McMillan was intended as the answer to this and other factionalism. He was, said the *Guardian*, 'a member in whom the most prejudiced place confidence'. They were inspired by that 'praiseworthy liberality' which had 'won him a name' in the district. The member had donated a silver cup to the horse racing committee; it would be presented to the winner of an annual race between horses bred in the district. A goldfields resident wrote from the high country that he would be more grateful for roads.

Horse racing was one of McMillan's passions, as it was with many of his fellow squatters. In 1860 the racing club made him judge at the annual spring races. It was not his only honour or his only interest in these very respectable days. He was president of the Caledonian Society. To demonstrate their concern and their largesse the squatters of Gippsland formed an Agricultural and Horticultural Society in 1859 and ran regular contests to encourage improved breeds of cattle, sheep and vegetables. McMillan was a founding member and vice-president.

But the prosperous man of 1860 was virtually in penury by the middle of 1861. He lost four of his five holdings in North Gippsland, keeping only a mountain run at the junction of the Mitchell and Wentworth rivers called Tabberabbera. Somehow he had accumulated huge debts; in excess of £31,000, it seems, for that was what Kaye and Butchart said they 'paid' him. A number of writers have claimed that bushfires had ravaged his land and stock in the autumn of 1861. If they had it was not reported in the Gippsland newspapers, and nothing else supports the claim.

On the other hand there is evidence that he spent improvidently. It is possible that his estates ran down as he spent more time in Melbourne as a member of parliament. He might also have speculated unsuccessfully in gold shares, and invested more than he should have in mining. When Richard MacKay met him on a boat from Melbourne sometime after his resignation from parliament, he found McMillan 'most anxious in his inquiries regarding the new field on the Jordan, and the probability of its permanency'. The Jordan flows in the high country east of Omeo. If McMillan did not invest in mining there, he did stake a claim in the Crooked River field 60 kilometres or so up the Mitchell from Tabberabbera. It is possible that he found the field, but it returned him nothing.

When J. D. Lang instructed his flock on the question of gold he encouraged them to think of God as a banker and Australia as a vault. God had put the precious metal there 'as in a bank of deposit, thousands and perhaps tens of thousands of years ago, that it might be searched for and found, and drawn forth, and turned to account by intelligent, enterprising and energetic men'. Angus McMillan took little convincing. He spent the best part of his last four years in the Gippsland Ranges, grafting his way through the bush in what this time was a fruitless effort to reconcile private and public interest. But in the end he could not turn Providence to account and even he must have sometimes wondered if God was running a bank or a raffle.

If he could not master Providence it stood to reason that McMillan would never master capital. Here was a pastoralist who continued to observe such fundamentalist doctrines as sabbatarianism—albeit less strictly than he once had—and who clung to the idea, if not always the practice, that it was incumbent on a Christian to be charitable. There are too many examples of McMillan's selflessness to be ignored. On the scales of public and private interest he often erred on the side of his fellow man. He did not feed all his starving countrymen in Gippsland, but he certainly fed far more than anyone else in the district. He took care of poor Highlanders when they first arrived in Melbourne; employed them and fed them at Bushy Park; gave some of them plots at Stratford. If he was the leader of the Highland Brigade in the forties, it remains that he was one of the very few Europeans in the fifties who took a philanthropic interest in the Aborigines. No squatter in Gippsland had such a reputation for generosity. It was frequently said that he was generous to a fault.

Richard MacKay found him a lovable character even when his fortunes were low: 'He was full of Scotch humour,' MacKay wrote, 'and a great favourite with the ladies.' McMillan was not a lavish host, more of a chronic one. He was a compulsive story-teller, a composer of legends. The tradition of the ceilidh seems to have been maintained at Bushy Park. There was a hint of McMillan's character, and of his fate, in another observation of MacKay's; he recalled that McMillan had been 'particular in his desire to know if he spoke Gaelic'.

McMillan was 'improved'. He was too well educated in English and animal husbandry to be mistaken for a Gaelic barbarian, but he was never as worldly as the likes of Lachlan Macalister, Robert Thomson or William Pearson. He was still afflicted with Highland modes of thought long after they had become affectations among the Highland gentlemen of Gippsland. The unfashionable and unprofitable notion of loyalty to one's superiors and to one's people seemed to have stayed with him. He remained somewhere between a Briton and a Highlander. Equally, he was always at least as much a servant as a gentleman. He was never a masterless man.

The nearest Angus McMillan came to being master

was in the bush. Ultimately his pride lay in that. No-one doubted that in his maturity Angus McMillan was a true bushman. He seemed to be forever in the scrub. William Pearson said McMillan was 'always more or less exploring'.

It was therefore fitting that when he was on desperate times in 1864 the Victorian government found work for him in the hills of Gippsland cutting tracks between the gold fields, from which men like William Pearson were profiting greatly. He saw in his task something in the nature of exploration. It reminded him—if he ever needed reminding—of his great exploits. He began a journal; wrote of setting out for the 'unknown fastnesses of Gippsland'; talked about laurels and honours, and of being 'the first European that ever broke ground in this far-famed land'. Notions of loyalty and leadership came to his mind: 'A party of explorers should be like one family,' he wrote, and the family should look on the leader 'as a Father and the leader should behave towards them as he would his children'.

McMillan cleared tracks from the Omeo fields to the Jordan and on to the Crooked River—435 kilometres in all. It was very tough country and more than once he thanked Providence for rescuing the party from fearful 'breakneck' places. He also paid his respects by not keeping the journal on Sundays, and on one occasion at least he fined a man sixpence for swearing. When they were not sliding down ravines into the headwaters of the Macalister or the Dargo, they were beating their way on all fours through dense and, as winter approached, damp scrub. Leeches almost consumed one of his companions one day. In April they worked in gales and snow.

For all the physical hardships, however, there are prolonged passages in McMillan's journal which suggest that he was at peace in the bush. He seemed to belong there, and there can be no doubt that he believed that the salvation of his self-respect, if not his fortune, lay in this work.

In May things began to go wrong. He complained of the faithlessness of his men. From 18 May he began to write much less. Five days later he wrote, 'not able to follow the men, being attacked by Rheumatism . . .' The next day he was 'still unable to move'. It was the same on the twenty-fifth. Then there was nothing until 3 June when he started home. On 5 June he wrote in the same faded ink which had first appeared on 28 May, 'I have suffered fearfully on the road.' It was the journal of a dying Victorian explorer.

McMillan was 'a good and useful man', the Minister for Roads and Bridges said, 'but he was no bookkeeper'. He overdrew on the funds the government had granted for his work in the high country. He did not return vouchers for his purchases, so the government dishonoured his cheques. He overdrew to an extraordinary extent and was obliged to sell his last asset, a share in a mine called the Pioneer, to pay his debtors.

Angus McMillan spent the New Year, 1865, in the Club Hotel in Sale. The hotel's day book does not record the presence of his wife and children—it was as if they had ceased to be a part of his life. He also spent the first 23 days of February at the Club Hotel, and several days in early March. In the first 10 days of May he was there again. 'On his eyelids was the shadow of death,' the *Gippsland Times* said later. Since the New Year he had run up a bill for more than £67 at the Club Hotel.

On 18 May he died in the hotel at Iguana Creek, about 24 kilometres south of Tabberabbera. At least one other Highlander was there—Simon Gillies was the publican.

Another Highlander signed the death certificate. Dr Thomas Macalister of Sale declared that McMillan had died of endocarditis. Macalister must have been treating McMillan for his rheumatism and was probably not surprised by his death—rheumatic fever causes endocarditis. Macalister would have heard the murmur in his heart.

There was no need to hold an inquest. The death certificate said what was necessary. It gave Christina's maiden name as MacDougald, put the second son's age forward a year (the name and age of the first son has been inked out) and McMillan's occupation was declared to be 'Sheep farmer'. Presumably they thought it sounded better than 'Bushman'.

McMillan's body was taken to Sale some 64 kilometres away. The funeral was a lavish affair—full of 'fruitless vanity' the Puritans would have said. Sale closed down for the afternoon while at least 200 people followed the hearse to the grave. Even P. C. Buckley came up from the Ninety Mile Beach. Login read the Presbyterian service, then someone read the service of the Oddfellows—the organisation of men which seemed to materialise in every pocket of the capitalist world. The 'grave was speedily filled up, and all that remained on earth of Mr McMillan had passed among men', reported the *Times*. 'Done my business at Sale then came home d.f.,' wrote Buckley.

When Paul Strzelecki died in London in 1873, the London *Times* numbered among his many achievements in the fields of science, philanthropy and exploration, the discovery and mapping of 'that valuable tract of country known as Gippsland'. Not everything they said about him was untrue. He had done great work administering relief on the west coast of Ireland during the famine. He had interested himself in many philanthropic causes. Florence Nightingale, Sydney Herbert and William Gladstone were his friends. The Royal Society had made him a Fellow, Oxford University made him a Doctor of Civil Law, the Queen made him a KCMG, and they all made him an Englishman.

Strzelecki had no belief in an afterlife: he wanted no altars to be built to him. He wanted to be judged by his contemporaries. He died in his house in Savile Row on 6 October, just a few days after receiving a letter from Gladstone telling him in passing that the Queen had recently expressed a wish to meet the famous 'count'.[2]

It must have hurt Strzelecki to hear that the Queen wished to meet him when he was unable to rise from his bed. But Strzelecki had received more than his share of credit among Australian explorers, and what he lacked in altars after his death was amply compensated by laurels in his own lifetime. Angus McMillan's life and death were cast in the other mould of Australian explorers. A cast-off agent of the pastoral interest, he had just come in from the bush when he died. Like John McDouall Stuart and Ernest Giles he died poor. Like them he had not been able to settle in society. In the end nature had a victory over all three.

Nevertheless, in Sale the *Gippsland Times* decided to make a hero of McMillan, and the *Gippsland Guardian* did the same in Port Albert. Both newspapers declared that he was the discoverer of Gippsland and revived the tale of Strzelecki's usurpation of the title. The writers made no mention of what killed McMillan. The *Guardian* said he had been in poor spirits in the past but seemed in recent days to have been lively and confident. The *Guardian* believed that it was probably the result of an accident he had had while cutting tracks. A pack horse had rolled on him and he had not recovered from his injuries.

That story became the legend. One hundred years later

2 Strzelecki did not marry Adyna Turno. They met in Geneva in 1868 but, understandably, the spark had gone.

it was official. The fall in the Moroka Valley had caused 'severe internal injuries. He set out for Bairnsdale but reached only as far as Iguana Creek, where he died in Gilleo's Hotel a few hours later'.[3] It was the most appropriate end if not the actual one. Rumours about McMillan still persist in Gippsland. Among the old families and the local historians there are some for him and some against him. Some say he might have died of drink, others that he killed himself; even that he died in a brawl at the hotel and that he and an Aborigine who also died in the mêlée are buried a few metres up the road from the hotel.

Conclusions about McMillan's death tended to depend on estimates of his life and not everyone in Gippsland was handed down the legend of his virtue. Only one interpretation has been enshrined. The *Gippsland Times* more or less laid the basis of it the day after the funeral. The *Times* painted biblically: 'The silver cord has been loosened, the golden bowl broken, the pitcher broken at the fountain, and the wheel broken at the cistern.' In Melbourne the *Age* saw a message for Australia as a whole, declaring that he should be regarded by all as 'a martyr to his zeal for his adopted country'. The *Gippsland Times* obituary said that his works spoke for him more than the most eloquent pen.

Subsequent generations, however, have found it necessary to continue to speak for McMillan, and to leave monuments to fix his legend in history.

Gippsland is now dotted with cairns to mark the way of the pioneer; some of them bear a relief of the Highlander in his bonnet. They are convenient picnic spots, and

---

3 The quotation is from the *Australian Dictionary of Biography*, which can hardly be blamed for the inaccuracies. The standard story of McMillan was told so often it was almost impenetrable and immovable.

instruct tourists in history: 'Angus McMillan passed this way', they say, and give the appropriate date and sometimes a small extract from his diary. McMillan's name is also honoured by an electorate, a stretch of water, a mountain, numerous streets, an annual memorial lecture, and a motel. The roadside obelisks don't utter at all to the people who picnic beside them. Like myth itself they immobilise the world. There is not the faintest echo of Skye to be heard, not a breath of McMillan's own mythical universe. To be preserved the hero must be disembowelled: the doubtful and ambiguous portions must be taken out along with any other matter which might compromise his virtue or complicate the lesson his life is meant to teach.

In Gippsland, like everywhere else in the empire, reality was fading fast in 1913. In the town of Sale a dignitary declared that Angus McMillan had gone out into the land of Canaan. Gippsland was better than the land of Canaan, another said. The citizenry were told that McMillan's spirit had been carried into the Boer War and that in any future conflict the same resolve would be taken to the defence of England, the country which had made 'such great sacrifices in the defence of freedom'. In all the enthusiasm the irony was lost.

REFERENCES

Chapter 1

General works on Scotland in the eighteenth and nineteenth centuries

The outstanding general work on Scotland to 1830 is T. C. Smout, *A History of the Scottish People 1560–1830*, William Collins, Glasgow, 1969. Despite their academic critics, John Prebble, *Culloden,* Penguin, Harmondsworth, 1973 and *The Highland Clearances*, Penguin, Harmondsworth, 1973, are evocative and invaluable. On crofting, James Hunter, *The Making of the Crofting Community*, John Donald, Edinburgh, 1976, stands alone. On the Highland clearances, Alexander MacKenzie, *The History of the Highland Clearances,* Inverness, 1883, and Eric Richards, *A History of the Highland Clearances: Agrarian Transformation and the Evictions 1746–1866,* Croom Helm, London, 1981, provide a wealth of detail, the latter of a more dispassionate kind than the former. Michael Hechter offers a radical view of the British conquest in *Internal Colonialism: The Celtic Fringe in British National Development 1566–1966*, Routledge & Kegan Paul, London, 1975. Edwin Muir, *Scottish Journey*, Victor Gollancz, London, 1935, is an elegant cultural overview, and he goes into a more specific region of the Scottish mind in *John Knox, Portrait of a Calvinist,* Jonathan Cape, London, 1929.

Highland folk life

The most comprehensive and authoritative account is probably I. F. Grant, *Highland Folk Ways,* Routledge & Kegan Paul, London, 1961, and there is additional material in the same author's undated pamphlet, *The Early History of the Highlands.* Valuable older works include Dunbar E. Dunbar, *Social Life in Former Days,* Edinburgh, 1866; James Logan, *The Scottish Gael: on Celtic Manners as Preserved Amongst the Highlanders,* Inverness, 1831, and D. Stewart, *Sketches of the Character, Manners and Present State of the Highlanders of Scotland,* Edinburgh, 1825. More recent, scholarly works I have drawn on here include Judith Ennew, *The Western Isles Today,* Cambridge University Press, Cambridge, 1980; T. C. Smout, 'Aspects of Sexual Behaviour in Nineteenth Century Scotland', in A. Allan MacLaren (ed.), *Social Class in Scotland: Past and Present,* John Donald, Edinburgh, 1976; and Hamish Henderson's suggestions about the role of women in the Celtic past in '"Infirm of Purpose! Give me the daggers!" Some Thoughts on Highland History', *Cencrastus,* Edinburgh, Summer 1980.

Travellers in the Highlands and Islands

Few who ventured there failed to write a book about it. This is a select list. Martin Martin, *A Description of the Western Isles of Scotland, 1695,* London, 1884; John L. Buchanan, *Travels in the Western Hebrides from 1782–1790,* London, 1793; Thomas Pennant, *A Tour in Scotland and A*

Voyage to the Hebrides 1774–1775, London, 1776; Edmund Burt, *Letters from a Gentleman in the North of Scotland 1754,* London, 1822; Samuel Johnson, *A Journey to the Western Isles of Scotland,* London, 1775; John Walker, *An Economical History of the Hebrides and the Highlands,* London and Edinburgh, 1812; John D. MacCulloch, *A Description of the Western Isles of Scotland,* (3 vols), London, 1819, and the same author's *The Highlands and Western Isles of Scotland* (4 vols), London, 1824. Thomas Browne took exception to MacCulloch in *A Critical Examination of Dr MacCulloch's Work on the Highlands and Western Islands of Scotland,* Edinburgh, 1826. Derek Cooper offers a collection of travellers' tales in *The Road to the Isles: Travellers in the Hebrides 1770–1914,* Routledge & Kegan Paul, London, 1979. Maurice Lindsay, *The Discovery of Scotland,* Robert Hale, London, 1964, and A. J. Younger, *Beyond the Highland Line: Three Journals of Travels in Eighteenth Century Scotland,* Burt, Pennant and Thornton, are useful works in a category similar to Cooper's. Robert Somers went to the Highlands during the famine of the 1840s and wrote his eloquent and moving *Letters from the Highlands,* London, 1847; Karl Marx and Frederick Engels never went there but fortunately they were not deterred by such considerations: Marx's comments on the Highlands, written in January 1853, can be found in Karl Marx and Frederick Engels, *Collected Works,* Vol. II, Lawrence and Wishart, London, 1979, pp. 486–94.

Local histories

The view from within was not always so clear or so candid as the view from without. Written by parish ministers, *The Statistical Account of Scotland 1791–1799* and *The New*

Statistical Account of Scotland 1835–1845 are not the strikingly analytic works their titles might suggest to a modern audience. However, they make infectious, if not compelling, reading.

Chapter 2

Skye

The MacLeod Papers, held in the Scottish Records Office, Edinburgh, particularly the correspondence between the MacLeods and their southern friends, agents, tacksmen and ministers on the Dunvegan estate, comprise an intriguing record of social and economic change on Skye. The Kirk Session Minutes in the Skye parish of Bracadale-Minginish help to fill out the human picture.

The 'Cult of the Picturesque'

The novels and poems of Sir Walter Scott are a good start of course, but formidable. See also Gerald Finlay, *Landscapes of Memory. Turner as Illustrator to Scott,* University of California Press, Berkeley, 1980. C. Leasingham Smith puts down his impressions in *A Journal of a Ramble in Scotland,* Cheltenham, 1835.

Crofting, kelping and improving

James Hunter, op. cit., is the outstanding work on all these subjects. For kelping, this chapter also draws on the *Report by the Committee of the Highland Society of Scotland upon the Manufacture of Kelp,* Edinburgh, 1817. John Girvin was an improver. See his *Address to the Landholders, Factors and Tenantry in the Highlands of Scotland for Preventing Emigration to Foreign Countries and Encouraging and Practising Industry in Fisheries, Agriculture, Manufactures, Especially for Planting Willows etc. for Hoops,* Edinburgh, 1803, which gives some idea of how comprehensive were his plans. David Low wrote two valuable treatises for his own age and for this: *Domesticated Animals of the British Isles,* Edinburgh, 1844, and *Elements of Practical Agriculture,* Edinburgh, 1834.

Social conditions

In addition to those cited for Chapter 1, two influential nineteenth-century works and one twentieth-century corrective should be noted. For the nineteenth-century see Donald Ross, *Real Scottish Grievances,* Glasgow, 1854; and the same author's *The Scottish Highlanders. Their Present Sufferings and Future Prospects,* Glasgow, 1852; and Donald MacLeod, *Gloomy Memories in the Highlands of Scotland,* Glasgow, 1892, which T. C. Smout, among others, says is altogether too gloomy. The corrective is Ian Levitt and T. C. Smout (eds), *The State of the Scottish Working Class in 1843: A Statistical and Spatial Enquiry based on data from the Poor Law Commissioners' Report of 1844,* Scottish Academic Press, Edinburgh, 1979; as well as Smout's *History of the Scottish People.* Redcliff N. Salaman's classic, *The History and Social Influence of the Potato,* Cambridge University Press, Cambridge, 1949, and Stig Joatinen, 'The Human Geography of the Outer Isles', *Acta Geographica,* 16, 2, 1957, provide useful insights into the social consequences of changes to traditional modes of agriculture.

Church of Scotland

The Record of the Home and Foreign Missionary Society reveals a good deal about the Church's perspective as well as its activities. Educational and missionary ambitions are expressed in the General Assembly's *Statement as to the Want of Schools and Catechists in the Highlands and Islands,* Edinburgh, 1825. A concern with form is apparent in both Walter Stewart, *Collection and Observation Concerning the Worship, Discipline and Government of the Church of Scotland,* Edinburgh, n.d., and the General Assembly's *The Form of Process Concerning the Sin of Fornication and Adultery, and scandalous carriage attending thereto,* Edinburgh, n.d. (*c.*1830). Under this heading it is worth adding the useful work of the Inverness Society for the Education of the Poor, *Moral Statistics of the Highlands and Islands,* Inverness, 1826.

Chapter 3

MacLeod Papers

The MacLeod Papers (boxes 61 and 66) and the *Reports and Correspondence of the Central Board for the Relief of Destitution in the Highlands* offer a peculiarly human view of the famine and emigration. Among the more significant documents in the MacLeod Papers are 'An Essay on the Late Emigration from the Highlands of Scotland, Giving an impartial account of the Causes and Rise of that fatal spirit and Humbly proposing some methods to stop its present fury; and to prevent its future return, By a Highlander', 1774; 'List of Householders' (on MacLeod's estate) *c.*1848; 'MacLeod's Address to his People', 26 December 1848;

correspondence with his factor, Robertson, Robert Brown, and various officers of the Central Board of the Relief Committee, Especially Sir Charles Treveylan; and correspondence between Emily MacLeod and various people on the estates.

Emigration

See Highland Emigration Society, *Emigration from the Highlands and Islands of Scotland to Australia*, London, 1852; Peter Ross, *The Scot in America,* New York, 1896; J. P. MacLean, *An Historical Account of the Settlement of Scotch Highlanders in America Prior to the Peace of 1783,* Glasgow, 1900; T. Douglas (Earl of Selkirk), *Observations on the Present State of the Highlands and Islands of Scotland,* London, 1805; Robert Brown, *Strictures and Remarks on the Earl of Selkirk's Observations*, Edinburgh, 1806; Colonial Office, *Commission for Emigration Respecting the Australian Colonies*, GD46/13/184; P. L. MacDougall, *Emigration and Its Advantages to Britain and Its Colonies,* London, 1848; William Cobbett, *Ten Letters Addressed to the Tax-Payers of England*, London, 1829; Alexander J. Ross, *Memoir of Alexander Ewing, D. C. L. Bishop of Argyll and the Isles,* London, 1877; Lord Cockburn, *Circuit Journeys*, Edinburgh, 1841.

Celts: their character and their prospects

Westminster Review, October 1841 and October 1860; J. Anderson, *Primeval Man,* Edinburgh, 1861; Duke of Argyll, 'Isolation, or the Survival of the Unfittest', *Nineteenth Century,* January–June 1889; Marx, op. cit., p. 531; Catherine Sinclair, *Scotland and the Scotch,* London, 1840.

Skye's military record

See Alexander Cameron, *History and Traditions of the Isle of Skye,* Inverness, 1871.

Highlanders in Australia

Eric Richards provides our only insight in 'Highland Emigrants to South Australia in the 1850s', *Northern Scotland,* 1, 1982.

Chapter 4

Frontier life in Australia

Few squatters were so introspective as Farquhar MacKenzie in his 'Journal', 1836, held in the Mitchell Library, Sydney. By far the best study of the Monaro, where MacKenzie had his sheep, is W. K. Hancock's *Discovering Monaro,* Cambridge University Press, Cambridge, 1972. The *Singapore* expedition is described by W. A. Brodribb in his *Recollections of an Australian Squatter,* Sydney, 1883, reprinted with Lavinia Hassell Bennett, *Account of a Journey to Gippsland,* Queensberry Hill Press, Melbourne, 1976. Bennett's account describes Hobson's overlanding journey to Gippsland in 1844. For McMillan's and other squatters' memoirs see T. F. Bride, *Letters from Victorian Pioneers,* Melbourne, 1898. Reverend D. MacKenzie, *Ten Years in Australia,* London, 1852, and the Quaker, James Backhouse, *Narrative of a Visit to the Australian Colonies,* London, 1843, offer the perspective of men of God. Backhouse's is particularly detailed. A somewhat opinionated Scottish adventurer,

G. F. Davidson, left us his view in *Trade and Travel in the Far East, or Recollections of Twenty-One Years Passed in Java, Singapore, Australia and China,* London, 1846. Two recent studies of the squatting experience testify to the diversity of frontier life: Paul de Serville's study of the immensely successful John Peter, *'Tubbo': The Great Peter's Run,* Oxford University Press, Melbourne, 1982, and Judith Wright's look at her own ancestors' struggle in fringe country, *The Cry for the Dead,* Oxford University Press, Melbourne, 1981, which brilliantly describes just how brutal it could be. For squatting life elsewhere in Victoria see E. M. Curr, *Recollections of Squatting in Victoria,* Melbourne, 1883 (2nd edn, Melbourne University Press, Melbourne, 1965). Curr offers interesting observations on life in Melbourne as well.

John Dunmore Lang

D. W. A. Baker's biography of J. D. Lang was published after this book—the same author's Introduction to Lang's *Reminiscences of My Life and Times,* Sydney, 1878 (?), reprinted, Heinemann, Melbourne, 1972, and his entry in the *Australian Dictionary of Biography* were the most authoritative accounts at the time of writing. Lang's outpourings were faithfully reported in his hometown, in the *Greenock Advertiser.* In Sydney, the *Colonist* and the *Sydney Gazette* debated his views.

Transportation and New South Wales society

For a Marxist analysis see R. W. Connell and T. H. Irving, *Class Structure in Australian History. Documents, Narrative and Argument,* Longman Cheshire, Melbourne, 1980. See also C. M. H. Clark, *A History of Australia,* vol. 3, Melbourne

University Press, Melbourne, 1968; J. Ritchie, 'Towards Ending an Unclean Thing. The Molesworth Committee and the Abolition of Transportation in New South Wales 1837–40', *Historical Studies,* vol. 17, October 1976.

Goulburn in Lachlan Macalister's day

There are two useful histories; Ransome T. Wyatt, *The History of Goulburn, New South Wales,* Lansdowne, Sydney, 1972, and *Charles Macalister, Old Pioneering Days in the Sunny South,* Goulburn?, n.d. The Macarthur Papers, vol. 95, 12991, Mitchell Library, New South Wales, contain correspondence with and concerning Lachlan Macalister and James Macarthur in the early years at Goulburn.

Perceptions of New South Wales

Barron Field, Judge-Advocate of New South Wales, edited *Geographical Memoirs of New South Wales* (by various hands) in 1825. Its influence in Britain appears to have been considerable. For a review see *Quarterly Review*, October 1825. It was frequently quoted in British journals over the next decade. The man who saw New South Wales through similar eyes was J. Fowles; see his 'Journal of a Voyage from London to Sydney' in the *Barque Fortune*, Mitchell Library, New South Wales.

The Kurnai tribes of Gippsland

A. W. Howitt's *The Native Tribes of South Eastern Australia,* London, 1904, and the Howitt Papers in the La Trobe Library, Melbourne, MS 9356, are by far the most extensive sources on the Kurnai. P. J. F. Coutts, *The Archaeology of Wilson's Promontory,* Australian Institute of Aboriginal Studies, Canberra, 1970, and the same author's *The Victorian Aboriginals 1800–1860. Readings in Victorian Prehistory,* vol. 2, Victorian Archaeological Survey, Melbourne, 1981, are much needed scholarly contributions. In *The Moth Hunters. Aboriginal Prehistory of the Australian Alps,* Australian Institute of Aboriginal Studies, Canberra, 1980, Josephine Flood discusses Aboriginal society in the high country of south-eastern Australia. For a discussion of traditional violence among the Port Phillip tribes see Beverly Nance, 'The Level of Violence. Europeans and Aborigines in Port Phillip', *Historical Studies,* October 1981.

Prehistory

Josephine Flood, *Archaeology of the Dreamtime,* William Collins, Sydney, 1983, and D. J. Mulvaney, *The Prehistory of Australia,* Penguin, Melbourne, 1975, are the best introductions for the layperson. For the debate on the antiquity of the Australian Aborigines see Rhys Jones and James Urry, 'Old Questions, New Answers. Some Thoughts on the Origins and Antiquity of Man in Australia', *Aboriginal History,* vol. 2, pt 2, 1978. Olive Pink is quoted in Ashley Montagu, *Coming Into Being Amongst the Australian Aborigines* (2nd edn), Routledge & Kegan Paul, London, 1974.

Chapter 5

Angus McMillan

Angus McMillan's 'Journal of a Cruise from Greenock to

New Holland', 5 September 1837–22 December 1837, is held on microfilm in the La Trobe Library, Melbourne, MS 9776, MF 145. An outline of the McMillan clan history can be found in Ian Grimble, *Scottish Clans and Tartans,* Paul Hamlyn, London, 1977. The Protestant mind is analysed by Phillip Greven in *The Protestant Temperament. Patterns of Child-Rearing, Religious Experience and the Self in Early America,* Alfred Knopf, New York, 1977, pp. 142–43.

Emigration

S. T. Coleridge was quoted for the benefit of emigrants in *Extracts from the Works of Various Authors for the entertainment and instruction of a party of emigrants on their voyage to Australia*, London, 1838. The writings of Sir Thomas Mitchell, which may have encouraged them to go, first appeared on his return from Australia Felix in the *Sydney Herald* and *Sydney Gazette*, 10 November 1836. His observations were later published as *Three Expeditions Into the Interior of Eastern Australia,* London, 1839.

Savages

For savages in 'lofty forests' see the *Record of the Home and Foreign Missionary Society,* July 1858, p. 159. For women and savage life see *Quarterly Review,* April 1824, p. 575; Buchanan op. cit., p. 111; *Fraser's Magazine,* March 1836, pp. 322–23. For Romans, Greeks, Maoris and Kaffirs see *Quarterly Review,* April 1824, pp. 57–8; *Blackwood's Magazine,* December 1837, p. 785; *Rambler,* May 1852, pp. 414–15; Alfred W. Cole, *The Cape and the Kaffirs: or Notes of Five Years' Residence in South Africa,* London, 1851, and Augustus Earle, *A Narrative of Nine Months' Residence in New Zealand,* London, 1833. For cannibalism see the *Record of the Home and Foreign Missionary Society*, October 1859, p. 251; *Quarterly Review,* April 1824, pp. 58–60; *Glasgow Herald,* 15 August 1837; *Quarterly Review,* September 1836, pp. 18–19, Alistair Hennessy, *The Frontier in Latin American History,* Edward Arnold, London, 1978, p. 43, J. C. Hall writing in Charles Pickering, *The Races of Man,* London, 1841; Alfred W. Cole writing in the *Rambler*, May 1852, pp. 411–12, and Sievewright's account of his experiences are published in A. S. Kenyon, 'The Aboriginal Protectorate of Port Phillip', *Victorian Historical Magazine*, March 1928. For phrenology see Richard Burton in *Journal of the Royal Geographical Society,* vol. 29, 1859; Horatio Hale, *Ethnography and Philology,* London, 1846, pp. 106–9; P. E. Strzelecki, *Physical Description of New South Wales and Van Diemen's Land,* London, 1845, pp. 342–3. Richard Burton is brought to life by Fawn Brodie in *The Devil Drives,* Penguin, Harmondsworth, UK, 1971.

Aborigines in the scale of civilisation

The works by Hale, Pickering and Strzelecki all take up this subject at some point, as do a number of the articles cited. See also *Quarterly Review,* January 1828, p. 29; *Westminster Review*, January 1841, p. 175 and Howitt, op. cit, p. 458. Mitchell's reflections on Aboriginal life and his note accompanying an Aboriginal skull can be found in the Mitchell Papers, vol. 7, Mitchell Library, New South Wales.

Frontier warfare

J. D. Lang wrote about the squatter's doctrine in *Cooksland,*

London, 1847. See also C. D. Rowley, *The Destruction of Aboriginal Society,* Penguin, Melbourne, 1970, p. 36. The extract quoted from Robert Montgomery Bird's *Nick of the Woods: a story of Kentucky*, London, 1837, was published in the *Greenock Advertiser*, 8 June 1837.

Chapter 6

McMillan's expeditions

McMillan's account of his Gippsland explorations has been published in a variety of places and in a variety of forms. It was probably written in 1853 at the request of the Governor of Victoria, Charles Joseph La Trobe. That letter, dated 25 August 1853, is held by the La Trobe Library, Melbourne, MS 10749; and was published in T. F. Bride, *Letters from Victorian Pioneers,* op. cit. By the time Richard MacKay published his *Recollections of Early Gippsland Goldfields,* Traralgon, Victoria, 1916, certain amendments had been made. Discrepancies also occur in the J. J. Shillinglaw Papers, La Trobe Library, Melbourne, MS 8910.

McMillan's accounts of his explorations are not contested in Kenneth Cox's amiable biography, *Angus McMillan, Pathfinder,* Olinda Public Relations Pty Ltd, Olinda, Victoria, 1972; Hal Porter's elegant *Bairnsdale,* John Ferguson, Sydney, 1977, nor in any of the following: Charles Daley, *The Story of Gippsland,* Whitcomb and Tombs, Melbourne, 1960; Charles Daley, 'Angus McMillan', *Victorian Historical Magazine,* March 1927, and T. A. MacLean, *A Dauntless Man,* Traralgon, Victoria, 1972. In a series of articles in the *Maffra Spectator*, 1944–46, and the *Gippsland Times,* 1947, and in his 'Official History of the Avon Shire', John Wilson disputed many of McMillan's claims.

N. A. Wakefield, 'Aspects of Exploration and Settlement in East Gippsland', *Proceedings, Royal Society of Victoria,* 82, 1969, considers all the claims.

Strzelecki

There are two biographies of Strzelecki in English: H. M. E. Heney's scholarly and extremely critical *In a Dark Glass: The Story of Paul Edmond Strzelecki,* Angus & Robertson, Sydney, 1961, and Geoffrey Rawson's laudatory *The Count, A Life of Paul Edmund Strzelecki, KCMG, Explorer and Scientist,* Heinemann, London, 1953.

Copies of Strzelecki's letters to Adyna Turno (in French) 1837–51 are held in the Mitchell Library, Sydney. A 3355. The Mitchell Library also holds his correspondence with James Macarthur and S. Donaldson, Macarthur Papers, A 2991.

Strzelecki's explorations and scientific work, as presented in his *Physical Description of New South Wales and Van Diemen's Land,* were reviewed in *Quarterly Review*, vol. 76, 1845, and *Edinburgh Review,* July 1862.

Strzelecki's explorations

Strzelecki's initial report of his journey through Gippsland appeared in the *Sydney Morning Herald*, 19 August 1841. The *Port Phillip Herald* celebrated his arrival on 2 June 1840 and Gisborne defended him against McMillan's supporters in the *Australian*, 24 July 1840. James Riley's account of the expedition is contained in his letters which have been published in C. R. Long, 'Gippsland Explorers', the *Age*, 2 April 1927; and 'The Young James Riley', *Victorian Historical Magazine,*

May 1961. The originals are held in the La Trobe Library, Melbourne, MS 9853. James Macarthur's description of the ascent of Mt Kosciuszko was published in the *Victorian Historical Magazine,* December 1941. The vexed question of Kosciuszko's conquest is discussed by Alan E. J. Andrews in his introduction to John Lhotsky, *A Journey from Sydney to the Australian Alps, undertaken in the months of January, February and March 1839*, Blubber Head Press, Hobart, 1979, and also by D. J. Jeans and W. J. R. Gilfillan, 'Light on the Summit: Mt William IV or Kosciusko?', *Journal of the Royal Australian Historical Society,* March 1969. For descriptions of the great forests through which Strzelecki passed on his way to Westernport, see John Adams, *So Tall the Trees,* Narracan Shire Council, Narracan, Victoria, 1978.

The dispute of 1856 and after

See the *Gippsland Guardian,* March and September 1856. J. J. Shillinglaw wrote in defence of McMillan with an extract from McMillan's 'journal', in the *Australasian*, 19 August and 15 September 1874. Bayliss put his case in the *Australasian*, 12 September 1874.

Port Albert

Jane Lennon, 'Squatters, Merchants and Mariners', MA thesis, University of Melbourne, 1975, is the outstanding work.

Chapter 7

The most extensive collection of material on Gippsland's

first decade of white settlement is that gathered by the Reverend George Cox in the early years of this century. Some of the material comprised written evidence but much of it was collected orally and transcribed. The collection, known as Cox's Notes, is held in the La Trobe Library, Melbourne. Between 1912 and 1923 Cox published more than 130 articles on Gippsland history in the *Gippsland Standard*. Cox thus left behind a most valuable if somewhat elusive resource.

Pioneer diaries of Gippsland

A microfilm copy of Patrick Coady Buckley's diary 1844–72 is held in the La Trobe Library, Melbourne, MS 6109; C. J. Tyers's diaries 1844–46 and letters 1855–63, MF 157–158; John Pettit's Letters to his father 1852–68, BL 418; and the King Papers A 3599 are held in the Mitchell Library, Sydney. The Port Albert Maritime Museum holds a great deal of valuable material including some letters of Robert Russell written during his brief stay in Gippsland in the early 1840s, and the Bond Store Journal which not only documents the settlers' transactions but suggests changes in their fortunes and status. The Sale Historical Museum holds some very useful 'Notes on Settlers' collected by a second-generation pioneer, Mrs Campbell Coulson.

Published diaries

George Dunderdale's *Australian Bush Tales* or *The Book of the Bush,* Ward Lock & Co., London, 1898 (republished in 1973 by Penguin as *The Book of the Bush)*, is a classic. F. J. Meyrick, *Life in the Bush 1840–47,* Nelson, London,

1939, is another fine example of the genre but without Dunderdale's literary skill. 'Garryowen' (Edmund Finn), *The Chronicles of Early Melbourne 1835–1852,* Melbourne, 1888, is full of vivid and opinionated descriptions of town and country. George H. Haydon, *Five Years' Experience in Australia,* London, 1846, is among our best descriptions of overlanding, and Haydon was sharp-witted as well. For A. W. Howitt's experiences in the region see Mary Howitt Walker, *Come Wind, Come Weather. A Biography of Alfred Howitt,* Melbourne University Press, Melbourne, 1971. R. U. Billis and A. S. Kenyon, *Pastoral Pioneers of Port Phillip,* Macmillan & Co., Melbourne, 1932 (2nd edition Stockland Press, Melbourne, 1974), gives details of squatters' holdings.

Church diaries

The extensive notebooks of the Reverend W. S. Login are in the possession of Mrs H. Cowie, Sale. Extracts from Login's notes were published by Mrs Cowie and John W. Leslie, in *The Wind Still Blows. Extracts from the Diaries of the Rev. W. S. Login, Mrs H. Harrison and Mrs W. Montgomery*, Sale, 1973. The accounts of their Gippsland experience left by Parson Bean and the Reverend Hales were published in A. E. Clark, *Church of our Fathers,* Sale, 1947. See also Charles Daley, 'Memoirs of a Pioneer Clergyman', *Victorian Historical Magazine,* June, 1944.

Articles and books on Gippsland pioneers

Among the best are: Charles Daley 'The Oldest Road in Gippsland', *Victorian Historical Magazine,* September 1918;

'The Early Days of Sale', *Victorian Historical Magazine,* March 1927; 'How the Hunters Came to Gippsland', *Victorian Historical Magazine,* March 1927; A. W. Grieg, 'The Beginnings of Gippsland', *Victorian Historical Magazine,* May 1912; I. T. Maddern, 'The Squatters in Gippsland', *Victorian Historical Magazine,* August 1965. Among the best local histories are John Adams, *The Tambo Shire Centenary History*, Bruthen, Victoria, 1981, and Davis Kemp, *Maffra. The History of the Shire to 1975,* Maffra, Victoria, 1975. Chester Eagle's *Hail and Farewell! An Evocation of Gippsland,* Heinemann, 1971, is a unique book written from a contemporary perspective but suggestive of Gippsland's past.

Port Phillip

Paul de Serville provided new insights into the colonial gentry in *Port Phillip Gentlemen,* Oxford University Press, Melbourne, 1980. For J. D. Lang's ill-fated prophecies about the colony see *Phillipsland*, Edinburgh, 1847.

Chapter 8

Conflict on the Gippsland frontier: diaries and letters

C. J. Tyers's letters and diaries in the Mitchell Library comprise one of the few authoritative accounts of conflict with the Aborigines in Gippsland. The journal of George Augustus Robinson (microfilm in the La Trobe Library, Melbourne) is discussed by George Mackaness in 'George Augustus Robinson's Journey Into South Eastern Australia', *Journal and Proceedings of the Royal Australian Historical Society,* vol. xxvii, 1941. The Reverend John Bulmer's papers are held in the La Trobe Library, Melbourne.

Articles on the conflict

Until Peter Gardner began his work on the subject there was little more than the article by 'Gippslander' in *The Gap*, Bairnsdale, 1925, and A. S. Kenyon, 'The Aboriginal Protectorate of Port Phillip', *Victorian Historical Magazine,* March 1928. Gardner's articles are 'Massacres of Aborigines in Victoria', *Historian*, October 1975; 'The Pre-White Population of the Gippsland Aborigines', *Journal of the Royal Australian Historical Society,* June 1978; and 'The Warrigal Creek Massacre', *Journal of the Royal Australian Historical Society,* June 1980. Since this book was published Gardner has also published, *Gippsland Massacres. The Destruction of the Kurnai Tribes*, Ngarak Press, Ensay, Vic. 1993. See also Phillip Pepper and Tess d'Anargo, *The Kurnai of Gippsland*, Hyland House, Melbourne 1985.

W. J. Cuthill made an extensive collection of documents and articles on the white woman. It is held in the La Trobe Library, Melbourne, MS 10065. The undated statement of J. MacLeod to A. W. Howitt referred to in this chapter forms part of the Cuthill collection. See also Cuthill's 'The White Woman with the Blacks in Gippsland', *Victorian Historical Magazine*, August 1960. Peter Gardner has helped to sort the matter out in 'The Journals of de Villiers and Warman. The Expedition to recover the Captive White Woman', *Victorian Historical Journal,* May 1979; and added a telling footnote to the story in 'A Melancholy Tale, Thomas Bunjeleene, the Civilised Blackman', *Victorian Historical Journal,* May 1981. 'Garryowen' discussed the case at length in *The Chronicles of Early Melbourne*, op. cit, pp. 602–11. For white women in America see Leslie A. Fiedler, *The Return of the Vanishing American,* Jonathan Cape, London, 1968.

Race relations on the Australian frontier

In *The Other Side of the Frontier,* Penguin, Melbourne, 1982, Henry Reynolds makes a case for extensive and ingenious black resistance on the Australian frontier. That thesis was proposed by Fergus Robinson and Barry York in *The Black Resistance,* Widescope International, Melbourne, 1977. For Victoria see M. F. Christie, *Aborigines in Colonial Victoria 1835–36,* Sydney University Press, Sydney, 1979. For Myall Creek, see *Letters from Government Officers,* 28 April 1838; and 'Despatches Relative to the Massacre of Various Aborigines of Australia in 1838 and Respecting the Trial of Their Murderers', 2 August 1839. J. D. Lang wrote about the Reverend Schmidt's reports of poisoning in Queensland in *Cooksland,* op. cit.

Chapter 9

Strzelecki

Strzelecki's work in Ireland is discussed in the report of the British Association for the Relief of Distress in Ireland, London, 1849, and in Cecil Woodham Smith, op. cit. For Strzelecki's associations in London, see Heney, op. cit.; letters to Florence Nightingale, British Library, 45798, ff.26, 36, 39 and correspondence with Gladstone, 1856–73, British Library, 44385, f.335; 44397, ff.125, 164, 199; 44398, ff.22, 93, 195, 316; 44399, ff.16, 295; 44410, f.194; 44419, ff.202, 260; 44440, f.147. For Strzelecki's emigration work see Heney, op. cit, and Macarthur Papers, AZ 9340, vol. 38, pp. 28–84, Mitchell Library, New South Wales.

Gold

John Dunmore Lang put down his thoughts on the gold rush in a compilation of various authors, *The Australian Emigrant's Manual; or a Guide to the Gold Colonies of New South Wales and Port Phillip,* London, 1852.

Angus McMillan

McMillan's political career left little trace except for reports in the *Gippsland Times* and *Gippsland Guardian* at the time of his election campaign in 1858. He made no speeches in the parliament. The parliament however debated his widow's entitlement to a government grant: see *Victorian Parliamentary Debates,* vol. 11, July 1865, pp. 1148, 1163–64, 1174, 1183.

The dispute about the site for an Aboriginal mission is discussed by P. D. Gardner in 'Ramahyuck Mission Controversy', *Aboriginal and Islander Identity,* January 1979.

The La Trobe Library, Melbourne, holds the 'Journal of the Leader of the Alpine Expedition', 9 March 1864–6 June 1864, on microfilm, MS 9776, MF 145, and McMillan's letter to his friend H. Shillinglaw, dated 8 October 1864, MS 8910, both of which are records of McMillan's sufferings in his last years.

McMillan was the subject of two cheerful novels: Tarlten Rayment, *In the Valley of the Sky*, Whitcomb and Tombs, Melbourne, 1938, and Stanley D. Porteus, *Providence Ponds. A Novel of Early Australia,* Australasian Publishing Company, Sydney, 1951.

INDEX

INDEX

INDEX

INDEX

Also by Random House:

Goodbye Jerusalem

Night Thoughts of a Labor Outsider

Bob Ellis

I wound up as usual in Beazley's office. The Deputy Prime Minister had a .303 rifle on his lap and was waywardly pointing it and laughing in his high infectious share-misery way. He looked like a sadly jocular amalgam of Falstaff and Fatty Fin. I asked him how his count was going in the West where his seat was threatened. 'Oh, I'll lose,' he said heartily. 'There's no way I can win.' …

Tim Fischer, long and gangly, appeared hat in hand in the doorway like the young John Wayne and craved to be admitted, as the next Deputy Prime Minister, to his new office. 'Come in, Tim,' said Beazley, 'have a cup of tea.'

We trooped out and watched the tall preposterous figure amble in, his body language, passing me (G'day Bob,' he said to my alarm), like a supporting actor from On Our Selection …

A portrait of the heart of the True Believers …
For over three decades Bob Ellis has trod the fringes of the corridors of power. Here he gives a personal insight into the tribe that is the Australian Labor Party: the personalities, the quirks, the fabled anecdotes and the grand ideals. *Goodbye Jerusalem* is a reflection on the

nature of Labor politics in Australia, its flaws, its heroes, its victories and its bitter defeats.

'It records ... the laughter and the tears that really did occur in Labor politics ... This is a highly emotional, highly biased but highly truthful account of some of the lesser known incidents in Australia's political history.'
Neville Wran at the book's launch,
quoted in *Sydney Morning Herald* 4/3/97

'If for nothing else—not the eloquent snapshots of some historical moments, the gut wrenchingly emotional eulogies to dead and dying friends, the revelations of unguarded conversations with both Labor and Liberal figures—read Bob Ellis's new book for its scarifying, frequently hilarious and uncannily precise descriptions of both friends and enemies...

The writing, at its best, is as brilliant, lucid, powerful and bitchy as Gore Vidal, the vignettes of the nights in politics where you get a 'blast of wild treachery and weirdness that not even the hard boys can handle' as sparkling as the master of the campaign trail's fear and loathing himself, Hunter S. Thompson... He has crafted with words the overpowering sense of melancholy, linked to the Coalition's enormous victory, which all Labor True Believers carry in their hearts. But Ellis skilfully weaves a thread of redemption through the dark tapestry.'
Sally Loane, *Sydney Morning Herald*

'... a fascinating read, a collection that will delight and madden in equal measure.'
Susan Geason, *Sun-Herald*

'Bob Ellis belongs firmly to the great tradition of eccentric intellectuals who have brightened and inspired the Labor side of politics ... He is an amusing storyteller, at times an acute observer, and his prose at its best is sharp and original ... he is a man driven by gut feelings, and his gut feelings about the Labor Party should be heeded very seriously by that party as it strives to rebuild.'
Dennis Altman, *Sunday Age*

'What power gives and what it takes away is a prime concern of the book, a business that Ellis knows intimately, if vicariously ... *Goodbye Jerusalem* takes a profoundly serious and patriotic view of Australian politics or, more particularly, of the possibilities that Labor offers for the growth of the country ... Of such rhetoric we need to hear much more.'
Peter Pierce, *Australian Book Review*

'... a great read ... also wildly funny ... deserves to become a cult classic.'
Mungo MacCallum, *Republican*